Beer and Society

Beer and Society

How We Make Beer and Beer Makes Us

Eli Revelle Yano Wilson
and Asa B. Stone

LEXINGTON BOOKS
Lanham • Boulder • New York • London

Published by Lexington Books
An imprint of The Rowman & Littlefield Publishing Group, Inc.
4501 Forbes Boulevard, Suite 200, Lanham, Maryland 20706
www.rowman.com

86-90 Paul Street, London EC2A 4NE

British Library Cataloguing in Publication Information Available

Library of Congress Cataloging-in-Publication Data

Names: Wilson, Eli Revelle Yano, author. | Stone, Asa B., author.
Title: Beer and society : how we make beer and beer makes us / Eli Revelle Yano
 Wilson and Asa B. Stone.
Description: Lanham : Lexington Books, 2022. | Includes bibliographical references and
 index.
Identifiers: LCCN 2021056367 (print) | LCCN 2021056368 (ebook) |
 ISBN 9781666904338 (cloth) | ISBN 9781666904352 (pbk)
 ISBN 9781666904345 (ebook)
Subjects: LCSH: Beer industry—United States. | Brewing industry—United States. |
 Beer—Social aspects—United States.
Classification: LCC HD9397.U52 W55 2022 (print) | LCC HD9397.U52 (ebook) |
 DDC 338.4/766342—dc23/eng/20220107
LC record available at https://lccn.loc.gov/2021056367
LC ebook record available at https://lccn.loc.gov/2021056368

Contents

List of Figures

Acknowledgments

As with the brewing of beer from grain to glass, this book represents a collaborative effort in the fullest sense of the word. Countless conversations with colleagues and friends—both in academia and in the beer industry—helped us fine-tune the recipe for this book. They also helped direct our research process and provide an essential layer of quality control for the (re)writing that now fills these pages.

We would like to begin by thanking the people in and around the beer industry who generously shared their time with us during interviews and field research. Some we have mentioned by name throughout this book. Many others we have not in order to preserve their confidentiality. We express our gratitude to everyone who met us for a beer to talk, took time out of their busy days to tour us through their brewhouse, struggled with us to navigate Zoom interviews, and let us hang out and soak up the atmosphere in their brewery taprooms (when it was safe to do so).

The idea of creating an interdisciplinary book on beer and society was neither the most obvious project we could have engaged in nor the easiest. It almost did not happen amid the swirl of the pandemic as well as myriad other academic and personal pressures over the past two years. Fortunately, several of our brilliant colleagues helped us dial in our intellectual pairings far better than we could have done alone. For offering feedback on early versions of our book chapters, we would like to thank Sarah Bennet, Maricarmen Hernandez, Elizabeth Korver-Glenn, Lambic Info, Maria Lane, Leslie Morrison, Erica Barreiro, Deisy del Real, Jennifer Schaller, Amy Zhou, Hajar Yazhdiha, Owen Whooley, and Rich Wood. We also thank Nate Chapman, Charlotte Feehan, and Shelby Chant for their support.

We are especially grateful to several colleagues who went above and beyond to offer extended feedback on our manuscript. David Brunsma, who recently coauthored *Beer and Racism: How Beer Became White, Why it Matters, and the Movements to Change It*, read through and commented on the full manuscript, pushing us to think deeper about how the history of beer is also connected to the history of racial inequality and oppression. Tahseen Shams challenged us to consider, among other things, a perspective we had overlooked: why the story of beer is still both relevant and fascinating to those who don't drink beer themselves. Phi Hong Su was our most steady-handed presence throughout our writing process as she proselytized "reverse outlining" each and every chapter in order to ensure that our arguments were on a solid foundation. Finally, Zachary Shank helped us bring our words on page to life through active, dynamic prose while also encouraging us to be as inclusive as possible with our language.

Courtney Morales, our editor at Lexington Books, has been a consistent source of encouragement as well as a steady editorial hand. From our early meetings and on through the production process, we are so grateful that Courtney helped guide our book writing journey while also making it—dare we say—fun. We also appreciate Matthew Valades for editorial support as well as the production team at Lexington Books that helped move this book along efficiently.

Throughout the writing process, we remained steadfast in our belief that members of the beer industry should have a say in a book that aims to say something about them, their workplaces, and their communities. During the final stages of editing, we organized an "industry peer review" to supplement Lexington Press' traditional peer-review process. We wanted to make sure our story was clearly written, engaging to nonacademics, and, most of all, fair and accurate. We want to extend our special gratitude to our industry reviewers: Diego Benitez, Ezekiel Gomez, Natasha Souther, and Rian Van Nordheim for offering their in-depth feedback on the arguments and facts presented in each chapter. All remaining errors are our own.

The winding journey to completing this book may have been shared by many, but as with any endeavor, our personal support teams were our own. Asa would like to express their gratitude for all their chosen family who has provided them with emotional nourishment while a series of unprecedented environmental, climate, and social justice crises coincided with this project. Bahinīharu's utter trust even in the midst of the storm has always been more consistent than any International Pale Lagers in their wee fridge, Aiden's continuous validations have been as *gezellig* as his farmhouse ale with beautifully whipped meringue on a rainy day, and no beer in the world would ever be as warming as Cristian's embraces. Special gratitude goes out to Mark for his unwavering confidence in them, which has been clear and unmistakable like his favorite American IPA. His dry sense of humor has never failed to be soul lifting. Asa extends their gratitude to Jean and his family for their generosity and friendship that led to their pivotal moment. After all, they never would have pursued their scholarship in beer without their fateful visit to Brasserie Cantillon during their public brew day.

Eli would like to thank his parents, Scott and Christine, foremost, for never flinching—well almost never—at the idea of him writing a book on drinking beer. Instead, they encouraged him to pursue fresh intellectual ideas and complex social stories about beer in tandem. Eli is also convinced that this book would lack a crucial layer of flavor—that extra hop addition or specialty malt in the grain bill—were it not for his wife Laura's consistent presence alongside the project. Showing gratitude to one's partner in life is obligatory, but Laura deserves so much more than that. Not only did she accompany Eli on many of his beer-related research trips, she also challenged him to rethink the possibilities of diversity and inclusion initiatives within the beer industry. Eli still cherishes the day he met Laura—at the beer bar where he worked, a full decade ago.

Introduction

Exploring the Social World through Beer

Let's get something out of the way before we get started. Perhaps you are wondering if this is the right book for you. If you reached for this book because you enjoy drinking beer, or if you are curious to learn how beer can help us better understand the social and cultural world that surrounds us, then dear reader, you have come to the right place.

Scan your memory for the first time you popped open a fresh bottle of your favorite beer (or another beverage you prefer). How did you first discover that tantalizing drink? Was it a happy accident, a brand that caught your eye because of its colorful label art as you strolled through the aisles of your neighborhood store? Or did you search for it after scrolling through an Internet-based article titled something like "10 Beers to Try Before You Die." Perhaps you were at a party and a close friend handed you a cold one with a nod of encouragement (and a little peer pressure). Who are you usually with and what are you doing when you take that sip? Alternately, when would you *not* drink beer and opt for something else? Context matters here. Because, as we will see, our social environment structures the personal relationships we have with beer—and each other.

However you choose to respond to these thought exercises, your answers will point to the fact that our relationships with beer are deeply sociological and psychological; our drinking practices are not entirely our own. Through the lens of beer, we can observe what is both fascinating and deeply frustrating about our society. Beer is a cultural object we collectively invest with meaning—it is embedded within a cultural fabric that varies with time and place. Yet beer is also produced within a society that remains deeply divided along lines of race, gender, class, and other social statuses—a society in which power and influence flow from social hierarchies and institutional structures. We as humans make beer, but beer also makes us by functioning

1

as a window into who we are as individuals and as members of these larger social groups and sociological patterns.

Until recently, people didn't give beer much serious thought at all. Compared to its more "sophisticated" alcoholic cousins, such as wine and Scotch, beer has had far fewer words spilled about it by those seeking to elevate or reinforce that beverage's culturally elite status through proper tasting techniques, designations of provenance, and celebrations of generations-old family recipes and production methods. Instead, in pop culture beer is often couched in one of three narratives: (1) *Beer as a Dangerous Intoxicant*, (2) *Beer as a Man's Drink*, or (3) *Craft Beer as Hipster*. To be sure, each of these narratives has some truth to them. First, beer is undoubtedly a dangerous psychoactive substance. Over 95,000 people die from excessive alcohol use every year, and many more are injured as a result of the careless actions of those who are intoxicated. According to the Centers for Disease and Control, alcohol is the leading cause of preventable death in the United States. Beer also affects us psychologically in ways that can be both pleasurable and reckless, and the results of both are externalized in the social world. Second, drinking beer continues to be more closely associated with men than other genders. This *gendered* framing of beer consumption is not new or unique to the United States: it is men who are usually the ones "throwing back a cold one," whether in movies, TV shows, or sexist beer advertisements.[1] By contrast, women are either absent from these scenes, portrayed in subservient roles, or portrayed as the "cool girl." Many iconic scenes from Hollywood films—such as John Belushi's character from *Animal House* chanting "Toga!" while crushing a can of beer on his head, or Will Ferrell's character dropping to one knee to do a "beer funnel" in front of a raucous fraternity crowd—reinforce a powerful image of beer drinking (guzzling?) intricately tied to ideas about heteronormative masculinity.

Finally, the image of craft beer drinkers as effete hipsters is the newest addition to the canon. As a Budweiser commercial from 2015 depicted, craft beer is replete with bearded young men wearing jeans and flannel sitting around sipping beers that don't taste like "real" beer (according to Budweiser) due to the addition of fruit, spices, or other flavors not found in pale lagers. This, of course, is a highly stereotyped image of craft beer that overlooks important nuances within this social scene—just as the first two narratives do in different ways.

Clearly, dominant cultural representations of beer and beer drinkers represent only a small slice of our complex relationship with this beverage today. For example, amid the continued market dominance of large, corporate beer producers—Big Beer, for short—there are parallel efforts underway to cultivate beer connoisseurship, preserve historical beer styles, revive regional beer cultures, and diversify who makes and drinks great beer. This book is about how we construct and give meaning to beer both individually and collectively. We aim to illustrate that what goes on beyond the beer glass is just as rewarding to consume as the flavors swirling around it.

HOW DO WE MAKE BEER?

Let us begin with the basics. Beer is a remarkably simple creation in terms of its primary ingredients and core brewing processes. To make beer, you first mix malted grains and hot water to convert starch in the malted grain into sugars. After separating the spent grains from the sugary water called wort, you boil it and add hops for bitterness, flavor, and aroma. After quickly cooling the wort, you pitch in yeast, which starts the fermentation process that converts sugars into alcohol and carbon dioxide. Though people dedicate their lives to perfecting this craft, when stripped to its basics anyone can make beer, or at least something vaguely recognizable as beer.

However, at a deeper level, understanding how we "make beer" goes well beyond material ingredients and fermentation science. It requires taking stock of beer's immaterial components—the stuff of the social, cultural, and economic *world of beer*. Understanding the world of beer requires examining how beer is produced, circulated, and consumed.[2] Today's leading breweries are capable of delivering fresh beer around the globe with remarkable consistency and quality; the journey of any beer from raw ingredients to glass involves a web of ties between farmers, brewers, importers, distributors, retailers, and government regulators. Through the process of bringing beer to the market to be bought and sold, beer becomes *embedded* in society as an economic commodity as well as a cultural object, something imbued with shared significance on multiple levels. Further, ideas about beer originate not only from industry-driven marketing campaigns but also from beer consumers, through social media (such as popular online platforms like Untappd or Beer Advocate) as well as casual conversations in local beer "scenes" within bars, breweries, festivals, and backyard parties.[3]

While the modern brewing industry is often celebrated as a triumph of innovation, technology, and business ingenuity, a closer look at the brewing industry must also reckon with who has historically been excluded from participating. In this sense, beer can illustrate how forces of social inequality get reinforced—and sometimes challenged—in our society at large. Consider the genesis story of the U.S. craft beer movement, a topic we return to in greater detail in later chapters. Most accounts of the rise of craft beer in the latter half of the 20th century point to the actions of a small number of intrepid brewers and brewery entrepreneurs, such as

Jim Koch (founder of Boston Beer Company), Ken Grossman (founder of Sierra Nevada), Fritz Maytag (founder of Anchor Brewing Company), and John Hall (founder of Goose Island Brewing).[4] As the story goes, each of these individuals followed their unwavering passion for bringing flavorful, small-batch beer to the public. Each stuck to their conviction about opening a brewery despite facing considerable adversity—not least of which was the lack of precedent for running a small brewery in the United States during this era. While these pioneers rightly deserve credit for their early and highly influential achievements that helped springboard the craft beer movement in the United States, it is important to recognize the *structural advantages* that helped underpin their success. Each of the "founding fathers" we just named is a white, college-educated man that was raised in a well-to-do family. These characteristics reflect intersecting privileges in our society associated with whiteness, upper-middle-class resources, and masculinity. This helped each of these craft beer entrepreneurs fuse their brewing aspirations together with access to financial resources, support from well-connected friends, and a snug fit within cultural assumptions about who people typically expect to work in beer. While these factors alone may not explain why it was Jim Koch who *specifically* launched the Boston Beer Company after leaving a lucrative career in corporate consulting, they do help explain why it was educated, cisgender heterosexual (cis-het), white men *categorically*, rather than Black, Indigenous, and People of Color (BIPOC), women, LGBTQIA+ people, or members of the working class that managed to blaze a path forward for craft beer. In other words, understanding the way the world of beer has developed cannot be divorced from a larger conversation of how social power and entrenched inequalities based on intersectional statuses have shaped this process at every step.[5]

HOW DOES BEER MAKE US?

From our relationship with beer to our drinking environments, beer influences the way we think about ourselves. It is a highly evocative filter to our experiences as well as a signal that we give off to others about who we are. Both are evident when we consider the *psychology* of beer—how beer influences our cognition, mood, and decision-making. Beer has neurological effects on the human brain: it releases a flood of endorphins, the so-called feel-good brain chemicals that in turn influence how we interact with those around us. This is what that makes drinking beer and achieving a "beer buzz" such a pleasurable activity for many people. Of course, the role that alcohol plays in lubricating social interactions and heightening emotional responses can work in both desirable and undesirable ways. On the one hand, recent research shows that consuming alcohol can elevate our mood by alleviating anxiety; alcohol can improve our memory and cognitive functions when consumed in moderate amounts.[6] Similarly, drinking beer can be highly evocative: the effervescence of a crisp Pilsner, the brilliant copper hue of a German *Altbier*, or the intense citrus and piney flavors of a West Coast–style India Pale Ale can immediately transport us to a different time and place and temporarily away from the stress of our daily lives. However, drinking alcohol can also lead people down a dangerous path toward exaggerated emotional expressions and substance dependency. By decreasing serotonin levels, beer can exacerbate feelings of depression and isolation. The ways in which drinking beer can influence our behavior are not always negative. Nor are they always under our control.

Consuming beer influences our *social identity* in other ways. As the saying goes, "you are what you drink," which has more to do with what beer we choose to drink rather than how much of it we consume. Whether we intend it or not, our choice of beer signals to others about the kind of person we are and what else we stand for.[7] For example, expressing a preference for mass-produced pale lagers in a room full of hardcore beer enthusiasts might get people talking about (and judging) that person's taste in beer. By contrast, as sociologist Michael Ian Borer describes, popping the cap on a limited release barrel-aged stout at a "bottle share" is likely to garner one a tremendous amount of cachet among this same crowd. These examples illustrate how our expressions of social identity through beer, and others' reactions to these identities, depend on social context just as they do ideas about what constitutes "good" and "bad" taste. At a professional football game, someone opening that same ultrarare bottle instead of opting for a draft pour of ubiquitous pale lager will almost certainly lead others around to think of that person as a bona fide beer snob.

Beer also signals who "we" are collectively. How a society engages with beer through norms, practices, and values reveals something about that culture more broadly as well as the economic system that underpins it. Consider the mainstream culture of beer in the United States during the mid-20th century. In the decades that followed World War II, the United States experienced a steady decline in the number of breweries in operation; by 1970, fewer than 100 breweries existed nationwide. This did not happen by accident. By mid-century, commercial beer production was dominated by a handful of large corporations making beer that was almost impossible to tell apart from one another in terms of flavor and color. Beer had become consistent, widely available in retail stores, affordable to the average American—and completely homogeneous. These trends were not unique to beer during this time. The homogenization of consumer products was also evident in the food sold in supermarkets (Twinkies and Wonder Bread got their start around this time), the suburban tracts where the American middle-class resided by the millions, and in many other consumer goods ("a television in every house"). It was during this era that brands like Budweiser, Miller, and Pabst cemented their status as American's cultural icons. Seen from this lens, the recent growth of craft beer in the United States—along with rising interest in preserving "real ale" in Britain—represents a noteworthy cultural shift. It suggests that brewers have reignited their interest in traditional methods for crafting beer in smaller batches (rather than mass-producing it using heavy machinery), and that a growing proportion of beer drinkers are opting for products that they feel represent authenticity.[8] Both the way beer is produced and consumed reflect deep-set, yet also highly contested, beliefs about who we are and what we stand for.

OUR UNIQUE PERSPECTIVE

A good tour guide helps enchant the place you are visiting. They make it more captivating by showing you new ways to see it, understand it, and, ultimately, experience it. As authors of this book, we see ourselves as tour guides leading you toward a deeper appreciation of how beer and society are deeply intertwined. Allow us to briefly introduce ourselves and our unique perspective on the world of beer as "insider outsiders" that will inform the pages that follow.

Eli is a sociology professor who brings together his research expertise on race and labor issues with nearly ten years of experience working in and around the craft beer industry as a Certified Cicerone®. Asa is a psychology researcher with an Advanced Cicerone® who has researched and taught the intersection of beer and society worldwide. Throughout this book, we bring sociological and psychological insights together with our own up-close industry experience, which we have interspersed throughout these pages through personal vignettes. This book is also the product of empirical research. In order to learn as much as we could about what people in and around the world of beer experience on a daily basis, we conducted a total of twenty in-depth interviews with industry workers, made dozens of visits to breweries and other beer establishments around the country, and engaged in numerous informal conversations with industry professionals and avid beer enthusiasts alike.

We have written this book so that its content will be engaging for a general reader interested in learning about the social, psychological, and cultural dimensions of the world's most popular alcoholic drink.[9] We focus mostly on the United States, allowing us to go deeper into local contexts and controversies that frame key issues. We have also designed this book to complement college courses in psychology, sociology, and food studies. We provide a *critical perspective* on how beer and society are connected in ways that are at once deeply personal and framed by complex economic systems, contested cultural values, and social inequalities. We have minimized technical language and academic jargon wherever possible and let the people who have devoted their professional lives to beer do most of the talking.[10] That said, in no way are we able to cover all of the potential topics that beer touches on, which would require a multivolume encyclopedia (Garrett Oliver's *Oxford Companion to Beer* is a fantastic place to start).

Through beer, we learn about the way society is organized socially and culturally—bumps, bruises, and joys, all. We believe that beer and the people who have dedicated their careers to it can play a role in bringing about change to society, such as through advocating for greater social inclusivity in the workplace and a deeper sense of cultural appreciation. We highlight breweries, advocacy groups, and other industry leaders who are taking bold steps to fuse the craft of brewing and selling beer with the creation of (new) spaces that invite social dialogue and promote diversity, equity, and inclusion. While these practices have not always been evident in the world of beer in the past, they can help define its future—because we make beer, and beer makes us.

A BRIEF SOCIAL HISTORY OF BEER

Imagine how much more interesting high-school history class would have been if we learned that some scholars believe that the creation of early civilization was really about humankind's quest to brew beer better. Our ancestors have consumed versions of beer-like fermented beverages for nearly as long as humans have been forming groups and farming the land. Beer production itself, along with agriculture, is a primary reason why early humans decided to establish sedentary communities and transition away from nomadic lifestyles.[11] Brewing beer required consistent access to ingredients, such as grain, water, and time (hops were a later addition, and yeast was not discovered until the 1800s). Beer in its simplest form is the fermented by-product of grains soaked in water over time. Soaked grains yield a sugar-water solution that yeast cells can metabolize, giving off alcohol and carbon dioxide. Once this process is complete, other ingredients can be added to the beer to make it more palatable, or to keep it from spoiling quickly.

For centuries, beer served as an important social and cultural glue for early human societies. It was used as a component of many social rituals ranging from the celebration of harvest season to the commemoration of religious ceremonies. Beer was also the subject of veneration itself. Ancient hymns and painted pottery from the Sumerians and Egyptians commonly depict vessels used specifically for beer. In these scenes, the vessels used to hold beer were often wielded by or placed alongside powerful and important leaders. The Hymn to Ninkasi, written down around 1800 BCE and dedicated to the Goddess of all creation and overseer of brewing, remains among the oldest identified pieces of writing in the world.

Historians believe that beer was a nutritional component of the human diet in many ancient societies. Made from hearty grains such as wheat and barley, beer would have contained many of the basic nutrients necessary to sustain life. Beer was also safer to drink than water.[12] As early as the 6th century in Europe, beer was regularly being brewed and consumed by monastic monks, who would use the proceeds generated from the sale of beer to provide for themselves. These monks would also drink beer while engaging in ritual fasting. No wonder some scholars believe that the alcoholic properties of beer may have contributed to early recollections of religious experiences!

Throughout history, the process of brewing beer has been integrated into the daily rhythms of social life all around the world. The ingredients used in beer recipes reflect local tastes, native ingredients, and prevailing techniques of the day. For example, before the widespread use of hops to flavor beer, which began around 1100 in modern-day Germany, brewers used a mixture of herbs and honey to flavor their fermented malt beverages. From small additions of heather and bog myrtle to yarrow and juniper berries, brewers took advantage of what was locally available to make traditional beers such as *Sahti* in Finland and *Roggenbier* in southern Germany.

The task of brewing beer has long been assigned to specific groups of people in society, usually those of a subordinate status. Slaves, for instance, were thought to have been used to brew beer in ancient Egypt (just as they were used for many other duties involving physical labor). Following the medieval period in Europe, brewing beer was considered a domestic task, much like baking bread or preparing meals. As such, in England prior to the 17th century, brewing "ale" (beer without hops) was considered women's work, done by women "brewsters."[13] Brewing beer took place within the private home and on a small scale, intended for daily consumption by family members.[14] During this time beer had to be brewed regularly and consumed quickly; it was not until the invention of refrigeration in the 18th century that beer could be reliably transported in any scale.[15] Brewing beer thus reflected a gendered division of household labor in European society: women brewed beer because the task could be done indoors and with ingredients that were stored and prepared in the same space, such as bread. Importantly, brewing was also a task that garnered little reputation and status during this time.

Only recently have men come to dominate brewing in the Western world. Over the course of the 17th, 18th, and 19th centuries, beer became an increasingly commercial product made in large quantities using specialized equipment, and sold profitably in the market. As beer production moved from the domestic sphere to the factory, brewing shifted from a humble practice associated with women to a profitable, commercial one dominated by men. To be sure, many women continued to brew beer for household consumption well into the Industrial Revolution. Some also transitioned to brewing and serving beer commercially, albeit on a small scale, in Taverns and Inns that dotted the countryside. These "Ale Wives" ensured that guests had access to fresh beer made on premise in these establishments.[16] However, by the time an entrepreneurially minded German immigrant named Augustus Busch opened his first commercial brewery in St. Louis in 1877, brewing on an industrial scale was a trade firmly done by men in Europe and the United States.

Men also dominated the public places where beer was most often purchased and consumed by the turn of the 20th century. Bars and saloons functioned as places where working-class men would go after work and before returning home.[17] In the United States, neighborhood saloons dotted many city blocks; the working-class men who were regulars at these establishments were often on a first-name basis with the barkeep. As historian Madelon Powers notes, working-class men enjoyed comradery with one another while drinking at these venues, which also helped them temporarily escape from their repetitive daily routines at work and at home.[18] While this pattern of gendered beer consumption in public spaces was not unique to the United States during this era—in Japan, the ritual of heading to bars for several drinks after work was also done almost exclusively by men—it is clear that beer served as a social glue and bars and saloons an institutionalized place of (alcoholic) consumption during this period of American history. Rather than standing apart from everyday society, what happened in these places reflected and reinforced the social organization of working-class life. Until it all came to a halt.

The Great Shutdown

Beer as we know it in the United States nearly came to an end in the early 20th century. While the consumption of alcohol has long had its detractors for a variety of moral, social, and religious reasons, by the end of the 19th century, temperance movements in the United States and Europe had begun to organize anti-booze protests and public condemnations of the alcohol industry. Teetotaler groups such as the Anti-Saloon League became advocates of the outright ban of alcoholic beverages in the United States. The movement was fueled by broader changes in society. As Powers notes, the stigma surrounding alcohol increased during an era when it was being consumed (1) outside the home and in public venues; (2) mostly by men, in the company of other men; and (3) alongside the rise of factory work that involved long hours and hard, repetitive work. For many workaday men, drinking alcohol was both a form of social entertainment after work and a way to cope with the hardship of daily life during this era.

These new norms of alcohol consumption did not sit well with factions of society that saw this behavior as a moral threat. By 1910, the tide against alcohol had gained political traction in the United States—just as it had in other Western nations such as Finland, Canada, and Iceland. The election of a pro-temperance U.S. congress and president (Woodrow Wilson), stoked by the United States' entry into World War I and prioritization of wartime efforts, gave teetotalers a powerful political platform for their message.[19] The landmark federal decision in 1920 to prohibit the production, transportation, and sale of alcohol in the United States, known as Prohibition, was a decision never supported by the majority of working-class men. Rather, it illustrated who had political power to control the industry through laws and regulations (we discuss this in chapter 5). As history has shown, Prohibition suppressed but did not eradicate the nation's appetite for drinking beer and other forms of alcohol. Instead, the sale and consumption of beer moved underground into the black market and out of government regulation.

The shutdown of the domestic brewing industries in the United States and elsewhere in the world was catastrophic for brewers. Of the 1,200 commercial breweries in the United States that were in operation prior to the passage of the 18th Amendment, nearly 500 would close over the next thirteen years. Only the strongest and best-capitalized breweries were able to survive by pivoting their business away from beer while using the equipment and facilities they already had. For example, Schlitz, Blatz, Pabst, and Anheuser-Busch began making "Near Beer," a carbonated product that looked like beer but contained less than 0.5% alcohol by volume.[20] Other breweries shifted their focus toward manufacturing "malt syrup" as an alternative sweetener using the same malted barley that would have gone into brewing.[21]

Prohibition also had profound ripple effects throughout the world of beer from the consumption of beer to its supply chain. As has been well-documented by historians, the sale of beer and other alcoholic beverages came under increasing control of extralegal actors: smugglers, unsanctioned "speakeasies" and barkeeps, and hidden storage and distribution facilities. It is difficult to know how many American breweries were directly involved in this underground market. In other words, Prohibition moved the sale and consumption of alcohol underground and outside of government oversight. Meanwhile, hop and malt producers in the United States, key industry suppliers, had to adjust their business plans quickly. Luckily, since neither were directly involved in the production of alcoholic beverages, their operations were spared from mandated closures. According to historian Peter Kopp, while hop growers in Willamette Valley, Oregon, one of the nation's largest hop production areas at the time, initially stalled following the passage of Prohibition, they were able to expand into key export markets in Europe, Mexico, and South America. Sales volume of hops from Willamette actually increased during Prohibition despite the domestic market for hops slowing to a trickle.

The era of Prohibition also contributed to the narrowing of the American palate for beer. Prior to the 1900s, the vast expanse of neighborhood taverns and pubs with modest brewing operations attached resulted in a wide range of beer styles being brewed all over the country. Depending on the region, immigrant tradition, and brewer preference, some breweries served English porters and stouts to their local clientele, while others made Hefeweizens and Vienna-style amber lagers. But the beer style that would ultimately dominate the U.S. market and by extension American taste buds was the gold-hued, effervescent German pale lager known as Pilsner. Pilsner was, unsurprisingly, the flagship style of nearly all industrial-sized breweries by the turn of the 20th century, such as Anheuser-Busch, Coors, and Pabst. As these large brewing companies began to expand outward beyond their home markets, smaller breweries were forced to close down or consolidate in order to remain competitive. The high-watermark for the number of breweries in the United States was over four decades *before* Prohibition, in 1873. Beer was quickly becoming big business around the globe, and mass-produced German-style pale lagers were the product of choice. By the time major Prohibition laws around the world were being repealed in the 1930s, the beer landscape had changed. For surviving American breweries, for instance, the doors to the beer market were flung open, although state-level restrictions, such as Blue Laws, remained in some cases for decades (as we discuss in chapter 5). Breweries with the greatest command of resources and business savvy were able to capitalize quickly. Big Beer—loosely defined as large, corporate beer companies that mass-produce beer—saw their profits skyrocket as small breweries folded or consolidated operations. In the four decades following the repeal of Prohibition, corporate control of the beer industry increased and the total number of breweries dwindled even further until only seventy-six breweries existed in the United States. By the time Fritz Maytag released his first batch of "Steam" beer in the late 1960s, Budweiser was already the leading beer brand in the country by a large margin. The corporate domination of the beer industry was even more absolute in other parts of the globe. In South America, Mexico, and Europe, mass-produced light lagers accounted for three out of every four beers sold. The moment was ripe for a change.

The Rise of Craft Beer

As a market commodity, beer could not have got more homogenized by the 1960s. Most beer sold around the world was a pale lager that was light in flavor, color, and body. Heavily marketed and mass-produced, pale lagers ruled the roost (or, more accurately, the supermarket shelves, where the majority of all beer is sold in the United States). Beers such as Budweiser, Heineken, and Carlsberg were technical achievements in terms of their consistency, but together they represented only a tiny slice of the diverse regional styles, brewing techniques, and local beer traditions that had characterized centuries of beer production and consumption. Aside from a few imported curiosities (e.g., Guinness Stout), by mid-century, the number of beer brands available in most markets could be counted on one hand.

The industry was ripe for a change. As organization scholars Glenn Carroll and Anand Swaminathan note, the state of market consolidation in the beer industry allowed opportunities for specialized producers to offer a wider variety of beers geared toward satisfying consumer tastes that were unmet by the sameness of the beers on store shelves.[22] The industry was structured in a way such that small startup breweries were in a better position to offer a wider variety of beer styles than large monolith corporations. The first brewery to spark interest in "microbrewed" beer was Anchor Brewery in San Francisco. Anchor was an old beer brand in decline when the brewery was bought by Fritz Maytag in 1965. Instead of attempting to imitate the pale lagers that were dominating the beer market, Maytag decided to sell and market "Steam" beer based on the company's pre-Prohibition recipe made with a lager yeast fermented at higher temperatures for a distinctive aroma and flavor. Following Anchor's lead, several smaller commercial brewery operations launched on the West Coast, the first of which was New Albion, opened by Jim McAuliffe. At this point, however, the craft beer movement was still slow to take hold; small-batch brewing was a novelty rather than a noteworthy trend.

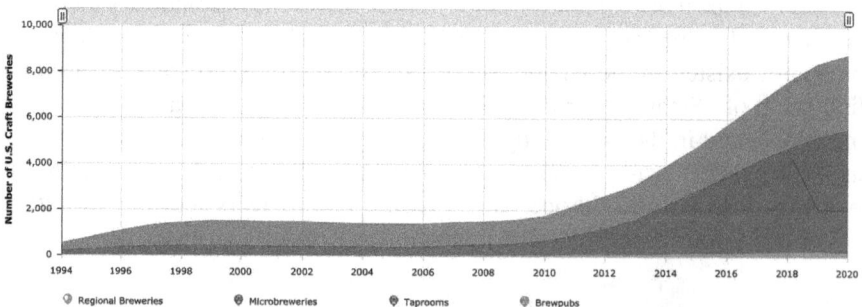

Figure 0.1   The Number of Microbreweries in the United States Has Increased Rapidly Over the Last Few Decades, Especially during the Period from 2010 to 2020. *Source: Courtesy of Brewers Association 2020.*

Another barrier to the growth of craft breweries in the United States was that homebrewing had, since the Prohibition era, remained illegal. This meant that the very process of brewing on a small scale was restricted by law, and the equipment and training manuals needed to do so were hard to find. As a result, Jack McAuliffe, the founder of New Albion, the nation's first microbrewery since Prohibition, needed to be much more than just a brewer entrepreneur to get his operation started. He also needed to be a welder, politician, businessperson, general handyman, and amateur engineer all at once, since little of this infrastructure existed prior.

The year—1978—that President Jimmy Carter signed bill HR1337 making homebrewing legal was a watershed moment. It allowed homebrewers, the de facto minor league system for craft beer, the basic legal rights to begin to assemble and accumulate social and technical knowledge related to homebrewing beer.[23] Several other "early promoters" further stoked interest in craft beer, including industry advisors such as Michael Lewis, a professor of brewing technology that advised Jack McAuliffe, beer writers such as Michael Jackson (not *that* one), and homebrewer-entrepreneurs such as Charlie Papazian. Papazian's *Zymurgy* magazine, dedicated to the craft and culture of homebrewing, was founded in 1978, the same year homebrewing was legalized. Homebrewing has since blossomed into a robust culture and practice. Of the estimated six million homebrewers worldwide, one million of them are located in the United States, many of whom join local associations that allow them to share their knowledge with others.

Much has changed in the world of beer in the four-plus decades since "microbreweries" first gained in popularity in the United States. The craft beer movement now has global momentum. For years, American brewers and beer fans had to look to Europe for technical knowledge about brewing and stylistic diversity. Today, the arrow of influence also points the other direction. The 8,000 craft breweries in the United States (as of 2020) far exceeds the number in any other country (the United Kingdom is second, with just under 2,300); American brewers are widely seen as the leading edge of innovation in beer (see Figure 0.1) Beer styles popularized in the United States, such as Hazy IPAs, Pastry Stouts, and Kettle Sours, are now brewed in countries as far flung as New Zealand and Thailand. Small brewers in Italy, France, and Japan are making craft beer their own by developing new traditions, reviving old ones, and using local ingredients.

Craft beer has also faced challenges. Small breweries continue to face pressure from corporate-owned beer companies seeking to gain in market share and squash business competitors. In 2011, Anheuser-Busch's purchase of Chicago-based Goose Island Brewing Company sent shockwaves throughout the craft beer industry and raised concerns about whether the golden era of craft beer was coming to an end. More recently, the global pandemic caused by COVID-19—still ongoing at the time of this writing—has wreaked havoc on the economic viability of small brewing companies. Many of these operations are highly dependent on face-to-face customer interaction and local traffic and thus were directly impacted by government-mandated temporary closures of "on-premise" business.

In the last few years, more U.S. craft breweries have begun to look beyond beer with their businesses and toward social issues sweeping the country. Dozens of prominent breweries, alongside industry collectives such as the Brewing Change Collaborative in Minnesota and Cheers to Change in New Mexico, have made conscious efforts to support racial justice, gender equity, and LGBTQIA+ inclusivity in their workplaces and communities. While support for these efforts is far from uniform and has faced pushback, the industry's ongoing relationship to current social movements is poised to shape the future of the world of beer—a topic we return to later in this book.

AN OVERVIEW OF *BEER AND SOCIETY*

Whether developing an appreciation for beer or anime or opera, sociologists note that the process of becoming a "fan" follows a similar sequence of actions.[24] First, you must learn how to engage with that activity by understanding its prevailing techniques, processes, and rituals. Demonstrating this basic competence leads other people to begin to acknowledge and accept you as a fan. This in turn deepens your own identity and engagement, as you move from being a neophyte to a true "insider." It takes time and concerted effort to develop an appreciation for the social and cultural dimensions of beer—and by extension, how our broader society is organized. Let this book be your guide.

We begin with the deeply personal and proceed outward. Chapter 1 introduces the reader to what we have called "beer psychology," in which we examine our internal relationship with the beer we drink. Beer influences everything from our implicit mental processes to our explicit behavior. We are often not fully aware of this influence. Drawing on recent psychological research, we show how beer influences our thoughts and actions and how our thoughts and actions impact our appreciation of beer.

Chapter 2 focuses on the consumption of beer as an interpersonal process. We begin by asking: Who drinks what beer and why? Our preference for one beer over another is not arbitrary; rather, it tells us something about our other tastes as well as the social groups we belong to. Because we consume beer in deeply social ways, these ways of consuming reflect the cultural norms and hierarchies that pattern the society around us.

Have you ever walked into a brewery and wondered, why does everyone here seem to be a bearded white dude? Chapter 3 surveys the *social organization* of the beer world. It sets out to explain patterns of *who* does *what*—and why—in the world of beer, which has everything to do with issues of race, gender, sexual orientation, and social class. At the same time, most breweries in the United States are not racist or sexist establishments run by overtly prejudiced people. Instead, we argue that a subtler system reinforces the normative *whiteness* and *maleness* of craft breweries today—one steeped in economic privilege, social connections, and cultural tastes. We consider the steps needed to break down these barriers based on race, gender, and sexual orientations, informed by breweries that are leading the way for meaningful social changes.

Chapter 4 examines the business of beer by taking the reader behind the scenes to showcase how the modern industry really operates—and why large, multinational beer companies continue to thrive despite the growth of craft beer. The strategies used by Big Beer in their attempts to dominate the industry are far from the same as those used by small breweries looking to maintain their piece of the pie by appealing to values of authenticity and craft. This is a story of capitalism and business competition, but also about how multiple market logics coexist. We detail how beer companies produce, advertise, and distribute beer in highly strategic ways.

Competition may be heating up between breweries, but by what rules is the game itself played? How did these rules come about, anyway? Chapter 5 examines the regulations that structure the beer industry and how regulations continue to shape the nature of beer production and consumption. Today, U.S. states continue to vary widely in how they tax and regulate beer. While consumers are largely oblivious to the tangle of laws facing brewers and other beer companies, behind the scenes these laws are subject to heated battles played out at the courthouse that can literally mean life or death—profit or business failure—for many small breweries.

Throughout human history, the place of beer within society has been characterized by both tradition and tension. Chapter 6 explores the cultural complexity surrounding modern beer. Beer as a cultural object is imbued with meaning and ritual at once global and particular. The way we think of beer is framed in particular ways by key organizations. What does it mean, for instance, for a beer to be brewed "authentically" or for one beer to be considered of higher quality than another? We describe how cultural knowledge about beer involves constructing claims by leading authority groups in the industry. This chapter surveys these internal struggles within the beer world that have grown more heightened as beer makers grapple with a fundamental question: who are *we* and what does this mean for the products we make?

The book's concluding chapter, along with its epilogue, documents an ever-evolving connection between beer and society through contemporary trends shifting the world of beer today. We draw attention to the intersection between large-scale movements for social and economic justice and the world of beer. These movements have brought fresh voices into the fold that are helping the industry reckon with the systemic exclusion faced by members of oppressed groups based on race, gender, and sexual orientation. While recent efforts to push for social inclusivity in the industry have resulted in promises for real change, other efforts, such as better employment conditions and unionization in brewery workplaces, have struggled to achieve sustained momentum.

Our book ends with an epilogue grappling with the widespread disruption that the COVID-19 pandemic has caused in the beer world. During 2020 and much of 2021, government-mandated closures of many taprooms and brewpubs—followed by a cautious return to in-person business—created unprecedented challenges for the beer industry. As the crisis continues to reshape the way beer is sold, produced, and consumed, we highlight some of the resourceful ways small breweries have adjusted their operations to not only keep their businesses afloat but also lend support to other local organizations in their communities.

Your first drink should be nearly finished now, so let us take stock. A rich world of beer exists from grain to glass and beyond. This book will help you gain a deeper appreciation for its many intertwined dimensions. We began by asking you to think about your favorite beverage; we provided some of the social history that stands behind these suds. Yet as individuals, how are our emotions and cognitive decision-making processes reflected in what we drink? What can be learned about our identities, values, and interpersonal relationships? These are the questions we turn towar in the next two chapters.

Let's begin our next round.

NOTES

1. For more on how we interpret the social world through binary gender "frames" that are socially constructed, see: Ridgeway, Cecilia L. 2011. *Framed by Gender: How Gender Inequality Persists in the Modern World.* Oxford: Oxford University Press.

2. The idea of a "world" of interrelated people and activities comes from Becker, Howard S. 2008. *Art worlds: updated and expanded.* Berkeley, CA: University of California Press. We also draw on the concept of a "field," which links together actors, structures, practices, and meanings within a given field, such as beer was popularized by Pierre Bourdieu. See Bourdieu, Pierre. 1993. *The Field of Cultural Production.* New York: Columbia University Press.

3. Borer, Michael Ian. 2019. *Vegas brews: Craft beer and the birth of a local scene.* New York: New York University Press. Borer conceptualizes this blend of consumers and producers of craft beer as a "scene."

4. Chapman and Brunsma refer to this founding story as the "hero narrative" of U.S. craft beer. Chapman, Nathaniel, and David Brunsma. 2020. *Beer and racism.* Bristol: Bristol University Press. See also Acitelli, Tom. 2013. *The audacity of hops: The history of America's craft beer revolution.* Chicago: Chicago Review Press; Hindy, Steve. 2014. *The craft beer revolution: How a band of microbrewers is transforming the world's favorite drink.* New York: Palgrave MacMillan.

5. Throughout this book, we have tried to use inclusive terminology to describe social statuses and identities such as gender, race, and sexuality. These statuses always exist intersectionally: we each have a gender identity just as we do a racial identity, sexual identity, and so forth. However, because these statuses are not always fully described in existing research nor are readily disclosed by all individuals we talked with while researching this book, we have chosen to describe people in this in ways that highlight the status(es) that are most relevant to our particular analysis.

6. Reas, Emilie T., Gail A. Laughlin, Donna Kritz-Silverstein, Elizabeth Barrett-Connor, and Linda K. McEvoy. 2016. "Moderate, regular alcohol consumption is associated with higher cognitive function in older community-dwelling adults." *Journal of Prevention of Alzheimer's Disease, 3*(2): 105–113.

7. Goffman, Erving. 1967. *Interaction Ritual: Essays on Face-to-Face Behavior.* New York: Pantheon Books.

8. Borer 2019, p. 12; Koontz, Amanda and Nathaniel Chapman. 2019. "About us: Authenticating identity claims in the craft beer industry." *Journal of Popular Culture, 52*(2): 351–372.

Elliot, C. S. 2018. "Consuming craft: The intersection of production and consumption in North Carolina craft beer markets." University of North Carolina at Chapel Hill. Dissertation.

9. For beer industry professionals, our evidence-based insights can also serve as a resource for expanding one's breadth of knowledge about the industry and how it relates to larger social groups and structures in society.

10. In order to preserve the confidentiality of our interviewees, we refer to specific people and breweries using pseudonyms throughout this book unless (1) we were given explicit permission to use their names; or (2) the quote or other data comes from secondary sources.

11. Craft Beer & Brewing. "The history of beer." Accessed 2/8/21: (https://beerandbrewing.com/dictionary/UqfrcsPoAI/).

12. Sewell, Steven L. 2014. "The spatial diffusion of beer from its Sumerian origins to today." Pp. 23–29 in *The Geography of Beer*, edited by Mark Patterson and Nancy Hoalst-Pullen. New York: Springer.

13. Bennett, Judith. 1996. *Ale, Beer, and Brewsters in England.* Oxford, UK: Oxford University Press.

14. Bennett 1996.

15. Ogle, Maureen. 2007. *Ambitious brew: The story of American beer.* San Diego: Harcourt.

16. Craft Beer & Brewing. "Ale Wives." Accessed 2/8/21: (https://beerandbrewing.com/dictionary/C1O0mFMSGP/).

17. Beer was not the only kind of liquor offered at these establishments: whisky was in fact the most popular alcoholic beverage in the United States up until the late 1800s.

18. Powers, Madelon. 1999. *Faces Along the Bar: Lore and Order in the Workingman's Saloon, 1870-1920*. Chicago: University of Chicago Press.

19. Acitelli 2013; Ogle 2007.

20. As Ogle (2007) notes, near-beer was initially popular in the early years of Prohibition but sales had flatlined by the end of the 1920s.

21. Stack, Martin H. "A concise history of America's brewing industry." *EH.net*. Accessed 7/1/21 (https://eh.net/encyclopedia/a-concise-history-of-americas-brewing -industry/).

22. Carroll, Glenn and Anand Swaminathan. 2000. "Why the microbrewery movement? Organizational dynamics of resource partitioning in the U.S. brewing industry." *American Journal of Sociology, 106*(3): 715–762; Elzinga, K. G., Tremblay, C. H., and Tremblay, V. J. 2015. "Craft beer in the United States: History, numbers, and geography." *Journal of Wine Economics*, *10*(3): 242.

23. Legislation passed to repeal Prohibition policies occurred both at the federal and the state levels. The last states to legalize homebrewing were Alabama and Mississippi, in 2013.

24. Becker, Howard S. 1953. "Becoming a marihuana user." *American Journal of Sociology, 59*(3): 235–242; Benzecry, Claudio E. 2009. "Becoming a fan: On the seductions of opera." *Qualitative Sociology, 32*(2): 131–151.

Chapter 1

Beer Psychology Is Totally a Thing

"What is your favorite beer?" As a psychologist and a beer sommelier, this is one of the most frequent questions I get asked. My answer is always the same: "one that pairs with the given moment." Instead of treating beer as the sole protagonist, I prefer to shed light on the intersection of beer and psychology, where the intricate flavors, aromas, and textures of beer meet the power of the human brain to shape our understanding of the world around us. My favorite part of beer always has been more than beer itself. From its power to evoke emotions and memory to its integral role in our social lives, beer reveals who we are—and how who we are can change based on our interaction with beer.—Asa

As social creatures, we enjoy talking about our common interests. "What is your favorite ___?" is one of the simplest ways to get to know others and begin the process of transforming ourselves from strangers into acquaintances. Mutual self-disclosure, or the back-and-forth sharing of personal information with one another, brings people together and elevates their sense of belonging.[1]

But to go deeper into the psychology behind this question and why it matters, we must go back to 1994, when Paul Rozin at the University of Pennsylvania and Rozin's then PhD student Willa Michener answered the question, "what satisfies our craving for chocolate?" Not chocolate itself, it turns out. Rozin and Michener found that it was not the physiological content of the chocolate but our sensory experience that satisfies our chocolate cravings.[2] For the first time, a psychological study demonstrated that we perceive chocolate as something more than what makes up the chocolate itself. In the years following this experiment, research has explored the role that psychological forces play in our perception, understanding, and experience of a wide variety of foods and beverages. For example, experimental psychologist Charles Spence noted the following about wine drinking:

> [t]he perception of wine itself and the wine-tasting experience more generally have been shown to be influenced by everything from the weight of the wine bottle through to the sound made by its closure and the glass from which it is drunk, to the wine's visual appearance and the multisensory environment/atmosphere in which it happens to be consumed.[3]

Our perception of wine, like our perception of chocolate (or, as we will show, beer), is more than the sum of its parts. The ideas, memories, and emotions we associate with objects or activities play a crucial role in how we experience them.

Whether selecting, tasting, or evaluating beer, psychology aids our understanding of the "why?" and "how?" of our personalized experiences. This is what we refer to as beer psychology.[4] To be sure, the respective definitions of beer and psychology are quite straightforward: beer is a fermented alcoholic beverage brewed with water, malts, hops, and yeast; psychology is the scientific study of mental processes (thinking) and behaviors (doing). Beer psychology marries the two, giving us a framework for making sense of our relationship with beer through a psychological lens. A fundamental premise of beer psychology is that a complex interplay among biological, intrapersonal, interpersonal, and environmental forces influences our perception and ultimately contributes to our personal experience with beer. Beer psychology also acknowledges that while genetic and hereditary factors make up the hardwiring of our relationship to beer, environmental and social factors impact key dimensions of this relationship. All of these factors come together in unique ways that do not always reach the level of our conscious awareness. This is why the fine-grained details of our experiences often feel unique to our personal circumstances. Let us examine how this works.

THE PSYCHOLOGY OF BEER SELECTION

Our experience with beer begins long before we take our first sip. It is the result of many decisions we've already made, both conscious and unconscious. To drink beer, we must first select one specific beer. Before that, we must choose to drink beer among a variety of alcoholic beverages. Even before that, we must choose to consume alcohol in the first place. While it may seem as simple as reaching for what's in our fridge at the moment, beer selection is not just about the single observable action of grabbing a specific beer or the qualities of the beer itself. It is about a series of decisions strung together and, from a psychological standpoint, all these decisions revolve around a single frame of reference: you.

The Subjectivity of Our Reality

In a way, all of us live in our own reality, even when we share our moments with others. We transform the objective conditions of our surroundings into our subjective reality of perception through our identities, values, attitudes, and experiences.[5] As a result, we interpret the same space of objective reality differently from each other. Asa's experience traveling with their partner Mark illustrates this point:

> *My partner and I stopped by an unassuming bottle shop at the corner of a small strip mall in Nebraska during a road trip. It looked like any other bottle shop that I've been to before, but this one turned me into a kid in a candy store with their amazing selection of imported bottles of beer I that hadn't seen outside of Europe. I couldn't help but point and gawk at all the bottles I'd take home with me and how I'd enjoy them. "It would be a gastronomical vacation without having to travel!" I exclaimed. I began planning a series of beer-paired dinner nights and putting together invitation lists right on my mobile phone. "That's what beer friends do, right?" I turned to my partner, assuming he would be as excited as I was. What I didn't expect to encounter was his signature "oh boy" smile and "calm down" gesture. He's as much of a beer lover as I am, so I was surprised to see him not filling a shopping cart himself.*
>
> *"How about picking just 5 or 6 of them that you really like?" he said. "They're not exactly cheap, and we've got pretty limited space in the car. We need to think about how to get them home safely, too, remember? We don't have a cooler with us, so we don't want to ruin them. Besides," he continued. "I think you want to leave some beer for other people to discover and enjoy too, don't you?"*

The theory of planned behavior helps us understand why people behave the way they do—including times when they behave differently.[6] According to this theory, our behavioral intentions are influenced by three factors: attitudes toward behavior, subjective norms concerning the behavior, and perceived behavioral control. Our beliefs about the positive or negative outcomes of our behavior influence our attitude toward that behavior. That day at the bottle shop, Asa was singularly focused on their belief that buying beers would lead to their joy. Their partner Mark was focused on a very different set of concerns, which included the price of the beers, transportation of the purchased bottles, and how this might impact other potential buyers. Asa and their partner's respective beliefs about what buying beer from the bottle shop would mean (their "planned behavior") ultimately led them to perceive the act of buying beer very differently.

Our actions are similarly influenced by subjective norms, or what we believe others will think or do. In the story above, Asa anticipated that their friends would do the same as them and buy interesting beers to share. This encouraged them to buy beers liberally. On the other hand, their partner believed that other people would be considerate of others who might want to access those beers. Because of this, he advocated limiting the number of bottles they purchased. Lastly, our beliefs about our control over external factors influence our behaviors. Getting beers safely home was not Asa's primary concern that day in the bottle shop, but it certainly was their partner's. According to the theory of planned behavior, we only engage in the target behavior when our perceived control is strong enough.[7]

In short, each of us interprets the objective reality around us based on different cues based on who we are, what we value, and how we learn to interpret our environment. This leads to our own subjective reality of a given situation which is then validated or challenged by others around us. This has profound implications that go beyond how we experience beer because our subjective realities differ based on our social position in society as a function of our race, gender, sexual orientation, class, and other statuses (we explore these themes in more detail in the next chapter). The beer in front of us may have the same objective characteristics, but the way we interpret that beer speaks to who we are as well as how our subjectivities are patterned by our social environments.

Paradox of Overchoice

Contrary to popular opinion, having more options is not always better when it comes to making choices. During her TED talk titled "The Art of Choosing," Sheena S. Iyengar explains:

> Americans tend to believe that they've reached some sort of pinnacle in the way they practice choice. They think that choice, as seen through the American lens best fulfills an innate and universal desire for choice in all humans. [. . .] For modern Americans who are exposed to more options and more ads associated with options than anyone else in the world, choice is just as much about who they are as it is about what the product is. Combine this with the assumption that more choices are always better, and you have a group of people for whom every little difference matters and so every choice matters.[8]

Research shows that having an abundance of options can impair our smooth mental processing leading up to a given decision. This is known as *overchoice*. When there is an overwhelming number of options, sorting through all this information is cognitively demanding. Our brains want relief from this strain. This can cause us to opt out of the controlled information processing altogether by leaning on automatic information processing or falling back on what is familiar and easy.

Our attention is a cognitively limited resource; we are not capable of processing all the available options without losing our focus. This is why our choices are also influenced by the presentation of available options, including how these options are sorted and categorized for us by others. Many businesses attempt to address overchoice (whether they understand this concept or not) by guiding our selective attention while minimizing other possible options. The benefits of doing so for the business are obvious, but it can also help ease the process of decision-making for the consumer, too. Research suggests that our limited cognitive capacity can process only four categories of similar items or chunks.[9] Actively grouping, or chunking, can reduce our cognitive demand by reducing hundreds of individual options into a handful of categories. At a brewery, for example, this could be "light & fresh," "hop forward," "Belgian & sour," and "malt forward" (see Figure 1.1). The store may sell hundreds of different beers, if not thousands, but we are able to process this information relatively efficiently because of cues the store provides for us. Other ways businesses help consumers manage overchoice is by posting product quality scores, having specials, and providing product samples on premise to orient our attention to specific items for sale.[10]

Such cues can ease the problem of overchoice by doing some of the filtering process for us. They nudge us to select specific beers over other possible options. This process is, of course, double-edged: it can contribute to a shift in our mindset from a cautious and conservative consumer to a more impulsive and indulgent one.[11] While we may enjoy a less stressful decision-making experience when making a purchase, we are also vulnerable to overspending. Or simply making decisions that do not reflect the careful processing of information on our own terms. Our selective attention makes certain options more vivid; it can intensify our emotions surrounding those options.[12] Yet because of our limited cognitive capacity, we are frequently overwhelmed by too many options, leaving us searching for other available cues to guide our choices.

Personal Values and Internal Dilemmas

Research shows that many of us value products and experiences we believe to be "authentic" and made with integrity.[13] We base our decision-making on products that signal authenticity in part because of what these products say about us and what we stand for.[14] However, our perception of authenticity

TAPLIST

<u>Light & Fresh</u>   Hop Forward   Belgian & Sour   Malt Forward   Guest Cider   Wine

Light & Fresh

The Most Interesting Lager In The World	$5	**Stay Goalden**	$6
Brewed With Saaz Hops, Vienna And Pilsner Malts, And A Hint Of Flaked Corn.		This refreshing Golden Ale is an homage to New Mexico United and the Somos Unidos Foundation.	
*Mexican Lager	5.0%	15 IBUs*		1.00 of each pint goes to the Somos Unidos Foundation.	
		*Golden Ale	5.0%	20 IBUs*	
Perle Haggard	$5		
Sweet Malt, Straw, Honey, Floral, Earthy, With A Noble Hoppy Crisp Finish.		**There's No I In Steam**	$6
*German Pilsner	5.1%	32 IBUs*		Bready malt flavor balanced with a clean hop bitterness. Hella quaffable hybrid lager/ale	
2020 GABF Gold Medal Winner!		*California Common	5.8%	40 IBUs*	

Figure 1.1   A Tap List at Ex Novo Brewing Co. in Corrales, New Mexico, Exemplifies How a Beer Menu Can Ease Overchoice by Grouping Beers into Descriptive Categories. *Source*: www.exnovobrew.com.

is highly malleable and subject to external influence (such as the branding efforts of companies, as we discuss in chapter 4). For one, we tend to associate the authenticity of a product with its overall quality. Research shows that people perceive the "naturalness" of handmade products as a sign of their quality and are willing to pay more for these products.[15] This has a complex interplay with our own psychology. When we select beers that we consider authentic, we are more likely to rate our experience with that beer higher.[16]

The desire to choose authentic beers can conflict with our desire to stand out from the crowd. Research shows that how we see ourselves in relation to a group setting influences our beer choices. We may order a different beer from others in the group in order to present ourselves as suitably unique.[17] Melissa Dahl, deputy editor of the magazine *The Cut*, humorously writes about our desire to signal uniqueness:

> You know that thing where you're out to drinks with friends, and you'd very much like an IPA—but then the first person to order chooses an IPA, and you feel like you can't order the same thing, because that would be weird? So you order an amber ale instead. The drinks arrive, and you unhappily sip the second-choice beer you already regret ordering.[18]

As individuals and as group members, we desire to strike a balance between being too much like everyone else and being too different. Psychologists refer to this give and take as optimal distinctiveness, which captures our simultaneous and opposing need for inclusion and differentiation.[19] If selecting the same beer signals that we have something in common, choosing different beer signals that we are distinct from others in the group in a way that highlights our own individuality. This, too, has its limits: we want to select things that make us subtly stand out but not so far as to lead others to think we don't belong as members of that group.

THE PSYCHOLOGY OF BEER TASTING

Thus far, we have illustrated how psychology can help us make sense of the many decisions and cognitive processes that go into getting beer in front of us. It only gets more interesting from here. In what follows, we explore the world of neurogastronomy using a psychological lens. We do so by following a standard beer tasting format: starting with vision and then moving to olfaction, taste, and auditory influence.

The Power of Visual Influence

For many of us, our initial experiences with a given beer are heavily influenced by visual information.[20] We tend to experience what we expect to experience based on what we see. We process information that confirms our existing beliefs about that beer, object, person, or just about anything else for that matter. Imagine a glass of dark brown–colored beer. What aromas do you expect from this beer? Nuttiness, perhaps? Maybe notes of caramel and toffee? As soon as we conjure a mental image of this beer, our brains begin to imagine its aromas, flavors, and even mouthfeel based on our prior experiences. If we believe a dark brown beer to have notes of nuts, caramel, and toffee, we tend to pick up those notes. In psychology, this phenomenon is called *confirmation bias*. We tend to look for information that supports our preexisting beliefs by actively seeking and processing information that supports those beliefs. We tend to disregard information that contradicts those beliefs. Similarly, visual cues like beer color also impart a psychological effect known as *priming*. Priming occurs when our perceptions of beer color influence the flavors we expect to taste. As functionally useful as priming can be for our brain's ability to integrate new information, priming can lead us to be surprised when things turn out not to fit our expectations. This is why beer styles like Golden Stout (light golden-hued beer with deep cocoa and coffee flavors) and black IPA (dark-colored beer with impactful hop flavors) betray our expectations and play with our senses. By perceiving a beer's color, we interpret the sensory information via bottom-up processing based on a combination of sensory input and our prior knowledge, experiences, and beliefs. In the case of the aforementioned beer styles, we are forced to adjust our mental bank of what a golden-hued or black-hued beer can taste like in light of new information.

Visual cues are thus an extremely important component of how most people taste beer. In one study, researchers prepared two samples of the same beer with different artificial coloring, yielding one pale beer and one dark beer. Based on color alone, participants indicated that they expected the dark beer to be more bitter, have a higher alcohol content, be fuller bodied, and be more expensive than the pale one.[21] Our association of dark beer and bitterness yields powerful preconceptions that in turn influence our expectations about a beer's flavor (though not necessarily our *experience* of that flavor, as one recent study found).[22] By contrast, pale-colored beer can produce a very different set of associations, which correspondingly shape our experience of beer with that coloration.

The shape of the glass we drink out of also influences our perception of its contents. A tall slim glass can show off the brilliant pale gold of a Pilsner along with its effervescence; a snifter glass (with a wide bottom and smaller opening) can concentrate the aromas of beer, especially pungent beers such as dry-hopped double IPAs and imperial coffee stouts. To be sure, this is not the only reason beer is served in characteristic glassware around the world, which also has to do with culture, tradition, and even the regional availability of certain materials. Psychologically speaking, however, the shape of glassware affects our individual engagement with beer itself in both conscious and unconscious ways. For example, one study showed that participants drank a lager from a straight glass 60% slower than from a curved glass, while another study indicated that people perceived a beer as more intense and fruitier served in a glass with curved sides than in a glass with straight sides.[23] Another study revealed that curvature of the glass increased the perception of intensity and fruitiness in beer.[24] Whether we pay active attention to the glassware we taste beer in or not, the visual differences in beer that they create directly influence our experience with that beer.

The Expressiveness of Olfaction

Our ability to smell has long been the least valued and appreciated of the human senses.[25] This is partly due to the myth that our sense of smell is underdeveloped compared to other animals and that smell, in the words of one researcher, "operates in opposition to a disembodied rationality that makes humans civilized and distinct from other mammals." In other words, our ability to smell does not portray us as more civilized than any other species in the animal kingdom.[26] Further, many introductory psychology textbooks barely go into detail about our human senses beyond the visual and auditory systems, which only reinforces the existing hierarchy of senses.

Let us correct the record. Our sense of smell is so expressive that it influences many aspects of our lives in ways that do not reach our conscious awareness. For example, scientific evidence suggests that we communicate nonverbally through our body odor and that certain emotions like fear and disgust can be contagious.[27] This function of smell may aid our survival by triggering a reflexive fight-or-flight response in the face of danger. Some research also suggests that we may be able to smell others' genetic information through their body odor, and we are more likely to be attracted to those with different immune systems over those with similar immune systems.[28] Our sense of smell may even modulate our perception of physical pain: in one study, the sweet odors of banana were found to lower the unpleasantness of physical pain.[29]

Unlike any other sense, our olfaction possesses the power to evoke emotions and trigger biographical memories. When we sniff a glass of beer, its aromas, in the form of odorant molecules, travel through the nasal cavity into the olfactory system. Received signals are sent to the olfactory cortex and then distributed to two different avenues. The first pathway is to the frontal cortex, where our perception is consciously processed. The other is to the limbic system, including the amygdala and hippocampus, which processes emotions and memories. Because humans are capable of identifying about ten thousand different aromas based on forty million distinct olfactory receptor neurons, it is the smell that makes our experience with beer highly evocative.

Many of us have had the experience of perceiving a familiar aroma that you can't quite put your finger on. This gap between "I know what that aroma is" and "I don't know the word for that aroma" happens because much of our experiences are processed implicitly (unconsciously), while our expressions are made explicitly (consciously). The former guides our experience with given sensory stimuli without always reaching the level of our explicit knowledge. For example, Asa's childhood experience growing up near the coast in Japan profoundly influenced their perceptions of aroma:

> *Growing up by the coast, I'm quite familiar with the scent of the ocean. I couldn't articulate what it smells like to me, but I knew it was more than "salty" like many simply describe it. I've been away from the beach I grow up with for years, but I have such an emotional connection to that scent. My partner and I once ended up at this beautiful restaurant called Lokal in Praha, Czech Republic. I ordered my first glass of Pilsner Urquell with the Mlíko pour ("a glass full of wet foam with just a bit of beer at the bottom").[30] Just with the first sniff, my childhood memories came rushing back to me and wrapped me with the sense of utter ease like "I'm home." At first, I didn't know what was*

happening—nothing does that except the scent of the ocean, which was nowhere
in sight. I brushed this feeling off at that time, but Pilsner Urquell has reminded
me of home ever since. It wasn't until much later that I learned the science
behind this connection: the sulfur coming out the ocean is DMS [Dimethyl
Sulfide], which is also commonly found in some Pilsners.[31] *The power of beer to*
evoke our memory and emotions never ceases to amaze me.

Whether with smell or other senses, research has shown us that our intu-
itions often have meaning, especially when we have prior experience or
expertise related to the subject.[32] In some ways, our intuition is closely tied to
our implicit knowledge that links smell, emotion, and memory. For Asa, this
manifested in their immediate sense of familiarity with a certain beer, which
evoked memories of living by the ocean. This is also why beer professionals such as Bill Simpson, who is the executive director of Cara Technology
Limited (a leading manufacturer of beer flavor standards), teach their trainees
that we should listen to our inner voice when learning to evaluate beer flavor.
Because about 80% of what we consider flavors comes from our sense of
smell, our beer experience can be both evocative and emotional—even if we
cannot always put words to these experiences.

The Relativity of Taste

When we taste beer, we are using our taste receptors located on the tongue
as well as the esophagus, cheek, and epiglottis to gather information about
the beer. Taste, in conjunction with aroma, results in the flavor we perceive
in that liquid. Taste perceptions vary widely among individuals, which contribute to the variability in eating and drinking preferences among different
people.

The variability in taste between people has also led to "human vs.
machine" debates about how breweries should assess the flavor in their
beer, known as beer flavor analysis. Many breweries use sensory panels to
conduct evaluations of their beer. However, the subjective nature of human
sensory perception means that some brewers prefer to use lab-based chemical
analyses of their beer. Research is inconclusive on which is more effective
for breweries.[33] Human sensory panels are widely considered to be an accessible and effective tool for beer analysis in many professional beer settings.
Many of those trained to gather and interpret these data, such as Liz Pratt, an
Amsterdam-based sensory analyst, are aware of the differences between the
objective parameters of a beer and the subjective perceptions of it:

We can absolutely send a sample through GC (Gas Chromatography) and find
out exactly what compounds are in each beer, but that doesn't tell us what those

compounds do to our sensory organs in concert with each other, and therefore, doesn't tell us about the experience of the beer. We can demonstrate this with two cans of crushed tomatoes. Add salt to one and then compare the taste with the other. My workshop participants often perceive the tomatoes without salt to be fresher and more sour, but GC cannot detect this change in taste perception.[34]

When the ultimate goal of the sensory panel is to control beer quality to ensure optimal beer experience for consumers, human sensory analysis can play a crucial role for commercial breweries. However, we don't have to be a sensory analyst to experience the distinction between the objective characteristics of beer and the subjective qualities of beer, either. Find two different styles of beer with the same International Bitterness Units (IBU), and compare their bitterness. Even with the same quantitative bitterness of 40 IBU, we would perceive the bitterness of a German Pils and an Oatmeal Stout differently because we experience the beer as a whole and not a sum of its parts. Our perceptions of taste change depending on the interaction of flavor compounds with our human palates. While technologies can aid our understanding of beer, humans process information beyond mere mechanical inputs and outputs.

Auditory Influences on Expectations

Sounds may not be the first sense many people think of when they think of how they experience beer. But sound can provide us with valuable information about the attributes of the beer we are about to drink. Cues of sound—pops, crackles, hisses—build our expectations about what flavors we are likely to experience. As psychologists Charles Spence and Qian Janice Wang put it, "the sounds of beverage opening and pouring, even the sound of the carbonated beverage sitting in a drinking vessel, provide information concerning the physical properties of a drink."[35] Researchers have also discovered a number of other ways that the sound of beer influences our perceptions of a beer's quality (as well as other attributes). For instance, a recent study titled "Searching for the Sound of Premium Beer" found that people associate the sound of a bottled beer being opened with higher beer quality when compared to the sound of a canned beer being opened, and that the louder a sound a beer makes when opened the higher its perceived quality.[36]

Our emotional associations with sounds can also shape our beer tasting experiences. That is, sounds occurring around us when we drink beer can be just as influential as those resulting from it. For example, one study showed that music with positive emotion was not only associated with an increased perception of sweetness in beer but also an increased perception of value. On the other hand, music with negative emotion was associated with enhanced bitterness and an increased perception of alcohol content.[37] The volume of music being played while we drink works in similar ways. One study suggests that loud music can disrupt our sensory system by impairing our ability to detect sweetness and sourness.[38] While music does not shape the beer itself, the rhythms and textures of sound shape our perception of beer and therefore how we interact with it.

BEER AS A SHARED EXPERIENCE

Many of us enjoy eating food or drinking beer in social settings, where the featured food or drink becomes the centerpiece for our interactions with others. Taking part in this social experience can also alter our very relationship with that food or drink itself. For example, one study showed that participants rated a piece of chocolate more highly when they tasted it with another person than when they tasted it alone. In a subsequent study, participants rated an unpleasantly bitter chocolate less likable when they tasted it with another person. These studies show us that sharing an experience with someone amplifies how we perceive that experience, whether positive or negative.[39]

Shared social experiences also influence our behavior. We tend to choose what we eat or drink based on the choices that others make. We tend to eat and drink more when in the company of friends and family. This illustrates what psychologists call *social modeling*, shaping our behavior to match that of others. We are particularly likely to engage in social modeling when we want to affiliate with others or perceive ourselves to be similar to them.[40] In this sense, who we are influences our food and drink choices, and in turn, we signal who we are through these choices. Our choices also have an implicitly gendered dimension, as well as racialized and classed dimensions (we explore this in greater detail in the next chapter). What we drink situates us in relation to those around us as well as larger social stereotypes. As sociologist Megan Nanney explains,

> When we think about beer, we typically think of masculinity. [. . .] Women are 15 times more likely to be suggested a beer that is attributed to femininity, so sours or fruits, rather than being recommended a dark roasty beer or something that's considered a real beer.[41]

To break such gender stereotypes, some women signal their identity by intentionally selecting beers that are considered masculine. As we drink beer socially, our individual choices always take on new meaning within interpersonal contexts.

The Dark Side of Beer

As a social lubricant, beer can enhance our shared experiences with others by curbing our social anxiety and lowering inhibition. The Japanese tradition of *bōnenkai*—an end-of-the-year gathering to forget the troubles of the passing year and look forward to the coming one—involves alcohol consumption precisely for this reason. Yet the shared consumption of alcohol can also have potentially dangerous consequences, for the group dynamics of drinking socially can lead to drinking more than we would otherwise, and behaving in ways that we wouldn't ordinarily.

Beer is a psychoactive drug that alters our mental processes and behavior. Its potentially negative impact on our physiology, cognition, and behavior can be illustrated through alcohol myopia theory. Alcohol myopia limits our information processing capacity and leads to an attention deficit. This can manifest as impaired cognitive functioning and impaired motor skills, which in turn can increase the likelihood that people engage in short-sighted, impulsive, and potentially risky behaviors, such as drinking and driving or unsafe sex.[42] Alcohol's role in limiting cognitive functioning, lowering information processing capacity, and creating attention deficits also mean we focus on certain information more than others. This is one of the reasons why drinking alcohol can make us more likely to respond to provocative cues in a hostile situation, sometimes escalating into violence.[43]

Alcohol is not an essential ingredient for beer to act as a psychoactive drug because we perceive beer as something more than what makes up the beer itself. Research shows that we feel and act inebriated when we believe we consumed alcohol because of the placebo effect.[44] Because of this, non-alcoholic beer can influence our mental processes and behaviors similar to alcoholic beer if we *believe* we have consumed alcohol. Beer, like other alcoholic beverages, does not necessarily cause harm on its own. It is in how we interact with it individually and collectively that can lead to dangerous outcomes—just as it can also facilitate positive forms of social engagement. Both are ever-present dimensions of our relationship with beer. Whether alcoholic or not, responsible drinking calls for mindful examinations of the interaction between alcohol and us.

When we started this chapter we asked about your favorite beer. Your answer speaks directly to how beer and psychology are connected. When we tell others about the beer we're drinking, we often assume a shared understanding of what this experience means, including what it feels like and tastes like. This chapter challenges that assumption. Our individual relationships with beer are constantly in flux, shaped and reshaped by the world around us. Social contexts color this relationship, directing our attention and spurring on specific behaviors.

Psychology can be our guide as we make sense of these experiences. More specific to our purposes, *beer psychology* provides us with a mental toolkit that allows us to deepen our relationship with beer while also enriching our understanding of the way we process information as social beings.

To be sure, there are objective measures that we can use to categorize and quantify beer. These measures include the Standard Reference Method (SRM) and the European Brewery Convention (EBC) for colors, alcohol by volume (ABV) for strength, IBU for bitterness, gravity as an indication of apparent attenuation, and even precise chemical compounds measured by a GC. However, we do not experience beer based on these measures alone. Instead, we translate each of these dimensions of beer through our own subjective filters.

Everything from our personal backgrounds to social norms to environmental stimuli influences how we interact with beer. Tasting beer evokes our memories, perceptions, and emotions just as it activates our neurological switchboard of human senses. This heady mixture is more complex than any one chemical compound in beer or physical response to the drinking of it. As beer psychologists, this is something we should embrace instead of trying to diminish. Becoming a more informed beer drinker means recognizing our fallibility as objective tasters and instead appreciating our tasting experience as a manifestation of who we are, who we are with, and what is around us. Regardless of brand or style, the best beers always pair with the given moment.

Having unpacked our psychological experiences with beer, we can now venture into the social meaning of beer and beer drinking. As we shall see in the next chapter, the social implications of drinking beer go much deeper than the liquid itself. The act of consuming beer evokes distinct kinds of social identities and groups that in turn map us onto the social world and its existing hierarchies in very different ways.

NOTES

1. Collins, Nancy L., and Lynn Carol Miller. 1994. "Self-disclosure and liking: A meta-analytic review." *Psychological bulletin, 116*(3): 457–475.

2. Michener, Willa, and Paul Rozin. 1994. "Pharmacological versus sensory factors in the satiation of chocolate craving." *Physiology & Behavior, 56*(3): 419–422.

3. Spence, Charles. 2020. "Wine psychology: Basic & applied." *Cognitive Research: Principles and Implications, 5*: 1–18.

4. We draw inspiration from Spence (2020) who coined the term "wine psychology."

5. Rivaroli, Sergio, Jörg Lindenmeier, and Roberta Spadoni. 2019. "Attitudes and motivations toward craft beer consumption: An explanatory study in two different countries." *Journal of Food Products Marketing*, *25*(3): 276–294.

6. Ajzen, Icek. 2020. "The theory of planned behavior: Frequently asked questions." *Human Behavior and Emerging Technologies*, *2*(4): 314–324.

7. Ajzen 2020.

8. Iyengar, Sheena S. 2010. "The art of choosing [Video]." TED Conferences. Accessed 7/1/21 (https://www.ted.com/talks/sheena_iyengar_the_art_of_choosing).

9. Cowan, Nelson. 2001. "The magical number 4 in short-term memory: A reconsideration of mental storage capacity." *Behavioral and Brain Sciences*, *24*(1): 87–114.

10. Malone, Trey, and Jason L. Lusk. 2019. "Mitigating choice overload: An experiment in the US beer market." *Journal of Wine Economics*, *14*(1): 48–70.

11. Betancur, Maria I., Kosuke Motoki, Charles Spence, and Carlos Velasco. 2020. "Factors influencing the choice of beer: A review." *Food Research International*, *137*: 109367.

12. Mrkva, Kellen, Jairo Ramos, and Leaf Van Boven. 2020. "Attention influences emotion, judgment, and decision making to explain mental simulation." *Psychology of Consciousness: Theory, Research, and Practice*, *7*(4): 404.

13. Hicks, Joshua A., Rebecca J. Schlegel, and George E. Newman. 2019. "Introduction to the special issue: Authenticity: Novel insights into a valued, yet elusive, concept." *Review of General Psychology*, *23*(1): 3–7.

14. Beverland, Mike B., and Farrelly, F. J. 2010. "The quest for authenticity in consumption: Consumers' purposive choice of authentic cues to shape experienced outcomes." *Journal of Consumer Research*, *36*(5): 838–856. We return to this idea in the next chapter in more depth.

15. Cinelli, Melissa D., and Robin A. LeBoeuf. 2020. "Keeping it real: How perceived brand authenticity affects product perceptions." *Journal of Consumer Psychology*, *30*(1): 40–59. For more information on authenticity and branding, see Fritz, Kristene, Verena Schoenmueller, and Manfred Bruhn. 2017. "Authenticity in branding – Exploring antecedents and consequences of brand authenticity." *European Journal of Marketing*, *51*(2): 324–348. doi:10.1108/EJM-10-2014-0633; Frizzo, Francielle, Helison B. A. Dias, Nayara P. Duarte, Gabriela Rodrigues, and Paulo H. M. Prado. 2020. "The genuine handmade: How the production method influences consumers' behavioral intentions through naturalness and authenticity." *Journal of Food Products Marketing, 26*(4): 279–296.

16. Domínguez-Quintero, Ana M., M. Rosario González-Rodríguez, and Jose L. Roldán. 2019. "The role of authenticity, experience quality, emotions, and satisfaction in a cultural heritage destination." *Journal of Heritage Tourism, 14*(5–6): 491–505.

17. Ariely, Dan, and Jonathan Levav. 2000. "Sequential choice in group settings: Taking the road less traveled and less enjoyed." *Journal of Consumer Research*, *27*(3): 279–290.

18. Dahl, Melissa. "The annoying psychology of how your friends influence the beer you order." *The Cut.* Accessed 2/1/21 (https://www.thecut.com/2016/09/the -annoying-way-your-friends-influence-the-beer-you-order.html). "https://www.the- cut.com/2016/09/the-annoying-way-your-friends-influence-the-beer-you-order.html" https://www.thecut.com/2016/09/the-annoying-way-your-friends-influence-the-beer -you-order.html.

19. Leonardelli, Geoffrey J., Cynthia L. Pickett, and Marilynn B. Brewer. 2010. "Optimal distinctiveness theory: A framework for social identity, social cognition, and intergroup relations." In *Advances in experimental social psychology* (Vol. 43, pp. 63–113). Academic Press.

20. Research shows that sight is the sense most valued by people, followed by hearing, touch, taste, and smell. See: Enoch, Jamie, Leanne McDonald, Lee Jones, Pete R. Jones, and David P. Crabb. 2019. "Evaluating whether sight is the most val- ued sense." *JAMA Ophthalmology, 137*(11): 1317–1320.

21. Reinoso-Carvalho, Felipe, Silvana Dakduk, Johan Wagemans, and Charles Spence. 2019. "Dark vs. light drinks: The influence of visual appearance on the con- sumer's experience of beer." *Food quality and Preference*, 74: 21–29.

22. Van Doorn, George, Justin Timora, Shaun Watson, Chris Moore, and Charles Spence. 2019. "The visual appearance of beer: A review concerning visually- determined expectations and their consequences for perception." *Food Research International*, 126: 108661.

23. According to researchers, the exact reason for the increase in drinking volume from a straight glass is not entirely clear. Researchers speculate that it may have to do with our differential ability to moderate our drinking speed given differently shaped glassware. See Attwood, Angela S., Nicholas E. Scott-Samuel, George Stothart, and Marcus R. Munafò. 2012. "Glass shape influences consumption rate for alcoholic beverages." *PLoS One, 7*(8): e43007.

Mirabito, Adrian, Marcus Oliphant, George Van Doorn, Shaun Watson, and Charles Spence. 2017. "Glass shape influences the flavour of beer." *Food Quality and Preference, 62*: 257–261.

24. Mirabito et al. 2017.

25. Enoch et al. 2019.

26. McGann, John P. 2017. "Poor human olfaction is a 19th-century myth." *Science, 356*: 6338.

27. De Groot, Jasper H., Monique Smeets, Annemarie Kaldewaij, Maarten J. Duijndam, and Gun R. Semin. 2012. "Chemosignals communicate human emotions." *Psychological Science, 23*(11): 1417–1424.

28. Wedekind, Claus, Thomas Seebeck, Florence Bettens, and Alexander J. Paepke. 1995. "MHC-dependent mate preferences in humans." *Proceedings of the Royal Society of London Series B: Biological Sciences, 260*(1359): 245–249.

29. Riello, Marianna, Maria Paola Cecchini, Alice Zanini, Miguel Di Chiappari, Michele Tinazzi, and Mirta Fiorio. 2019. "Perception of phasic pain is modulated by smell and taste." *European Journal of Pain, 23*(10): 1790–1800.

30. https://www.pilsnerurquell.com.

31. We credit Linsay Barr, the co-founder of DraughtLab, for this insight. See DraughtLab Instagram Post https://www.instagram.com/p/CDwr6AqpApB/?utm _source=ig_web_copy_link.

32. Remmers, Carina, Sascha Topolinski, and Johannes Michalak. 2015. "Mindful (l) intuition: Does mindfulness influence the access to intuitive processes?" *The Journal of Positive Psychology, 10*(3): 282–292.

33. For instance, comparing sensory evaluation and chemical evaluation methods, one study concluded, "Sensory analysis could be replaced with chemical/statistical analysis on an appropriate data set and for a distinct beer brand." See Ocvirk, Miha, Natasa K. Mlinarič, and Iztok J. Košir. 2018. "Comparison of sensory and chemical evaluation of lager beer aroma by gas chromatography and gas chromatography/mass spectrometry." *Journal of the Science of Food and Agriculture, 98*(10): 3627–3635.

34. Throughout this book, we refer to people we interviewed using a mixture of real names and pseudonyms based on their expressed preference along with other considerations of confidentiality. People referred to using a first and last name, such as Liz Pratt, are real names. Those referred to by first name only are pseudonyms.

35. Spence, Charles, and Wang, Qian Janice. 2015. "Sensory expectations elicited by the sounds of opening the packaging and pouring a beverage." *Flavour, 4*(1): 1–11.

36. Almiron, Paula, Francisco Barbosa Escobar, Abhishek Pathak, Charles Spence, and Carlos Velasco. 2021. "Searching for the sound of premium beer." *Food Quality and Preference, 88*: 104088.

37. Reinoso-Carvalho et al. 2019.

38. Spence, Charles. 2014. "Noise and its impact on the perception of food and drink." *Flavour, 3*(1): 1–17.

39. It's noteworthy that researchers controlled for the mere presence of others and reported that another person engaging in a different activity did not elicit the same effect of amplification, even if that person was in the same physical proximity. See Boothby, Erica J., Margaret S. Clark, and John A. Bargh. 2014. "Shared experiences are amplified." *Psychological Science, 25*(12): 2209–2216.

40. Cruwys, Tegan, Kirsten E. Bevelander, and Roel C.J. Hermans. 2015. "Social modeling of eating: A review of when and why social influence affects food intake and choice." *Appetite, 86*: 3–18.

41. American Sociological Association (2018, December 21). Bottling Gender. [Video]. YouTube. https://www.youtube.com/watch?v=xmTa-AABS2M.

42. For more information on effects of alcohol, see Petzel, Zachary W., and Jeffrey G. Noel. 2020. "Don't drink and drive, it's a prime: Cognitive effects of priming alcohol-congruent and incongruent goals among heavy versus light drinkers." *Journal of Health Psychology.* DOI: 1359105320934166; Field, Matt, Reinout W. Wiers, Paul Christiansen, Mark T. Fillmore, and Joris C. Verster. 2010. "Acute alcohol effects on inhibitory control and implicit cognition: Implications for loss of control over drinking." *Alcoholism: Clinical and Experimental Research, 34*(8): 1346–1352; Scott-ldon, Lori A., Kate B. Carey, Karlene Cunningham, Blair T. Johnson, Michael P. Carey, and MASH Research Team. 2016. "Alcohol use predicts sexual decision-making: A systematic review and meta-analysis of the experimental literature." *AIDS and Behavior, 20*(1): 19–39.

43. Giancola, Peter R., Robert A. Josephs, Dominic Parrott, and Aaron A. Duke. 2010. "Alcohol myopia revisited: Clarifying aggression and other acts of disinhibition through a distorted lens." *Perspectives on Psychological Science*, 5: 265–278.

44. Bodnár, Vivien, Krisztina Nagy, Adam Cziboly, and Gyorgy Bárdos. 2021. "Alcohol and placebo: The role of expectations and social influence." *International Journal of Mental Health and Addiction, 19*: 2292–2305.

Chapter 2

Who Drinks Beer—and Why

The first time I walked into the Denver Convention Center in 2009, I was shocked. It was during the annual gathering of beer lovers and industry professionals known as the Great American Beer Festival (GABF). Inside a vast room, rows upon rows of brewery booths were pouring beers I had never heard of before—despite the fact that I was a self-professed beer geek and a newly minted employee of a small brewery in Orange County, California at the time. Behind each booth were people wearing festival badges around their necks indicating that they were head brewers, brewery owners, and taproom managers from all around the country. As the festival attendees poured in, they filled the space with a jumble of motion, sharp laughs and hoops, and a sea of colorful pretzel necklaces of all shapes and sizes.

It was then that I noticed another striking pattern amongst those on both sides of the brewery booths. Nearly everyone at the festival seemed to be a White man between the ages of 25 and 50, sporting a bushy beard, jeans, and a brewery t-shirt or hoodie. I turned to the man standing next to me to mention my observation.

"Oh, you mean the uniform of craft beer?" He said. "Yeah. It's definitely a thing."—Eli

Who drinks *what* beer, and why? Beer may be the world's oldest and most popular alcoholic beverage, but the way that people have interacted with this beverage varies with time and place. Our *consumption* of beer, just like the consumption of food or coffee or wine, goes beyond the material substance itself to involve group norms, moral values, and social identities. These aspects of beer tell us about the person engaged in the act of beer drinking. They also give us insights into the social context where drinking takes place.

In the previous chapter, we looked at our relationship to beer in deeply personal terms. We examined how we perceive beer in ways not always conscious to us, and stemming from both our neurological makeup and surrounding environment. We now move further out into the social world to understand beer drinking as a fundamentally interpersonal activity laced with social implications. In its basic form, drinking beer is an activity that can bring us together. To drink socially functions as a collective ritual guided by group norms of behavior. This is what Eli's experienced at GABF, not only through the shared drinking of beer but the many other social norms of this festival, such as the wearing of pretzel necklaces and cheering after the sound of a taster cup clanking onto the hard cement floor.

At the same time, when we talk about *consuming* beer rather than just drinking it, we are drawing attention to beer's social and cultural properties that reflect distinct group norms, values, identities, and hierarchies. We experience the act of drinking beer on a personal basis, but many other aspects of beer consumption, such as our preferences in beer and how these preferences are interpreted by others, are *socially constructed* within a larger societal context. It is these dimensions of drinking beer that serve not only to bring us together but also to reinforce social differences and shore up existing group hierarchies. As this chapter helps us understand, the way we consume beer reflects who we are and where we stand within the existing social structure.

DRINKING BEER (INTER)PERSONALLY

We learn about beer and what to associate with the drinking of it from those around us. This means that our experiences, especially our early and formative ones, are a product of our immediate social environments.

Imagine someone is trying beer for the first time but is doing so under two very different hypothetical scenarios. In the first scenario, that person's friends and family members are actively engaged in trying new beers, learning more about them, and seeing how they stack up against other beers. They wax nostalgic about trips to *Oktoberfest* in Munich, Germany, and tour the Guinness brewery in Dublin, Ireland. Now consider another scenario. Imagine that few of that person's family and close friends do not drink beer at all. Some of them believe that beer tastes bad and isn't worth drinking, while others believe that drinking alcohol should be avoided for reasons of health, safety, religion, or finances (or a blend of multiple reasons). To practice behaviors they view more positively, they choose to enjoy other beverages with dinner.

The point is not to judge one scenario as objectively "better" than the other but rather to recognize how these two social contexts will shape that person's relationship to drinking beer in different ways. We can imagine that in the first scenario, the experience of drinking beer is one that person comes to look forward to; the act of sampling new beers garners positive reinforcement within their social network. Over time, they may learn to appreciate the difference between an American Pale Ale and an English Bitter, and sharing this knowledge with their friends. In other words, this person would be engaging in a process of learning how to *become* a beer drinker, and a certain type of one at that.[1] By contrast, in the second scenario, drinking beer is likely to remain something foreign and possibly even stigmatized owing to the same influences of family and peers we described above. As a result, that person may develop preferences that don't involve beer—let alone understanding the differences between types of beers.

These examples represent two extremes—we suspect that most people fall somewhere in the middle. But they illustrate a general principle that helps explain social patterns about who develops a taste for beer and also why people relate to beer very differently. Put simply, how we consume cultural objects such as beer is shaped by our *socialization* or the influence of people and social contexts around us on our attitudes, behaviors, and values. These socialization experiences are not randomly distributed in the population at large but in fact closely related to our social location with respect to gender, race, class, and more. People from different social backgrounds have unequal experiences in society as a function of how their (multiple) statuses are institutionalized. As a result, these experiences filter into our personal tastes and preferences—including our preferences for beer.

Let us consider how socialization works with respect to gender and beer drinking. In many societies, beer drinking continues to be coded as men's activity. Men are more likely to be visually represented in beer advertisements on TV or in movies drinking beer. They are also more likely to be treated as knowledgeable consumers of beer when they order a beer at a commercial establishment.[2] In many of those same beer advertisements, women are absent, positioned on the periphery, or highly sexualized. Too often, the names of beers themselves also reflect the sexist treatment of women (such as Flying Dog's "Raging Bitch" or Midnight Sun's "Panty Peeler") and the implied masculinity of both beer drinkers and beer makers. For these reasons, many women are dissuaded from expressing a personal preference for beer because they are conditioned to see beer drinking as unfeminine. They may feel less comfortable in public spaces of beer drinking that are occupied predominantly by men.[3] Women who do drink beer in these settings are often perceived by their peers who are men as the "cool girl," or greeted with expressions of surprise ("I didn't know you like bitter beers!"). Both reinforce the fact that women and their preferences for beer are not the default within these spaces. Nor are individuals who identify as gender nonbinary. This is because of the institutionalized ways in which gender is treated as a dyad (man or woman) in our society, as sociologist Cecilia Ridgeway notes.[4] Many beer drinking places are no exception, from gender-exclusive bathrooms to gender-exclusive social groups reinforcing gender binarism. These deeply gendered expressions of beer in our society end up influencing how each of us internalizes and expresses our own preferences—and makes sense of the preferences of others.

As with gender, class background and racial identity also pattern the way we consume beer. People from socioeconomically privileged backgrounds are more likely to be exposed to imported and craft beers than people from less privileged backgrounds, just as the former are also more likely to be exposed to other more expensive, luxury products such as fine wines and *Filet Mignon*. The wealthy aren't just more able to afford higher-end beers—which come with a higher price tag—they also patronize the kinds of establishments that have them on offer.

As sociologists Nathaniel Chapman and David Brunsma note, Black and Brown communities are far more likely than their White counterparts to see malt liquor and cheap beer brands being advertised in their neighborhoods and sold in nearby stores.[5] In these areas, it can be harder to locate these products based on assumptions by retailers and distributors that craft beers won't sell there. Further, for many people of Color, particularly those who are working class, the blend of price and cultural Whiteness surrounding craft beer acts as a power deterrent to drinking craft beer. What these examples show us is that persistent social inequalities in our society manifest in the world of beer as *gendered, classed, and racialized* patterns of consumption. We internalize preferences for beer based on who, and what, we've been exposed to.

Consuming Social Identity

As social psychologist Henri Tajfel famously described, our *social identity* is our sense of who we are as a function of our membership within existing social groups. We make assumptions about who other people are based on the cues available to us about the social categories they belong to. This includes a person's appearance as well as the things that person does, wears, says, and—yes—drinks. In this sense, the way we embody a given social identity is only partially under our own control because it incorporates how other people "read" us based in part on our preferences. People often make associations about others based on their preferred brand of beer. In this sense, we consume not just beer when we drink it but also distinct social identities. A humor article on *The Tab*, which attempted to characterize people's personalities and lifestyles by their choice in "trashy" beers, provides a tongue-in-cheek example of this process. About people who prefer Budweiser, the article states:

> Look, if Budweiser is your favorite beer, there's absolutely nothing wrong with that. In fact, if it is, you're probably quite literally the most average person in the world—and there's nothing wrong with that. But then again, there's nothing right with that either.[6]

Alternately, about Heineken drinkers: "You're in a co-ed business frat, your parents paid for you to travel round Europe last summer and you'll tell anyone who listens about that time you went to the Heineken experience in Amsterdam. Just drink a domestic beer, asshole." There are clearly all kinds of problems with the assumptions presented above. However, they do illustrate our very real tendency to infer group-based identities (and judgments) about one another based on something as simple as that person's beer preference.

In the dynamic process of establishing social identities, we come to perceive certain traits as those of in-group members ("us") and other traits as those of out-group members ("them"). This is how associations of race, class, gender, and sexuality can get wrapped into social identities. Back in 2009, most White, cisgendered, heterosexual men attending GABF might not have noticed that nearly everyone else at the festival looked, acted, and sounded similar to themselves. As members of the dominant social group at the festival, it would have been easy to miss the fact that part of the "groupness" of this crowd was premised on shared social characteristics just as much as a love of good beer.

Throughout the past few decades, the social identity of craft beer drinkers has been associated with Whiteness, masculinity, and middle classness (the "uniform" of craft beer, as Eli was told). This is due to the overwhelming presence of White men brewing and drinking the stuff.[7] In this context, women, BIPOC, and LGBTQIA+ people are less commonly perceived as "real" craft beer drinkers by members of the majority group (fewer beer geeks or experts). Instead, members of these nondominant groups stare down sexist, racist, and anti-LGBTQIA+ stereotypes—what Patricia Hill Collins calls *controlling images*—of their respective relationships with beer. Controlling images draw attention to the way people's gendered and racialized assumptions about others constrain the roles and identities that a person is able to inhabit. For example, sociologist Helana Darwin describes that women who drink craft beer are often trapped between two gendered identity narratives: they are seen as either the girlfriends or wives of "real" beer enthusiasts (men), or they are sexualized as "the cool chicks" who enjoy drinking strong, bitter, and "manly" beers.[8] Both uphold hegemonic views linking beer consumption to men and masculinity. While these rigidly gendered associations of beer drinking are beginning to loosen today in some senses (we return to this in later chapters), BIPOC, women, trans people, and gender nonbinary people who enter breweries or spaces of beer consumption are still less likely to be identified as part of the in-group as their White men peers.

In an attempt to navigate the overwhelming masculinity of craft beer, some women who drink craft beer today choose to assert identities as *beer lovers* who are *women*. By presenting themselves as knowledgeable and experienced beer drinkers, these women signal their gender identity through craft beer. Doing so has allowed at least some of these women to garner respect and acceptance among other craft beer drinkers.[9] Several organizations now support beer enthusiasts who have experienced othering and exclusion in craft beer spaces. For example, Girls Pint Out is a national nonprofit craft beer organization for women who drink beer. The organization, which now has 100 chapters in 40 U.S. states, provides a space for women to connect with other women through their educational, charitable, and social events.[10] Dani Fracassa, head of the Detroit chapter, explains, "[Girls Pint Out] exists to encourage women to be involved in the craft beer community and industry, come together and enjoy this thing that is here for us and to make us feel connected."[11]

A growing number of craft beer events aim to bring people who don't traditionally drink craft beer into the fold. This has required disrupting cultural assumptions that craft beer is for White men only and associated exclusively with White cultural expressions. Fresh Fest, for example, is a beer festival held annually in Pittsburgh, Pennsylvania, since 2018 that is explicitly geared toward increasing diversity and representation in the craft beer industry. As the nation's first festival celebrating Black-owned breweries, festival organizers seek to bring these breweries together with Hip Hop acts and other artists from the Black community. What these efforts have in common is a recognition that, for members of underprivileged groups, the barriers to identifying with craft beer go beyond money or exposure. These collective efforts seek to transform the gendered and racialized associations of craft beer—making the social identity of craft beer drinkers more inclusive of a wider range of people in the process.

WHO'S GOT GOOD TASTE IN BEER?

To further understand why people drink the beer they drink, we need to unpack the idea of taste. By taste, we do not mean our brain's gustatory perception of bitterness, saltiness, sweetness, sourness, umami (savory), and fat.

We mean the kind of taste that is a product of our social world, taste that is *socially constructed* rather than physiologically constituted. We evoke this distinction when we describe someone's taste in beer as "good" or "bad," sophisticated or otherwise. Taste captures how our consumption preferences stem from and embody a hierarchical system of cultural value. Put simply, not all taste preferences are created equal in our society.[12]

Having "good tastes" and other forms of elite cultural knowledge is what French sociologist and anthropologist Pierre Bourdieu calls *cultural capital*. According to Bourdieu, one acquires cultural capital through exposure to class-exclusive environments, such as by attending private schools or semi-annual events at an elite country club. It is within these elite spaces where "high-brow" forms of cultural knowledge are circulated and fine-tuned. It is also where these forms of cultural knowledge are given value. Those who possess cultural capital can exchange it for other kinds of advantages, such as access to economic resources or network ties to exclusive social circles. Having "good tastes" that others view as sophisticated is an expression of cultural capital, a signal that you fit in with an elite crowd.

Ironically, cultural capital is easiest to illustrate by making a traditional comparison between preferences for wine versus beer. For more than a century, fine wine has been associated with "high-brow" Euro-American tastes, something that elites sipped on in fancy glassware, paired with expensive dinners, and discussed using a particular rubric of value (e.g., vintage, region of origin, winemaking family). This image surrounding wine continues today, which is why most Michelin-starred restaurants around the world offer hundreds of bottles of wine on their wine menu and make sure to feature on their menu prestigious Napa Cabernet Sauvignons and Burgundy Pinot Noirs that command three- or four-digit price tags. Drinking high-value wines is more than a question of having enough money to buy them. It is a symbol of one's "cultured" tastes on display for others to see. By comparison, beer is a cheaper and more widely available beverage, one that has been historically associated with commoners and the working class. Within conventionally elite circles, such as what we've just described, to opt for a beer instead of a name-brand Napa Cabernet goes beyond the price tag. It says something about that person, their social location, and their cultural capital (or lack thereof).

Beer is, of course, far more differentiated in price and prestige today than the example above depicts. This means that one's preference for *certain* kinds of beers over others tells us about that person's cultural knowledge and their social background. Do you prefer to drink local craft beer or macro beer? Do you look forward to the release of a Wild Ale aged for twelve months in a Bourbon barrel or do you opt for a beer available at every grocery store? If you drink a light lager, is it made by a local brewery?

While none of these taste preferences are inherently right or wrong, they do come with distinct kinds of associations that vary depending on who is doing the observing. All of us have preferences for beer that we feel are deeply personal. But as we have been discussing, these preferences also get read by others and evaluated in ways that signal our place within the social hierarchy.

Understanding taste is about understanding how we internalize a system of value and the external consequences of those values. We learn from others to associate some beers as higher quality than other beers. One such distinction among beer drinkers is between those who prefer craft beer and those who prefer macro beers (i.e., products made by Big Beer). People on either side see this as a meaningful divide, a sign of group lines that represents divergent worldviews. To macro beer drinkers, craft beer drinkers may be perceived as effete and overly fussy. Yet to many craft beer drinkers, consuming "craft" products speaks to core beliefs about the value of handmade goods produced ethically over mass-produced products.[13] As Elizabeth Currid-Halkett notes, for members of today's "aspirational class" (characterized by a high level of cultural knowledge), buying craft beers produced in value-driven ways mirrors a preference for similarly produced items such as Third Wave coffee, organic skin care, and natural toothpaste.[14] While the objects of value themselves may vary, it is one's appreciation for their specialized production process or esoteric qualities that makes them desirable to elites.[15] This also marks a subtle change in what it looks like to have "good taste" today. Rather than being a snob who only drinks fine wine (the beer equivalent might be expensive, corked bottles of Belgian beer), today's "high-brow" consumers showcase their refined tastes by being "omnivorous": able to appreciate a wide variety of products.

Let's elaborate on the connection between taste in beer and cultural value in a different way. Consumers now have the option to buy a pale lager made by Big Beer (Coors Light) or one made by a local brewery (La Cumbre Brewing Company's "BEER"). Opting for the local option might yield a minor difference in flavor due to freshness and more expensive ingredients; it would also be more expensive. But the real difference between purchasing these two pale lager products can't be tasted in the liquid. It is about what buying each of these products says about us to others. In beer drinking, as in many other aspects of life, our preferences for certain goods and activities locate us within a larger social world composed of distinctly classed, as well as racialized and gendered, social groups. We interpret the choices and actions of others in light of these same factors. Taking note solely of the flavor of the beer we drink is like focusing our attention only on the stone flung in the middle of a pond: the ripple effects—larger and longer lasting—represent the social implications of one's tastes in beer.

BEER SCENES AND PLACE-MAKING

Thus far, in order to focus on *what* we drink we have set aside the basic fact that beer drinking always takes *place*—in a physical setting such as a bar, brewery, area of a city, sporting game, festival, or simply at home. Place matters for beer consumption in two primary ways. First, drinking beer brings people together in a literal sense, often in close proximity to one another engaged in a joint activity. In the process of coming together, we share in a social ritual dictated by the rules and norms of that place; we participate in something greater than ourselves (as sociologist Emile Durkheim would say). Second, consuming beer together can be a powerful form of *place-making* in itself. This process of place-making through the collective act of drinking transforms a physical space such as a bar, brewery, or entire city into what sociologist Michael Ian Borer calls a beer "scene," which he describes as "a collection of diverse people, places, and things devoted to or at least connected to a similar aesthetic disposition."[16] Beer scenes often have a particular character; they enchant the places where they occur with meaning.[17] Many famous destinations associated with beer drinking have their own distinct beer scenes that people both consume and coproduce through their participation.

Take *Oktoberfest*, in Munich, Germany, which occurs every year in late September. During this festival, roughly six million people from all over the world descend on the city to drink the gold- and amber-hued beers traditionally brewed in Munich. Tourists come to participate in festivities that spill onto the streets at all hours of the day; in doing so, they come to consume a version of German national identity itself.[18] *Oktoberfest* was originally founded as a public celebration of the marriage between King Ludwig I to Princess Therese of Saxe-Hildburghausen on October 12, 1810. The festival featured music and sporting events to go along with food and drink, steadily growing into a well-known annual celebration. Today, *Oktoberfest* is a social institution onto itself involving numerous rituals such as the beer barrel tapping, the costume and riflemen parade, and, of course, copious amounts of drinking from *Maß* (pronounced "mas," describing the amount of beer in a regulation mug, which is one-liter in modern times. It's also short for Maßkrug, a handled glass vessel seen in *Oktoberfest*), and, less commonly, ceramic *steins*, which are beer mugs made of stoneware. Munich may be many other things to many people, but it has become known globally among beer drinkers as the home of *Oktoberfest*, which stands as one of the world's cherished annual events.

Though it doesn't have quite the lengthy history as *Oktoberfest*, the Great American Beer Festival (GABF) has also grown into a distinct beer scene that brings together people who enjoy craft beer around the world.[19] The festival, originally founded by Charlie Papazian in 1982 in Boulder Colorado (it has since moved to Denver), is now the largest ticketed beer festival in the United States according to its organizers.[20] GABF is a celebration of all things craft beer. It includes a beer competition, educational panels, and a three-day event that most recently featured over 800 breweries pouring 4,000 different beers. Like *Oktoberfest*, what occurs during the week of the festival goes well beyond the official festival events. Local bars and restaurants hold countless special beer tappings, beer pairing dinners, and meet-and-greets. During GABF, beer drinkers transform the Denver city limits into a lively beer scene and the beating heart of this country's craft beer culture (see Figure 2.1).

Place-centered beer scenes need not always occur on such a grand scale as *Oktoberfest* in Munich and GABF in Denver in order to have a unique character. Two such examples are special beer release days at breweries and, more recently, regional beer festivals celebrating BIPOC in craft beer culture. Both illustrate in different ways a place-making process inscribed with collective meaning, symbols, and norms. During beer release days, beer drinkers are able to purchase a special beer that is produced in limited quantity or highly coveted by beer enthusiasts. These events are temporary gatherings within a larger gathering space (a brewery). The most prominent beer releases are known nationally, such as Dark Lord Day at Three Floyds Brewery

Figure 2.1   A Group Shot of Crafted X EDU Grant Winners at the Great American Beer Festival in 2019. The Authors, Who Were Awarded That Year, Are Second and Third from the Left. *Source*: Courtesy of New Belgium Brewing.

in Munster, Indiana, or the release of the newest hazy IPA from Monkish Brewing in Los Angeles. Breweries add further structure around release events by incorporating musical acts, offering specially available foods as well as other forms of entertainment for customers. Despite not being advertised to a wide audience, these social events can draw thousands of people to the brewery—a transient collection of people in-the-know, temporarily formed and disbanded soon after. The organic nature of these gatherings contributes to their perceived authenticity by beer fans.[21] Moreover, for these individuals, what happens in line while waiting to purchase the special beer is just as important a social ritual as obtaining the special beer on offer. Some people bring coolers of rare beers to share with other beer fans. They trade beers, pour samples, and fraternize over beer—all in the nondescript environment of a parking lot or alongside the back of a warehouse. To attendees, it is a chance to demonstrate their identity as a beer "geek," exchange specialized knowledge about beer, and revel in the groupness of it all.

If the implicit aim of beer release events is about exclusivity, beer events and festivals put on by Black and Brown beer drinkers often has the opposite aim. These events strive to leverage beer's capacity to bring people together to build inclusivity, particularly for those from under-represented groups, such as women and people of Color. Events such as Fresh Fest, in Pittsburgh, and ColdXela, in East Los Angeles, have succeeded in broadening the reach of craft beer scenes beyond White men. For example, Fresh Fest, founded by Ed Bailey, Mike Potter, and Day Bracey and held in a predominantly Black neighborhood of Pittsburgh, advertises itself through the slogan "Brew Culture × Drinking Partners."[22] It has grown steadily during its three-year run, gaining national attention and attracting a highly diverse crowd. Similarly, ColdXela, a homebrew festival held in East Los Angeles and put on by the nation's first "all-Latino" homebrew club, SoCal Cerveceros, advertises itself as the "largest gathering of Latino brewers."[23] Like Fresh Fest, ColdXela highlights a range of cultural events (music, food, art) that deviate from the cultural Whiteness of craft beer. With their grassroots founding, these types of events provide a blueprint for how place-making through beer can involve multiple kinds of meanings and expressions rather than represent a privileged cultural monolith.

BEER DRINKING SUBCULTURES

As we have described thus far, our individual relationships with beer are shaped by local contexts as well as societal forces. Yet within the broader landscape of beer, the distinct groups that beer consumers participate in can also take on distinctive character. We call these groups *drinking subcultures*, where the term "subculture" refers to groups that maintain their own internal social order within a larger group or society. Beer drinking subcultures have shared norms, meanings, and identities among those who participate in them. They can also have an outsized social and cultural influence within the broader world of beer drinking. Below, we detail three such beer subcultures: online beer communities, homebrewing clubs, and beer influencers.

Online Beer Communities

Online beer sites such as Untappd, RateBeer, and BeerAdvocate are places where members can interact with each other by discussing beer news, constructing lists of "best" beers, or debating over-hyped breweries at all hours of the day. Many of the most popular online beer sites are simple to join and count tens of thousands of beer drinkers as members, sometimes much more. With some variation, online beer communities cater to those with a high level of interest in beer drinking and some desire to share these interests with others. Through joining online beer communities, user-members also gain knowledge of how to communicate with others about these topics in site-specific ways, such as through the use of beer rating scales and specialized forums.

Online beer communities play a powerful role in constructing the value of certain beers and breweries and communicating this value to others. This form of beer knowledge is generated "from below," in the sense that it is formulated and circulated by beer consumers rather than trained professionals. This gives members a new platform to have their opinions and reviews about beers heard by a wider audience. Todd Alstrom, cofounder of BeerAdvocate, explains that when he and brother Jason founded their online beer community, consumers didn't have much voice in the market:

> Jason and I acted as that voice until we introduced the ability for others to join the site, post beer reviews and talk in our forums. We were social media before social media. We essentially empowered visitors to learn, share and advocate beer by using the website as a platform.[24]

In other words, the beer ratings generated by online community members on sites like BeerAdvocate represent a democratized system of value distinct from that of professional beer critics. For example, it was user ratings on RateBeer that first ranked Westvleteren 12 (formerly called "abt," which stands for Abbot), a Trappist ale from Belgium, as the "best beer in the world." It is a title that is now widely circulated about this beer among aficionados both amateur and professional.[25]

Aside from reviewing and discussing beers, beer trading is also a prominent activity within online beer communities. While beer trading is not necessarily unique to online beer communities, sites like RateBeer and BeerAdvocate took beer trading to another level by establishing member areas where beer "wants" and "haves"—known by the acronyms ISO ("in search of") and FT ("for trade"), respectively—could be posted.[26] Beer trading requires extensive knowledge of a beer's value as well as the norms of this subculture. Like trading other collectable items, beer trading is generally understood as the process of sending one or more beers to someone else in exchange for other beers. The idea is that both parties involved gain access to beers that they could not otherwise have procured through conventional means, such as purchasing them at a store. Beer traders can go to elaborate lengths to secure the beers they covet, which can involve sending representatives to wait in line at beer releases in order to ensure they are able to purchase limited release beers.[27]

Beer trading represents one of the most involved subcultural activities within the beer world—and also the most controversial. For one, to successfully trade beer requires a degree of beer-focused cultural capital, an understanding of which beers have value on the secondary market and which trading partners are trustworthy. Beer trading also requires knowing how to navigate shipping beer safely through the mail (most mail carriers, including USPS will not knowingly ship alcohol). As a beer subculture, beer trading has also received considerable pushback from consumers and industry professionals alike. For example, avid beer traders and beer resellers (not necessarily the same thing) have been known to buy all the supply of a single beer, only to turn around and resale or trade those beers for many times their initial cost. Non-trading beer drinkers may in fact have no idea that the most coveted beers from breweries right in their backyard are being bought out by avid beer traders because of the value the latter have to gain in the process. Some online sites have pushed back. Facebook, for example, shut down several high-profile beer trading groups, whereas breweries like Floodland in Washington have attempted to prevent people from buying their beers with the intention to resell them.[28] This has driven some beer trading groups further underground with a more exclusive membership criteria process. In any case, online beer communities will likely continue to represent some of the most invested beer consumers.

Homebrewing Clubs

Homebrewing clubs are gathering places for people to talk brewing, share ideas about equipment and recipes, and taste the beers made by fellow members. Over 2,100 registered homebrewing clubs exist in the United States, according to their parent organization, the American Homebrewers

Association (AHA), which aims to promote a community of homebrewers. As with other kinds of social clubs, homebrewing clubs give people the opportunity to come together with those who share similar interests. According to sociologists Diane Rodgers and Ryan Taves, homebrewers—as well as small-scale craft brewers—are connected through an "epistemic culture" (a shared web of knowledge) that appreciates homebrewing as both an art and a science.[29] For example, Brian, a member of the Dukes of Ale, the oldest homebrewing club in New Mexico, explains why he enjoys homebrewing:

> I could just buy beer, but I'd rather make it myself. I want to have my name on it. A lot of the things in my brewhouse I've made myself, too: like, I cut a keg open and that was my boil pot. I got a freezer and put that little collar on the edge of it so I could drill holes and make my own tap set up.

Homebrewers such as Brian enjoy tinkering with equipment and creating "DIY" recipes. Attending a homebrewing club offers these individuals a social venue to stoke their interests. Through meetings of the Dukes of Ale, Brian says he has gained an immense amount of knowledge about the process of homebrewing beer; he also gets to try beers he would never have thought to brew personally, such as beers made with prickly pear or wild ales made with seasonal berries. Brian is also able to share his own brewing passion with others who also possess similar interest. "One of the best parts is that no matter how unusual the beer you make is, if you bring it to a meeting, there is bound to be someone there that will try it and be like, 'this is great, how'd you make it?'" says Brian.

For Scott Carpenter, the vice president of Dukes of Ale and a twelve-year homebrewing veteran, being a member of this club is less about improving the technical aspects of his beer and more about bringing people together through the joy of homebrewing. Every year, Scott spearheads a homebrewing demonstration at a public festival held in the courtyard of a local science museum. "It takes a ton of work to organize," says Scott, "But I still love it when people come up to the booth and tell me, I had no idea you could make beer at home."

Being a member of a homebrewing club, however, requires investments of resources and time. For this reason, members of most homebrewing clubs in the United States tend to skew middle class, male, and White. Ricky "Ray" Rivera, who is Mexican American, saw this as an opportunity. Ray describes an early conversation he had with the man (Agustin Ruelas) that would end up becoming his fellow cofounder of an "all-Latino" homebrewing club:

> I'm telling him [Agustin]: "Hey, have you gone and checked out some of the other homebrew clubs? I've been online, and been checking them out. I noticed that there's really not club for Latinos. Do you know anything about that?" And he goes, "Yeah, man. Homebrewing and brewing is just a bunch of White guys

with beers." . . . It was just very clear to me that I wasn't seeing anybody else that looked like me. So that's where the idea was sparked, and I told him, "Hey, man. How about we start our own club?" I was like, "I don't know anything about a homebrewing club, but if there's other people like us, and we all could use the help. Maybe there's more that would be into it." (see Figure 2.2).

SoCal Cerveceros struck a nerve. The club has now grown to over 200 members and has received national attention. Members frequently brew beers using nontraditional ingredients that they grew up with, such as *jamaica* (hibiscus) and *tamarindo* (tamarind). A new generation of homebrewers are forging their own niche within a beer subculture that has historically been coded in Whiteness and masculinity. Through these types of efforts to reimagine homebrewing clubs, members of underprivileged groups are infusing this drinking subculture with new norms, values, and material expressions.

Beer Influencers

Social "influencers" who focus on beer, otherwise known as beer influencers, are a relatively new phenomenon that directly corresponds to the dual rise of social media and craft beer over the last two decades. Unlike homebrewers or online beer community members, beer influencers do not represent a defined subculture but rather a network of individuals who are exceptionally well-connected to a large group of "followers" on social media sites like Instagram and YouTube. Their influence within their respective networks can resemble that of a celebrity endorsement: based on the content of their posts, beer

Figure 2.2 The SoCal Cerveceros Homebrewing Club at a Member Outing. *Source*: courtesy of SoCal Cerveceros Homebrewing Club.

influencers make followers aware of new breweries and beer releases as well as beer events and other aspects of beer culture. Beer influencers generate discussion among their community of followers and play the role in bringing that discussion to a wider audience.

While beer influencers are by definition trendsetters, their relationships with beer as seen from their social media posts can range considerably. Many toggle between trying to stand out (one beer influencer who goes by the handle @louiebaton posts pictures of much-hyped beers placed within Lego scenes that he custom builds) while simultaneously contributing meaningfully to current conversations about the world of beer (the lightning-rod of attention on the Instagram account @ratmagnet, the handle of Brienne Allen, about sexual abuse allegations within the industry). The way beer influencers and the content they post are received, however, remains contingent on audience ("followers"). This has caused some beer influencers who are women to claim that they face sexist standards about how their posts are received, especially among audience who remains disproportionately men. On an episode of the podcast *Good Beer Hunting*, Megan Stone, who goes by the handle @isbeeracarb on Instagram, argued that influencers who are men can make posts without their shirts on, or pouring beer on themselves, without generating controversy while women who post the occasional photo of themselves holding a beer by a pool get their popularity unfairly attributed to being a "tits and ass" account. This double standard also causes the rich content about beer that women influencers create to be dismissed or overlooked. "We just want the same voice," she says, "if you are going to say something about women, why wouldn't you say something about the men doing that?"

Because of their increasing prominence in an era dominated by social media feeds, beer influencers serve as a *cultural intermediary* between beer consumers and professional breweries. That is, their role bridges these groups, translating messages back and forth. Beer influencers have the unique ability to make a public post about a beer they are drinking and command the attention of a large number of other beer drinkers in the process. This is precisely why some have attracted the interest of breweries that seek new ways to grow their business by generating hype among consumers who feel more "natural" rather than contrived. For example, one influencer named Edgar, a Mexican American man who goes by the handle @beerthuglife, explains that he regularly receives free beer in the mail from breweries all over the country. The expectation, rarely stated explicitly, is that Edgar will make a post about that beer that will subsequently be viewed by thousands of his followers. Recently, several breweries have gone a step further by reaching out to him to express their interest in brewing collaboration beers with his name on it. He now has over a dozen such collaborations under his belt, and is in the process of starting his own brewing label. Beer influencers thus take the consumption of beer and elevate it into a consumable aesthetic for all of social media to see. In an age of viral videos, the attention these individuals draw transcends the bounded communities of homebrewers or even the exclusive online forums of beer traders to influence the cultural landscape of beer consumption more generally.

In 2020, during the coronavirus pandemic, organizers for GABF made the difficult decision to move the popular festival online. In a scaled back format, the "virtual GABF" was highly successful in many senses: it was well-organized, professionally run, and went off without a hitch. Festival ticket holders received a brewery "passport" that granted them discounts at local breweries in the weeks leading up to the main event as well as access to two days of virtual programming featuring panels with famous and up-and-coming craft beer personalities from around the country. These efforts made what would normally be an expensive trip to Denver for beer drinkers far more inclusive and accessible than it has ever been in the past. Having attended this virtual event, Eli recounts his experience:

> *I was impressed by how easy it was to log in, pay my $20 for a pass, and participate in the virtual festival—all from the comfort of my living room. The "Brewing for Change" panels, which highlighted exciting new diversity and inclusion efforts in craft beer, were particularly inspiring to watch. These panels had a surprisingly intimate in feel: I felt like I was right there in the virtual offices and living rooms of well-known beer professionals.*
>
> *That said, the festival experience wasn't the same as I remember back in 2009. I missed the noise, the clanking of cups, the roars of laughter. I missed seeing people wearing brewery shirts I'd never heard of then fighting crowds to track down that brewery and try their offerings. Despite all of its flaws, frustrations, and exclusions, what I missed was the deeply social experience of consuming beer in person, together.*

From our taste preferences to the ways we drink beer with others, our relationship to beer reflects the complicated social world we live in. As this chapter has illustrated, consuming beer is a deeply social experience, a practice given meaning and value in groups. Consuming beer socially has the ability to make places into dynamic, memorable beer scenes—either virtually or in person. Beer can be the reason we gather, what we gather over, and what helps us enjoy gathering in the first place.

There is no single reason why we drink beer. Nor there is a universally "right" way to drink it in any objective sense. Rather, consuming beer takes on the meanings, values, and significance of its social surroundings. This is why distinct patterns of beer drinking reflect social inequalities in our society: what we prefer to drink *signals* to others about our position within a social world that is racialized, gendered, and classed.

What goes on within social groups of beer drinkers also shapes the world of beer from the bottom up. From influencers to online traders to homebrewers, engaging with beer provides people with an occasion to interact with others and form distinct subcultures around doing so. In each instance, the arrow of influence does not merely bounce among consumers: it can point back up toward the beer industry itself, driving new trends in both beer and beer drinking culture. This is especially true when consumers organize into larger groups (such as RateBeer or Untappd). It is also true when they connect beer to broader social causes, such as racial and gender inclusivity (such Fresh Fest and ColdXela have).

Beer drinkers remain an integral component within the world of beer. But what about the people who make, sell, and distribute beer for a living? Behind the scenes in breweries, jobs in beer require vastly different skills and day-to-day labor experiences. They pay different wages and result in unequal opportunities for recognition. They also reflect racialized and gendered patterns of employment, as we shall see in the next chapter.

NOTES

1. Becker 1953; Benzecry 2009.
2. Chapman, Nanney, Lellock, and Mikles-Schluterman 2018.
3. Darwin, Helana. 2018. "Omnivorous masculinity: Gender capital and cultural legitimacy in craft beer culture." *Social Currents, 5*(3): 301–316; Ridzik, Agnieszkam and Victoria Ellis-Vowles. 2019. "'Don't Use "the Weak Word"': Women Brewers, Identities and Gendered Territories of Embodied Work." *Work, Employment, and Society, 33*(3): 483–499.
4. Ridgway 2011.
5. Chapman and Brunsma 2020.
6. White, Rob, Harry Shuckman, Josh Kaplan, and Amanda Ross. "A definitive list of trashy beers and what they say about you as a person." *The Tab.* Accessed 7/1/21 (https://thetab.com/us/2017/09/08/what-your-choice-pisswater -beer-71630).
7. Withers, Erik T. 2017. "Brewing boundaries of white/middle-class/male-ness: Reflections from within the craft beer industry." In N. G. Chapman, J. S. Lellock and C. D. Lippard (Eds.), *Untapped: Exploring the cultural dimensions of craft beer* (pp. 236–260). Morgantown: West Virigina University Press.
8. Darwin 2018. See also Chapman, Nanney, Lellock, and Mikles-Schluterman 2018.
9. Chapman, Nanney, Lellock, and Mikles-Schluterman 2018.

10. For more, see Girls Pint Out. Accessed 2/2/21 (http://www.girlspintout.org/about/).

11. Quoted in WWJ News. "Craft Beer Conversation: Girls Pint Out Brings Women Together Over Brews." *WWJ Newsradio.* Accessed 6/01/21: (https://www.audacy.com/wwjnewsradio/articles/craft-beer-conversation-girls-pint-out-detroit).

12. Bourdieu, Pierre. 1984. *Distinction: A social critique of the judgment of taste.* Cambridge, MA: Harvard University Press.

13. Campbell, Colin. 2005. "The Craft Consumer: Culture, Craft, and Consumption in a Postmodern Society." *Journal of Consumer Culture, 5*(1): 23–42; Du Gay, Paul. 1996. *Consumption and identity at work.* Thousand Oaks, CA: Sage.

14. Currid-Halkett, Elizabeth. 2017. *The sum of small things: A theory of the aspirational class.* Princeton, NJ: Princeton University Press.

15. Peterson, Richard, and Roger Kern. 1996. "Changing highbrow taste: From snob to omnivore." *American Sociological Review, 61*: 900–907.

16. Borer 2019: 24; Deener, Andrew, 2012. *Venice: A contested bohemia in Los Angeles.* University of Chicago Press. For more on scenes and place-making, see: Deener (2012).

17. Paulsen, Krista E., and Hayley E. Tuller. 2017. "Crafting place: Craft beer and authenticity in Jacksonville, Florida." In N. G. Chapman, J. S. Lellock, and C. D. Lippard (Eds.), *Untapped: Exploring the cultural dimensions of craft beer* (pp. 105–123). Morgantown: West Virigina University Press.

18. DeSoucey, M. 2010. "Gastronationalism: Food traditions and authenticity politics in the European Union." *American Sociological Review, 75*(3): 432–455. See also: O'Carroll, Cliona. 2005. "'Cold beer, warm hearts': Community, belonging and desire in Irish pubs in Berlin." In T. Wilson (Ed.), *Drinking cultures* (pp. 43–64). Oxford, UK: Berg.

19. Borer (2019) describes GABF as a "trans-local" scene in that it links together multiple local beer scenes.

20. Great American Beer Festival. "FAQ: Attendees." Accessed 7/1/21: (https://www.greatamericanbeerfestival.com/info/faq/).

21. For more on how authenticity and place come together in beer scenes, see Borer 2019; Paulsen and Tuller 2017; Wallace 2019.

22. See: https://freshfestbeerfest.com/.

23. See: https://www.socalcerveceros.org/coldchela.

24. Shikes, Jonathan. "Q&A: Todd Alstrom Talks About Beer Advocate's Influence and his Move to Denver." *Westword*, August 6, 2013. Accessed 7/1/21: (https://www.westword.com/restaurants/qanda-todd-alstrm-talks-about-beer-advocates-influence-and-his-move-to-denver-5736577).

25. To be sure, beer writer Michael Jackson is widely credited for popularizing the *Great Beers of Belgium*—the title of his 1995 book—and bringing interest in Trappist Ales to an American audience.

26. There are now numerous websites and online platforms where beer trading is conducted, including websites like Beerexchange as well as beer trading groups on platforms such as Reddit and Facebook.

27. Borer 2019.

28. Pershan, Caleb. "Inside the members-only world of online beer trading." Eater .com, May 4, 2020. Accessed 7/1/21 (https://www.eater.com/beer/2020/3/4/21157606 /rare-craft-beer-trading-america-facebook-private-groups-invite-only).

29. Rodgers, Diane M., and Ryan Taves. 2017. "The Epistemic Culture of Homebrewers and Microbrewers." *Sociological Spectrum, 37*(3): 127–148.

Chapter 3

The Social Organization of Beer

The Way Things Are Now

"You know what, I could get into this," Charlie told his wife as they were driving home to New Mexico from a road trip in Arizona. He was flipping through a book on homebrewing for the first time, having purchased it on a whim at a retail store where they had stopped to rest. "My wife nodded at me like, okay honey, that's great. Good for you—*eyeroll*."

"No, you don't understand," Charlie told her. "Like, I could really, *really* get into this." That was fifteen years ago. Charlie, a White man in his late twenties at the time, was bitten by the homebrewing bug. He became, in his words, obsessed with brewing beer and perfecting his homebrew recipes. Charlie began devouring every piece of literature he could find on the topic of homebrewing; his weekends were spent brewing beer and tinkering with his equipment. Within a year, Charlie was entering his beers in amateur competitions and winning medals for his recipes. "One day it dawned on me that I was spending almost all of my spare time brewing, sometimes as much as 20, 30 hours a week," Charlie says. At his wife's encouragement, the idea of leaving his teaching job to open a small brewery started to take shape in his mind. But first, Charlie knew he needed professional experience in what would be for him an entirely new career. Fortunately, he was able to secure an apprenticeship with the most decorated brewer in the state. After a couple of years, Charlie and his wife managed to save up enough to put the money down to launch their own small brewery, River Bend Brewery. The brewery has grown every year since, while Charlie has become one of the most respected brewers in the southwest. His beers have won numerous medals at major national beer competitions such as the Great American Beer Festival.

For the past five years, Ricky has worked at Charlie's brewery on the distribution team, where he loads kegs and cases of beer into trucks and delivers these products to different retail accounts around town. Prior to getting a job at River Bend Brewery, Ricky, who is a thirty-three-year-old Native American man with a wispy beard and soft brown eyes, was struggling to find a job. "No one wants to hire you if you don't have a degree these days," he said. Ricky worked part-time as a security guard for a while, followed by a stint as a cashier at Burger King. He began taking college classes at a local community college that offers free tuition for Native Americans, and eventually earned an associate degree in accounting. But after another spell of unemployment, Ricky said he was willing to take just about any job in order to see a steady paycheck. He saw an ad posted for a delivery driver at River Bend and figured he didn't have anything to lose. He got a callback. "I thought I bombed the interview at first," Ricky recalls, adding that when he didn't receive word in the next few days he thought his fears were confirmed. However, two weeks later, he got offered the job.

At that time, Ricky had tried "fancy" beer only a few times in his life. It was not something he grew up with, nor was it the alcoholic beverage of choice among his friends and family. For Ricky, working at the brewery was just another job—at least at first. Five years later, Ricky still works on the "distro" team at River Bend. "The younger guys at the brewery now? They call me 'distro dad,' cuz I'm a little older than them. I'm like their dad," Ricky chuckles. He is proud of the role he plays in helping to ensure that beer gets to consumers while it is fresh and the draft lines are clean. He also acknowledges that much of what he does in the craft beer industry goes unrecognized by the public, even by the beer geeks he sees in the taproom that know all the beertenders by name. He's fine with that. Most days of the week, Ricky hangs out at the corner table in the brewery taproom after he finishes his workday, enjoying his "shift beer" alongside other members of the distro team, which at one time included his cousin that he grew up with on the nearby tribal reservation.

Carmela, a Latina woman in her late twenties, works in the Albuquerque-based taproom of one of the largest breweries in New Mexico. Before getting her front-of-the-house job at the brewery, Carmela spent several years employed as a server at a Thai restaurant fielding orders of *Pad Thai*, Spring Rolls, and *Tom Yum* soup to a modest lunch crowd. The tips she made averaged about $30 a shift. Carmela would have preferred more, but her focus was on finishing her degree in Foreign Linguistics at a public university across the street from the restaurant. "One day, a friend of mine came in and told me that a brewery had just opened nearby and she was hired to be the manager there," Carmela said. "My friend kind of asked me, do you want a better job?" The prospect of making better tips was Carmela's primary motivator, though working with her friend, a woman about her same age, was a nice perk, too. "I didn't know a lot about craft beer then, or about beer in general," she said. Over the next three years, Carmela proved herself to be a hard worker who was popular with guests. She was promoted several times, first from barback to beertender, where her job was to interact directly with customers, and, later, from beertender to assistant manager of the taproom.

Carmela has gained a deep appreciation for what her brewery offers to both workers and customers. "Being exposed to so many new types of beer, that is how I really started learning more about different styles and flavors of beer," she says. Carmela is now fluent in beer talk. She can rattle off the IBUs (International Bittering Units) and the finishing gravity of her brewery's core beers from memory. But this is not what Carmela takes pride in as a brewery worker. Instead, she sees hospitality as the main focus of her job behind the bar. "I want to make sure this place is inviting to all people—*especially* women and minorities. We are getting there for sure," she says. Then, upon glancing around at the roomful of White men drinking in the taproom, Carmela adds, "although, there is still a way to go."

Working in the craft beer industry these days can mean many different things to many different people. Charlie, Ricky, and Carmela all work in craft beer in the same city, though the jobs they do as brewers, delivery drivers, and taproom beertenders, respectively, result in very different labor experiences. Some brewery jobs are highly visible to the public and relatively well-paying, such as Charlie's role as head brewer and owner of River Bend. Other jobs operate behind the scenes and during off-hours, garnering modest wages, such as Ricky's job in distribution. Other brewery jobs still are focused on customer service, such as Carmela's position in the taproom, where the majority of money she will take home each day comes from tips, not wages.

Job descriptions and pay are not the only things that separate the workers profiled above. The differences embodied by Charlie, Ricky, and Carmela reveal how the *division of labor* within the industry is patterned by social characteristics, notably those of race, gender, and class. Taking stock of what sociologists call the *social organization of labor* within the beer industry helps us understand the persistent connection between job opportunities and social inequality today. Why is it that men, especially White, college-educated men, occupy the majority of higher-profile brewing jobs? Or that women who work in this industry mostly fill customer service roles within breweries? Why do BIPOC, especially men, operate in invisible, behind-the-scenes roles—if they find employment in craft beer at all? We approach these questions by starting with a basic conceptual premise: *who* ends up working *what* job is not accidental or arbitrary. Rather, it is the product of a complex interplay of social, economic, and cultural forces embedded in workplace practices and resulting in divergent employment opportunities for workers. These dynamics are just as relevant in breweries as they are in white-collar workplaces, Silicon Valley start-up firms, or almost any other type of labor setting.[1]

THE DEMOGRAPHICS OF THE
U.S. CRAFT BEER INDUSTRY

Today the vast majority of U.S. breweries are not "diverse" places to work. Men, particularly White men, continue to make up the majority of all brewery workers, which now tops 500,000 domestically. According to recent statistics from the Brewers Association, 92% of all brewers are men, and men own or co-own nearly every brewery in the country; only 2% of all U.S. breweries are sole-owned by women.[2] By contrast, women who do work in beer are overconcentrated in customer service jobs, where they represent a slight numerical majority (54%) in jobs such as beertender and server in brewery taprooms and brewpubs.

Most people who work in breweries are White, regardless of position. Eighty-nine percent of brewers identify as White, while the percentage of Latinx, Asian, and Black workers in the industry are each in the single digits (with slight regional variation), far less than their respective proportions in the population at large. Additionally, most Black and Brown men employed in breweries work in distribution jobs or in "non-brewing roles" in the brew-house, where the labor is more physical than creative or customer-oriented.[3]

Why do we see disparities of race and gender and, more implicitly, class, among those employed in the U.S. beer industry? Put simply: why is craft beer dominated by "bearded White dudes?" To be sure, these trends are not new in the beer industry. Each of the now-famous breweries launched in the 1970s and early 1980s was founded by White men. The generation of brewers they helped train were mostly White men, who would then go on to launch the next wave of small breweries.[4] Compared to a few decades ago, it is also true that more women, BIPOC, and LGBTQIA+ people work in craft beer today than ever before. But this alone does not tell the full story. Women and BIPOC, for instance, tend to be concentrated in service jobs and distri-butions jobs, respectively, while White men occupy more prestigious and creative positions as brewers and owners. Sociologists of work refer to this as job segregation by race and gender, which has both vertical (higher- and lower-ranking jobs) and horizontal (equivalent rank but categorically differ-ent) components. But how does this kind of job segregation happen? While we focus primarily on understanding how "bearded White dudes" come to dominate jobs in the industry, we also attend to why women like Carmela tend to work customer service jobs and working-class men of color like Ricky find themselves in distribution jobs. We uncover the forces of persistent labor market inequality that remain alive and well in craft beer—just as they are in many other types of work settings today.

UNDERSTANDING SOCIAL INEQUALITY IN MODERN WORKPLACES

The reason why cishet White men have historically dominated the most desirable jobs in our society used to be simple enough: other groups of people were formally and deliberately excluded from accessing these jobs in the first place. Up until the 1960s, refusing to hire someone based on their race, gender, or sexual orientation was an entirely legal practice in the United States. These institutionalized forms of exclusionary practices kept members of oppressed groups from accessing desirable jobs held by White men while simultaneously reinforcing the former's association with subordinate jobs involving frontline service tasks or "unskilled" physical labor. Meanwhile, hiring managers incorporated race and gender-based screening processes in their hiring decisions—practices that drew directly from their racist and sexist beliefs. *Formal discriminatory practices* thus kept many American workplaces White, with men in positions of authority and women in subordinated and part-time roles.

Times are different now, though inequality remains. Rising public outcry over discrimination in the workplace led to the passing of a series of anti-discrimination laws, most notably the 1964 Civil Rights Act. These acts made it illegal for employers to use a worker's gender, age, national origin, religion, or disability to make hiring or promotion decisions.[5] Following the passage of these laws, today all job applicants are *supposed* to be given a fair shake at getting hired based on their formal skills and qualifications rather than their social characteristics.

Legal protections have been an important step toward expanding opportunities for all people in the workplace because they reduce the use of overt standards used to exclude certain populations from getting hired. However, legal protections alone cannot eliminate the relative advantages and disadvantages that people of different backgrounds face in the labor market based on their race, gender, class, age, and other attributes. Many of these inequality-producing forces today are subtler and far less visible. For instance, employers can and do use unspoken standards to make decisions about job candidates that circumvent legal culpability.[6] Even well-meaning hiring managers can have their perceptions of a job candidate framed by underlying assumptions, such as the idea that women are "naturally" more nurturing than men (and best for jobs such as customer service or domestic work), or that men of color lack the "soft skills"—such as a friendly attitude or welcoming persona—to succeed at jobs that require them to interface with clients or work closely with coworkers.[7] Such perceptions become embedded in the way organizations and their leaders idealize traits associated with class-privileged, cishet White men, including their devotion to work as well as their hobbies and interests outside work.[8] Perceptions of group difference and hierarchy can also run deep. The implicit biases—attitudes toward certain groups, often unconscious—of managers can factor into hiring decisions that do not register as blatant bigotry, sexism, or ableism. For example, psychology studies show that people take longer on average to associate an image of a Black man's face with a positive adjective or a role of authority than they do a White man's face.[9] These kinds of implicit biases related to a person's perceived characteristics take concrete expressions in the workplace—especially when managers rely on informal standards to evaluate workers—which makes inequality within these spaces all the more difficult to eradicate.[10]

Another reason for the persistence of social inequality in today's workforce are the historical and cumulative disparities between groups with regard to access to valuable resources, such as economic capital, cultural capital, and social capital.[11] For instance, laws requiring the equal treatment of job candidates cannot amend the vast gap in resources that have accrued between Black families and White families over generations. Research shows that White families in the United States possess, on average, ten times the amount of wealth of Black or Latino families, measured in total assets such as home equity, stocks, and income, minus any debts. In the labor market, this means that White workers have greater opportunities to receive a better education, access high-quality training, and pay for formal credentials than BIPOC. Access to resources can also be the difference between someone being able to come up with the funds necessary to finance a brewery, either through family wealth or by successfully applying for loans by putting forth the possessing and the necessary collateral. More subtly, access to resources can also serve as a crucial safety net for workers. Resources can make that person more likely to take risks in order to advance their career, such as by agreeing to an unpaid internship for a time being in order to gain job experience or nurture key industry connections.

Social disparities also exist in social capital, or personal connections, which steer people into certain jobs and away from others in a variety of ways. On a broad level, social networks are related to the *socialization* process, or how we acquire our beliefs, values, norms, and behaviors. As described in the last chapter, the people that we are around influence our "tastes" for a variety of things, including our job aspirations. But since networks are clumpy—comprised of people with similar social characteristics—racialized and gendered networks contribute to our thinking about the kinds of jobs we believe suit us best and are attainable. Social networks can also help you get jobs in concrete ways. Research shows that friends, family members, and professional acquaintances can be extremely useful for both locating jobs and getting hired; *who you know* can be just as important as *what you know*.[12] However, because White men and women are typically more connected to business leaders and powerful people than BIPOC are, they are in a greater position to use their network ties to their employment advantage.[13]

So, what can we take away from this body of literature on social inequality in the workforce? While many modern workplaces feature well-meaning employers who abide by anti-discrimination employment rules, there remains a number of reasons why workers still experience divergent opportunities in their work lives tied closely to their social statuses such as race, class, and gender.

This brings us back to the craft beer industry. To be sure, many small breweries take pride in being welcoming, communal, family-run businesses that do not conform to stuffy and hierarchical social norms of the past.[14] No brewer or brewery owner that we know or have talked to for this book thinks that denying someone a job based solely on their race and gender identity or appearance is okay. Why, then, do we continue to see the majority of craft beer jobs, especially the most desirable ones, go to White men?

As this chapter illustrates, White men have greater access to brewery jobs than their women and BIPOC counterparts for three primary reasons: their access to economic resources, social networks, and their alignment with cultural expectations. Each of these factors alone contributes to the social organization of the industry by race, gender, and class. But when combined together, they give socioeconomically privileged White men a clear path to the most desirable jobs in craft beer. By contrast, women and BIPOC who enter craft beer are channeled into gendered and racialized jobs that have less authority and social recognition. This is not to say that brewery workers such as Ricky and Carmela do not enjoy their current jobs in the taproom and distribution, respectively—nor would they be any less capable of succeeding within the beer industry if given a fair chance at building skills and moving up. Labor stories like those of Ricky and Carmela simply reinforce the fact that in order for women and BIPOC to find their place in an industry dominated by White men they have to navigate cumulative barriers that involve economic, social, and cultural components.

CREATIVITY AND WHITENESS IN THE BREWHOUSE

White men who work in the craft beer industry like to joke that seeking a job at a brewery means one of two things: either you are comfortable not making much money in return for doing a job you love, or you have unrealistic expectations about what this line of work entails as a form of employment. What goes unspoken is that *choosing* to enter the craft beer industry, whether right or wrong, is a decision that would not be particularly attractive to many people. A brewhouse job doesn't look like a great job in the conventional sense that it doesn't offer lucrative earnings, plush benefits, or easy labor. Instead, White men emphasize that they initially sought jobs in beer for reasons that had little to do with any of these things. Being around craft beer was their "passion" before it became their job. Yet as we shall see, pursuing a line of work that aims to merge labor with leisure interests is a decision fundamentally enabled by privilege.

Many jobs in craft beer require high socioeconomic *inputs* while offering low economic *rewards*. For starters, developing a taste for craft beer is far more expensive than consuming macro-produced light lagers such as Bud or Coors. Whether it be a six-pack, a growler, or pint, a beer made in a small brewery is never going to be the cheapest option to purchase, and sometimes as much as 100% more expensive than a comparable Big Beer product (we detail why this is the case in the next chapter). While this cost premium does not deter those who are able to pay for a product they perceive to be of higher quality, people from socioeconomically oppressed backgrounds are far less likely to opt for this trade-off. Recall that Ricky, the Native American man introduced at the start of this chapter, said he had hardly experienced "fancy" beer growing up in a poor family on an Indian reservation; Ricky learned to associate beer solely with Big Beer brands that were the cheapest to buy and readily available at gas stations and the corner stores where he grew up.

Because White men are the ones who have the resources to develop a taste for craft beer, they are also the ones most likely to attempt to enter the industry for work. Think back to Charlie, the college-educated brewery owner who led off this chapter. While Charlie emphasizes how his "obsession" with homebrewing led him to the beer industry, seen from a sociological perspective, Charlie was already in a prime position to realize these career dreams due to his background. Being a professionally employed, educated White man from a middle-class family buffered his transition into the industry by allowing him to devote his spare time and resources to his homebrewing hobby. Charlie's access to economic resources also minimized the financial burden of setting up his homebrewing operation. Homebrewing equipment can cost hundreds of dollars, and the ongoing expense of brewing materials such as hops and malt add up quickly, especially when one is brewing 10-gallon batches every week as Charlie was. These socioeconomic advantages continue to pay dividends when White men transition to beer industry jobs. For Charlie, his relative financial security allowed him to feel comfortable taking a job as an assistant brewer making just above minimum wage (a considerable pay cut from his full-time teaching job). Doing so was, in his view, a crucial step in his career development: it allowed him to hone professional brewing skills before striking out on his own.

Charlie's subsequent transition to starting his own brewery also reveals how resources helped ease this undertaking. To be sure, opening a brewery requires a high degree of commitment, entrepreneurial ingenuity, and financial risk for anyone; there is no foolproof formula for ensuring your fledgling brewery will be successful. But being able to manage the costs involved with brewery start-up makes it precisely the area in which privileged White men, who have access to both financial capital and social connections, have their greatest advantage. Brewery costs can fluctuate based on a number of factors, including the selection of the brewery's location (noting local taxes and building codes), the type of equipment purchased, and optimal planning for brewery buildout.[15] The biggest factor that can ease these start-up challenges is one that few instructional guides mention: the ability to tap into personal and familial resources. Without these resources, we can imagine how much more challenging Charlie's path to opening a brewery would have been.

Eduardo, a Latino man raised in a working-class family, embodies these challenges. Eduardo says he aspires to one day open his own brewery, a goal that he has held onto while working as a shift brewer for the past decade at several breweries in the Albuquerque area. However, Eduardo fears his goal is still a long way off. He explains: "I would love to start a brewery one day, but unless I find some rich people to finance it, I have no idea how I'm going to come up with that money." Unable to access the same resources as his White male counterparts such as Charlie, Eduardo has settled for continuing to develop his brewing skills and creating recipes on his small homebrewing system, waiting for his big break within the industry.

What about simply finding a job at an existing brewery instead of starting one from scratch? Based on the modest wages of entry jobs in craft beer and minimal formal qualifications necessary, we might assume that brewery jobs would be widely available not just to White men but also to a wide variety of workers of every background. According to recent statistics, the average assistant brewer in the United States makes $14 an hour or $29,500 annually, well below the median earnings for American workers, while other brewhouse workers earn even less (for comparison, head brewers earn $50,000 to 60,000 according to industry insiders and recent statistics).[16] However, White men flock to these jobs for reasons that go beyond earning potential and speak directly to their "tastes" for this work: they enjoy the process of brewing beer, the act of tasting their handcrafted creations, and the prospect of socializing with others—mostly men—who feel the same. By comparison, people who have not developed these intangible interests in craft beer prior see little incentive to *seek* positions in the industry. This preserves the inner circle of White male workers who do this labor, particularly in creative bre-whouse jobs.

Roughly half of the brewers we spoke with told us that the easiest way to find work in a brewhouse is by initially working there for free. Many recalled either volunteering or simply hanging out at the brewery as a customer prior to getting offered a job there. David, a White man in his early thirties, recalls being so singularly motivated to work at his local brewery in Los Angeles where he was a regular customer that he would have taken any job that he was offered. Sitting at the bar, David soon befriended the owner of the brewery, who would often be walking around the brewery doing various tasks. Initially, the owner asked David to help out with small construction jobs and handy tasks around the brewery. Three months later, the owner offered him a job of washing kegs. None of these jobs paid much more than minimum wage, but David didn't care. "See that bathroom?" David tells me as we sit down for a beer at the brewery he works at. "I built that with my own hands. I've always loved taking apart and then re-building the pieces." David still makes less than $16 an hour while living in one of the most expensive cities in the country. But by engaging in extra work for minimal pay, he has achieved his goal of being a professional craft brewer.

Social Ties to the Industry

Social networks help to lock in place existing patterns of race, class, and gender inequality in the craft beer industry. This is because, as we mentioned earlier, networks are clumpy and tend toward *homophily*, better known through the expression "birds of a feather flock together."[17] Put simply, people tend to cluster together with other people who are similar to themselves. Social networks are a big part of why White men pursue, and often secure, brewing jobs in the industry (later we will see how networks also contribute to the kind of jobs that women and BIPOC work in beer).

Grant is in his mid-twenties and has scraggly brown-red hair. He works as a beertender at a popular local brewery in Albuquerque. Grant recalls the moment he decided to get a job in a brewery. "All my friends were drinking the stuff," he explains, "so I said, why not try to work here myself?" As a recent college graduate, Grant's goal with having a job was to have fun and work among friends. "I was basically working there anyway for free before I got the job, bussing tables and things to be helpful," he says. A couple of months after initially inquiring about a job there with the manager (he told his worker-friends to put in a good word for him), Grant was hired. Grant's network of contacts within the brewery proved useful in facilitating his own employment there, just as they had played a role in sparking his interest in the job in the first place.

Craft brewers often rely on social networks to build their knowledge of brewing informally. It is the knowledge that they say blends art, science, and experimentation. A White man named Fred has come to master all of these aspects of brewing, according to several of his brewer peers. However, for years, Fred initially found it difficult to figure out what to do and when to do it in the brewhouse. Fred said his ties to his White male colleagues in the industry have helped him learn. "I am able to call up so and so and ask him how he did it himself." Fred relies not only on extensive textbook knowledge about brewing but also social knowledge to help him navigate the early stages of recipe development and brewery troubleshooting. Now working as the head brewer of a fast-growing brewery in Albuquerque, Fred goes out of his way to make sure to help other fellow brewers should they reach out to him.

Social ties help White men like Grant and Fred advance quickly in the industry by streamlining the process of finding a job and developing skills that are otherwise difficult to learn. Their experience has also shaped their perspective on how the industry works. By moving from apprentices to peers to mentors, these men see the industry as highly communal and tight-knit, characterized by the sharing of information about job openings and occupational tricks of the trade. At the center of these social networks, Fred and Charlie have been able to pass on their knowledge of the industry to the next generation—and, however unintentionally, to other White men that look and sound like younger versions of themselves.

This is far less the case for women and BIPOC who work in the craft beer industry. While some say they have benefited from their social ties to White men within the craft beer industry, many of their closest ties are to other women and BIPOC in the industry who tend to be scattered among different breweries. These ties offer a valuable sense of camaraderie, if not necessarily an "in" to better jobs. For instance, a White woman brewery owner named Mary said that she has an ongoing text message thread between fellow women in leadership positions in the industry; they get together from time to time to hang out and talk shop. For Mary, not all of these conversations are about beer—and that's the point: these social gatherings normalize the presence of women in the industry even though they remain tokens within their respective workplaces.[18] A Black woman industry worker named Teresa recounted her experience connecting with other Black people in craft beer this way:

I think what is cool is that a lot of us have found each other . . .There is this one guy I met out in the Thousand Oaks area. And I was like, "what are you doing out here?" And he's the same age as my brother, very similar story. And I was like, "how is it for you out here?" And he's like, "honestly, it doesn't matter." But he got really excited to see me at a brewery, we both geeked out with each other.

Even if they are not fully locked out of industry networks, few women and BIPOC describe the kinds of readily available social networks that White men in the industry enjoy, where insider information flows freely. Instead, they work to build their own (see Figure 3.1).

Workers from oppressed groups thus see tremendous value in creating spaces and building up networks that specifically invite people in who are not White, college-educated, cishet, men. For example, one brewery managed by a woman of color holds queer meet-up events weekly, "women who love beer" nights each month, and local Hispanic and Native American-focused events each year. These efforts, which we return to in more detail later in this book, suggest that women and BIPOC seek to nurture their own social connections within the industry. While there are notable exceptions (Mary), unlike the networks of their White male peers, the networks of women and BIPOC in the industry are mainly among those employed in positions of less power and influence, roles that have historically limited their influence within the industry as well as in the labor market more broadly.

Figure 3.1   Kaylynn McKnight, Formerly the Head Brewer of Toltec Brewing Company, in Albuquerque, New Mexico. *Source:* Eli R. Wilson.

Displaying Preferred Tastes in Beer

Brandon, a White man in his forties, cares a lot about sourcing local, eating and drinking fresh, and respecting traditional methods of brewing. He emphatically differentiates things made the "right" way from lower quality versions of the same product.[19] Brandon's refined palate has led him to become one of the most respected head brewers in New Mexico: beer fans and professional peers alike admire the balance and structure of the beers he makes, which range from crisp *Kölsch* to tart fruit-infused sours. Brandon is quick to note that he had to cultivate his refined palate through extensive tasting and learning; he wasn't born with it. This is because, as we explained in chapter 2, developing and expressing the "right" tastes for beer is a social process rather than a physiological one and differentiated by access to cultural knowledge and economic resources. Possessing the "right" tastes, as a form of cultural capital, is something inherently unavailable to everyone. For example, several White men working in breweries recall having cultivated a taste for gourmet beer starting at a young age. One brewer recalled seeing his father drinking imported Belgian beers at the dinner table while he was in high school; another took pride in being the person who would bring beers no one had heard of to college parties where everyone else was drinking PBR and Natural "Natty" Light. In brewery workplaces, what you drink—and how you talk about what you drink—say a lot about if you belong there. Here, the material stakes of having "good" taste in beer can be significant: expressing proper taste for craft beer could be the difference between getting ahead in the industry or remaining in the lower ranks.

The same goes for having a passion for working in craft beer. For middle-class White men such as Brandon, expressing devotion to craft beer can be one way in which displaying "good" taste blends with a desired form of masculinity.[20] Doing so also signals one's social and cultural fit for employment in craft beer. This is because, according to many people we talked to for this book, the normative workplace culture in breweries remains a version of "bro culture." According to one woman who works as a shift brewer, the bro culture of craft beer means being comfortable with jokes involving sexual innuendo, drinking multiple "shift" beers during the workday, reveling in physical work, and being obsessed about all things craft beer. To the majority of brewery workers who are White men, none of this would seem out of the ordinary. But to this woman brewer, the cultural Whiteness and masculinity of her brewery workplace were immediately apparent. It was also exclusionary: she knew that she needed to either "deal with it"—figuratively rolling up her sleeves and dishing out crude jokes with the best of them—or leave.

"WOMEN'S WORK" IN THE TAPROOM

At first pass, in an industry dominated by men, the fact that one out of every two taproom workers today is a woman seems like an anomaly—perhaps a sign that the industry is rapidly achieving gender parity in terms of employment. Not so fast. Instead, the overconcentration of women in customer service jobs in beer (relative to their small overall numbers) reflects gendered values that surround this category of work in our society. As described earlier, customer service is *feminized* work deemed more appropriate for women than men. As a result, in breweries, employers—and often customers, too—are more likely to see women, particularly White, middle-class women, as a better fit for customer service roles rather than brewing or distribution jobs.

Brewery taproom workers who interact with customers are expected to provide a positive service experience for the latter. This means that making sure customers are happy and comfortable is at least as important a job skill as possessing detailed knowledge about the beer being sold. Customer service jobs require what Arlie Hochschild famously coined "emotional labor," which she defines as the management of feeling in order to foster the desired experience for customers. Customer service workers must keep guests satisfied through careful control over what they say and how they appear. Breweries are not alone in employing women in service capacities. For example, in restaurants, up until very recently, the job titles of "waitress" and "hostess" were considered standard job titles.[21] Because brewery employers expect that most women who apply for jobs in breweries will be applying to work in front-of-the-house capacities instead of in the brewhouse or in distribution, women who want to break into the ranks of brewer find themselves thwarted by cultural assumptions that these jobs aren't for them. For example, when we asked men brewers about why there weren't more women in the brewhouse, many reasoned that these jobs were too physically demanding for women. A White woman named Cora, who works as a head brewer in New Mexico, emphatically disagrees. Cora says there are many ways that women can learn to use proper techniques to accomplish all the physical requirements of professional brewing with ease. Instead, women are dissuaded from brewhouse jobs based on misguided, *gendered assumptions* about their lack of suitability for these roles. Cora should know: despite voicing her interest in brewing beer, she spent four years working as a host and server (read: women's jobs) before finally getting an opportunity to train in the brewhouse alongside a small team of exclusively White men.

The forces that pattern job opportunity and exclusion in the beer industry operate *intersectionally*. That is, they reflect simultaneous aspects of one's social location within existing status hierarchies of race, class, gender, and more. For example, the concentration of White, class-privileged women in taproom jobs is the result of not only gendered employment norms but also those of race and class. Many of these individuals, such as Ella, who work as a beertender, say they first developed a liking for craft beer while in college or while growing up in a family that enjoyed drinking local craft beer or premium "imported" beers. Ella says that her love for craft beer directly influenced her decision to pursue a job in craft beer. In order to secure a job in the industry, some women describe leveraging their connection to other women already working in beer. However, in nearly all cases, this pulls them into taproom jobs where these contacts are already employed.

For women, prior employment experience imparts a similar direction of influence. Recall that Carmela, the woman who led off this chapter, first got into the beer industry by transitioning from waiting tables to her taproom job. By doing so, Carmela was able to draw on her experience and bring her existing skillset in hospitality to the brewery (this was the case for Ella as well). Importantly, these gendered and racialized job experiences also inform how Carmela has learned to approach her job working on a staff of mostly White men. As a Latina woman, Carmela strives to make her brewery taproom feel more welcoming, inclusive, and safer for everyone, especially women and BIPOC. "Granted, you need some thick skin to work in an environment that is majority White and mal—and that is both workers and customers," says Carmela, "But the way I see it, it is also an opportunity to really make some positive changes around here."

THE INVISIBLE LABOR OF BEER DISTRIBUTION

Working-class men of color are most likely to find themselves employed in distribution jobs that are perceived to be the least desirable in the industry. The physicality of jobs delivering heavy kegs and cases of beer bears little resemblance to the taproom service jobs mostly worked by White women. Distribution jobs are also distinct from brewhouse jobs in that the latter rarely offer opportunities to engage in creative labor, such as by brewing beer and developing recipes, which is the primary attraction of this line of work for privileged White men. As a result, distribution jobs represent racialized and gendered employment in the industry where Black and Brown men are most likely to operate despite their limited overall numbers.

Daniel, a twenty-two-year-old Mexican American man with a high-school education, spends his days driving a truck for a local brewery in Albuquerque to make deliveries of kegs and cases of beer. Loading palates of these products is tiring and repetitive work. Daniel begins his days loading up his truck at seven in the morning. He averages ten- to eleven-hour shifts, driving from account to account on a set schedule making beer deliveries. "One time I was supposed to make a delivery to a town three hours away and I forgot my dolly," Daniel says. "It was a huge pain. That day took fourteen hours. I was exhausted by the end." Daniel may have been exhausted, but he has also come to expect that sometimes this is what his job will entail. He should know: at his previous job with a water distribution company, his hours as a driver were even longer. Daniel recalls averaging thirteen-hour days delivering 75-pound jugs of water to offices. "The difference was, over there, you would finish your shift and they would expect you back there ready to go the next morning." At the brewery, Daniel notes, at least he can have a beer on the house after he gets done delivering thousands of them. Daniel's previous work experience mirrors that of other BIPOC working in brewery distribution jobs. Ricky, who was described at the beginning of this chapter, was a private security guard and a cashier at Burger King before landing a delivery job at River Bend Brewery.

Despite the physical labor and sometimes long days of work, Daniel loves working at the brewery, which he says is his favorite job he has ever had. Upon getting hired, Daniel says he enjoyed the friendly welcome he received as a new employee. Now, months into the job, he relishes the camaraderie he has received from his brewery coworkers. "It's like a family here, man," he explains. "Like, my first day, everyone was all asking me how I'm doing, if I'm liking it so far. I've never had that before. At my other jobs, it's always been, work, work, work." Relative to what Daniel is used to, distribution jobs in breweries appear to be flexible, social, and imminently enjoyable (the free beer at the end of each shift certainly helps too). However, because drivers and other distribution workers spend less time around the brewhouse or taproom working, they sometimes do not have the opportunity to get to know their coworkers. Daniel, for instance, says he can never remember the names of the "ladies up front in the taproom." This speaks to not only the social differences between working-class men of color and their privileged White coworkers but also their exclusion from the core creative operation at the brewery.

To be sure, White men also work distribution jobs, just as they do every other job in an industry where they are the primary occupant. But the way these more privileged individuals approach their jobs differs from men like Daniel and Ricky as a function of their class and race position. For example, Nathan, a twenty-eight-year-old White man with a college education, explains his decision to accept a job as a delivery driver at a small brewery:

> I made the decision that I wanted to get into the industry any way I could. I told [head brewer] I'll do whatever they need me to do to get started. So that's how I got to delivering beer. But yeah, I want to get into the brewhouse. I'm already looking to move up, or maybe move on. I think management knows that.

Nathan accepted a distribution job as a foot in the door into an industry that he is passionate about.[22] While Nathan currently does the same job as Daniel, his goals within the beer industry are quite different. Daniel says he enjoys his distribution job for the employment conditions it offers him, whereas Nathan seeks to move into the brewhouse quickly or else he will be looking for another job. These two workers may labor in the same capacity for now, but due to factors both personal and deeply sociological, they will not remain there for long.

Many of the people who work in the craft beer industry such as Charlie, Ricky, and Carmela genuinely love their jobs. After all, this is an industry where, depending on your position, one gets to brew beer, talk about beer, and drink beer after work, often free of charge. However, the unequal capacities that workers with different social statuses find themselves laboring within reflect factors that go beyond formal credentials. White men continue to occupy the majority of all jobs in craft beer, and their numbers are particularly concentrated in creative capacities in the brewhouse. Meanwhile, a smaller number of women and BIPOC in the industry fill roles that are either lower in status and pay or less visible, or both, such as customer service jobs and distribution jobs. As we have described, this job segregation within the industry today reflects social inequalities in our society that exclude women and BIPOC from accessing more desirable jobs.

Why do these disparities of race, gender, and class persist in the labor market? We have shown that the answer lies in the cumulative, interlocking advantages that White men enjoy. They have access to economic resources and social networks and embody the gendered and racialized cultural ideals of this industry. These advantages make it easier for White men to find their way into the industry and eventually move into creative roles, especially that of head brewer and brewery owner. Larger patterns of social inequality today persist in spite of the good intentions of many individual actors; they persist for structural and systemic reasons, such as the entrenched economic inequality between racial groups, the binary and hierarchical gendered association of men—especially White men—with positions of authority in the industry and women with service roles. Few jobs in our society are race and gender-inclusive and are instead designated for people of specific races, socioeconomic statuses, or genders. These patterns speak to the fact that jobs exist within the contours of our larger society and attendant social hierarchies—bumps, bruises, biases, all.

It is important to recognize that the vast majority of people who own small breweries and choose to work in craft beer are not overtly racist or sexist or homophobic people; they do not actively choose to uphold systems of inequality. Quite the opposite. Nearly everyone we talked with while researching this book was kind-hearted, socially engaged in principle, and committed to what they do for a living. They also cared about their workers and wanted to see the industry grow in new ways. Many signaled support for getting more women and BIPOC involved as both consumers and workers by hosting "ladies nights," proudly etching Black Lives Matter on their storefronts, and partnering with local nonprofits to support the needy in their communities. But attempting to forge a more inclusive future also means understanding why things are the way they are *now* in order to begin to undo or even reverse these patterns.

Today there is more reason than ever to believe that change may be upon the world of beer, driven by forces both within and beyond the industry. From all-Latinx homebrewing clubs to pop-up cultural events led by BIPOC to women-led professional groups and mentoring initiatives, beer consumers and workers alike are signaling their willingness to realize social change, an important topic that we return to in the closing chapter. As more breweries commit to rethinking their hiring practices, customer outreach efforts, and workplace cultures, others will follow. An industry long known for Whiteness, masculinity, and heteronormativity still has time to re-craft a new narrative.

In order to better contextualize the experiences of workers and consumers in the world of beer, we need to examine the industry structures that frame these experiences. This requires understanding how the business of beer works, and how issues of power, entrepreneurial strategy, and market opportunity have simultaneously contributed to craft beer's rapid growth—as well as the continued dominance of Big Beer.

NOTES

1. Acker, Joan. 2006. "Inequality regimes: Gender, class, and race in organizations." *Gender & Society, 20*(4): 441–464; Ray, Victor. 2019. "A theory of racialized organizations." *American Sociological Review, 84*(1): 26–53; Tomaskovic, Donald, and Dustin Avent-Holt. 2019. *Relational Inequalities: An Organizational Approach.* New York: Oxford University Press.

2. The Brewers Association disaggregated their 2019 industry data into sole ownership by gender versus co-ownership. Seventy-seven percent of all breweries are owned solely by men, while another 22% are owned by men and women jointly (presumably husband and wife partners). This leaves less than 2% of all breweries sole-owned by women. We thank Bart Watson and the Brewers Association for sharing this dataset with us.

3. According to the Brewers Association statistics in 2019, a disproportionate number of Black and Latino brewery workers held jobs as "production staff (Non-brewers)," at 4.7% and 7.8% respectively.

4. Chapman and Brunsma 2020; Withers 2017.

5. At the time of this writing, there are still several notable exceptions to the list of categories that employers cannot consider when making hiring and promotional decisions, such as sexual orientation or gender identity. This continues to marginalize members of the LGBTQIA+ community. A recently proposed federal legislation called the Equality Act would extend more robust legal protections to this community and close gaps in our civil rights laws.

6. Moss, Philip and Chris Tilly. 2001. *Stories employers tell: Race, skill, and hiring in America.* New York: Russell Sage Foundation; Pedulla, David. 2020. *Making the Cut: Hiring Decisions, Bias, and the Consequences of Nonstandard, Mismatched, and Precarious Employment.* Princeton, NJ: Princeton University Press.

7. Moss and Tilly 2001; Ridgeway 2011; Waldinger, Roger and Michael Lichter. 2003. *How the other half works.* Berkeley: University of California Press.

8. Acker 2006; Rivera, Lauren A. 2012. "Hiring as cultural matching: The case of elite professional service firms." *American Sociological Review,* 77(6): 999–1022; Rivera, Lauren A. 2015. *Pedigree: How elite students get elite jobs.* Princeton, NJ: Princeton University Press; Wilson, Eli R. 2021. *Front of the house, back of the house: Race and inequality in the lives of restaurant workers.* New York: NYU Press.

9. A growing body of sociological research has illustrated persistent hiring biases in the United States due to race and gender among other social characteristics. For instance, employers have been found to use subtle cues to inform their hiring decisions with regard to a candidate's attitude, appearance, and their lifestyle preferences. See Moss and Tilly 2001; Neckerman, Katherine and Joleen Kirschenman. 1991. "Hiring Strategies, Racial Bias, and Inner-City Workers." *Social Problems, 38*(4): 433–447; Warhurst, Chis and Dennis Nickson. 2009. "'Who's got the look?' Emotional, aesthetic, and sexualized labor in interactive services." *Gender, Work and Organization, 16*(3): 385–404; Williams, Cristine L., and Catherine Connell. 2011. "'Looking good and sounding right': Aesthetic labor and social inequality in the retail industry." *Work and Occupations, 37*(3): 349–377; Wilson, Eli R. 2016. "Matching up: Producing proximal service in a Los Angeles restaurant." *Research in the Sociology of Work, 29*: 99–124.

10. Kalev, Alexandra, Frank Dobbin, and Erin L. Kelly. 2006. "Best practices or best guesses? Assessing the efficacy of corporate affirmative action and diversity policies." *American Sociological Review, 71*: 589–617.

11. For more on wealth disparities between Black and White families, see Oliver, Melvin L. and Thomas M. Shapiro. 1996. *Black wealth/white wealth: A new perspective on racial inequality.* New York: Routledge. For an excellent sociological study on race and social networks, see Royster, Diedre A. 2003. *Race and the invisible hand: How white networks exclude black men from blue-collar jobs.* Berkeley: University of California Press.

12. Granovetter, Mark. 1995 [1974]. *Getting a job: A study of contacts and careers.* Second edition. Chicago: University of Chicago Press; Mouw, Ted. 2003. "Social capital and finding a job: Do contacts matter?" *American Sociological Review, 68*(6): 868–698.

13. Royster 2003.

14. Borer 2019.

15. A whole cottage industry of book guides is now available on the market that provide information on how to open your own brewery on the cheap by finding more cost-effective, DIY ways to do nearly everything. Tom Hennessey's popular books on the topic, such as the *Brewery Operations Manual*, stress buying used brewing equipment, pouring sweat equity into the project, and taking advantage of friends and family who can help with construction, plumbing, and welding.

16. We base this on our own conversations with industry workers as well as the listed average earnings for an "Assistant Brewer" and "brewer" in the United States in 2020, according to ZipRecruiter. See www.ziprecruiter.com.

17. McPherson, Miller, Lynn Smith-Lovin, and James M. Cook. 2001. "Birds of a feather: Homophily in social networks." *Annual Review of Sociology, 27*: 415–444.

18. Kanter, Rosabeth M. 1977. *Men and women of the corporation.* New York: Basic Books.

19. For a similar discussion, see chapter 2 on the connection between elite consumption tastes and value derived from how these products are made.

20. Darwin 2018.

21. Hall, Elaine J., 1993. "Smiling, deferring, and flirting: doing gender by giving 'good service.'" *Work and Occupations*, *20*(4): 452–471. These jobs are now more commonly referred to by their gender-neutral terms of "server" and "host," respectively.

22. For a similar analysis of unpaid interns in the music industry, see Frenette, Alexandre. 2013. "Making the intern economy: Role and career challenges of the music industry intern." *Work and Occupations, 40*(4): 364–397.

Chapter 4

The Business of Beer

You've heard it before: the story of the Rise of Craft Beer. It goes like this:

Craft breweries are popping up all over the world following decades of corporate dominance within the industry. These small, independently owned operations have steadily gained market share while "fizzy yellow beer" declines in popularity. Every day, more consumers, particularly younger ones, are opening their eyes to the wonders of well-hopped ales and fruited sours that are made by a small but passionate team of brewery workers. Craft beer is the future of beer.

There is much to like about this narrative and what it represents. The Rise of Craft Beer has a moral ring to it to go along with a David versus Goliath vibe. However, consider an assessment of the industry told from a different perspective:

Today, Big Beer produces five out of every six beers sold around the globe. These brewing companies are owned by multinational conglomerates that are themselves the result of mega-mergers between regional beer companies. Big Beer's flagship products, pale lagers that are light in color and flavor, dominate global sales and remain unchallenged as the world's most popular style of beer. Despite an ever-changing world of beer, including the rise of smaller companies and trendy new styles, powerful businesses that are well-capitalized continue to thrive by design. Big Beer is still in control of the future of beer.

We can agree that this alternate story—one that depicts the unwavering dominance of multinational corporations over the beer market—is far less heartwarming than the one that preceded it. But it is just as true. These two narratives span the business of beer today, one that is stratified into *corporate* and *craft* segments, with the former wielding far more power within the industry than the latter. Both types of companies frame the way jobs are organized within the industry, as described in the previous chapter. They also jointly dictate the kinds of commercial products available to consumers. But in order to better understand how the business of beer affects the broader world of beer we have been exploring, we need to unpack how companies produce, distribute, advertise, and ultimately sell beer to consumers, and how these business strategies differ for Big Beer and independently owned craft breweries. In doing so we learn more about how "mass-produced" and "craft" styles of production differ in practice and principle—and why these distinctions are becoming increasingly blurred today.[1]

THE RISE OF CRAFT BEER IN AN ERA OF BIG BEER

Craft breweries today have transformed from small-scale curiosities to well-established economic and cultural forces. The specialty products they make are now sold on tap at professional sports games, offered on the alcoholic beverage menus at a wide variety of restaurants, and appear by the dozen on the shelves of supermarket chains. Hollywood film releases, such as *Drinking Buddies* (2013), feature people drinking craft beer and socializing in craft breweries as everyday activities (though it is worth noting that nearly everyone doing so in these movies is White and cishet). Even city officials have come to see craft breweries, along with other kinds of creative workplaces, as a boon to local urban economies and their revitalized (gentrified?) neighborhoods because of the role these businesses play in attracting affluent, educated people to the area.[2]

Sociologists and organizational scholars explain that the rise of U.S. craft beer in the 1970s and 1980s happened not only because of changing consumer tastes but because there was a gap in what was available in the market at the time. Large breweries were focused on mass-producing and mass-advertising cheap, light lagers to mainstream American consumers. This in turn opened the door for small, craft brewers to create and sell specialized brews to satisfy a smaller niche of beer drinkers who desired novel products.[3] Organizational scholars Glenn Carroll and Anand Swaminathan refer to this process as "resource partitioning," where, paradoxically, the *structure* of the beer market dominated by Big Beer during this era yielded a business opportunity for small breweries to thrive by differentiating themselves.[4] As a result, early craft breweries weren't necessarily drawing the same customers as Big Beer. Nor were they trying to mirror the latter's corporate business strategies, as this chapter will detail. Instead, in order to compete in the market, small breweries cultivated a craft brand identity that focused on the authenticity of their products. Craft has caught on. Four decades into the so-called craft beer revolution, the number of breweries in the United States has gone from less than 100 to more than 8,000—twice the number of breweries that existed during the previous high–water mark before Prohibition. Meanwhile, craft beer's share of the beer market has grown from less than 1% to nearly 14% during this time, while the most successful craft breweries are now distributed countrywide.[5]

Considering the popularity of craft beer today, we may wonder why small and independent breweries haven't been able to make a bigger dent into Big Beer's dominance. As the opening narratives in this chapter conveyed, craft breweries still make only one out of every six beers sold in the United States, while Bud Light and Budweiser still outsell all craft beers in this country *combined*—just as they have in past decades.[6] Big Beer's share of the global beer market today is also increasing. Fifteen years ago, ten firms accounted for just under half of all beers sold worldwide. By 2012, four firms accounted for 70% of the beer market.[7] Then, in 2016, the two largest beer companies in the world, Belgium-based AB-InBev and London-based SABMiller, agreed to merge into one giant company, which was at the time the largest business deal in modern history. The deal was so big that industry watchdogs decried the merger as an illegal monopoly, and international regulators held up the process in courts for months.[8] Nonetheless, since the dust settled on the merger, three out of every four beers sold worldwide are now produced by just two mega companies.

This story is not unique to beer. The concentration of a large share of the market in a small number of hands is known as *oligopolistic* control, which makes it difficult for new companies to enter the market and compete directly with large and extremely powerful businesses. The U.S. food and nonalcoholic beverage sector is dominated by a small handful of companies such as Nestle, Mars, and Coca-Cola; so is the airline industry, wireless carrier industry, and the music industry.[9] Moreover, the rise of large industrial breweries traces back to the mid-1800s, an era that saw the launch of many German immigrant-owned breweries with name brands still recognizable today, such as Anheuser-Busch, Miller, Pabst, and Schaefer. These breweries quickly began expanding their operations, beating out local competition, and growing their reach beyond the cities where they were founded. This ushered in the first era of intense competition in the beer industry. By 1870, 3,000 breweries were operating across the United States, though most of these breweries were small in scale and focused on a local clientele, much like the majority of craft breweries today. As larger companies moved into new markets, they caused many smaller operations to either fold or merge with other companies in order to stay competitive. By 1910, a full ten years before Prohibition, the number of breweries had decreased by half. Meanwhile, professional brewing was steadily becoming a full-scale industrial operation employing thousands of workers, mostly White men with union contracts, to mass-produce beer in large factory plants.

Prohibition caused further consolidation within the industry. This is because large and profitable breweries were better equipped than their competitors to weather these extremely difficult business times. To be sure, larger beer companies such as Anheuser-Busch, Pabst, and Schlitz also struggled: many were forced to adjust their business operations and repurpose their equipment to produce alternative goods (such as malt extract, "near-beer," and candy) with varying degrees of success.[10] However, in the decades following the repeal of Prohibition, large industrial breweries were able to steadily increase their control over the beer market. By the end of the 1960s—the same decade that saw washing machine heir Fritz Maytag launch the craft beer revolution by purchasing the failing Anchor Brewery in San Francisco—fewer than 100 breweries remained in the United States. For the average consumer, Big Beer *was* beer and its flagship pale lagers—such as Budweiser in the United States, Heineken in the Netherlands, and Sapporo in Japan—had become national icons.

STRATEGIES OF DOMINANCE, STRATEGIES OF CRAFT

Understanding how Big Beer dominates the world of beer begins with understanding that commercial beer is not only a cultural object but also a market commodity. Producing and selling beer professionally means carefully strategizing all aspects of the business of beer with an eye on profitability. Like other commodities, beer is subject to the cost and supply of ingredients, the dynamics of competition in the market, and consumer demand for specific kinds of products and brands. All of this means that breweries that learn to make their beers as efficiently as possible and sell them in large quantities to customers are in the best position to be successful. Further, the more that a company is able to exert control over the *commodity supply chain*, consisting of an array of raw ingredient suppliers, distributors, and retailers, the better their chances of success. In what follows, we profile how Big Beer and craft breweries manage four key areas of their business—the cost of making beer, business competition, relations with distributors, and branding—in ways that reflect their unequal position within the beer industry. Whereas Big Beer uses strategies based on mass-production and scale, craft breweries use strategies that reflect artisanal production as well as values of authenticity and independence.

The Cost of Making Beer

Like other industrial producers, Big Beer is able to leverage what economists call *economies of scale*, in which larger companies are able to gain a competitive advantage over smaller operations because of their size and volume of production. By purchasing the raw materials used for brewing in bulk, the price of these ingredients goes down; the same logic applies to producing beer in large quantities. In the past, these advantages were held in check partly by technological challenges. Breweries, like other manufacturers, had to overcome the dual challenges of distance (purchasing ingredients from faraway suppliers and later getting their products to faraway markets) and durability (ensuring the ingredients or beer didn't spoil).[11] These barriers have decreased over time due to improved transportation, refrigeration, and brewing techniques. In the 1800s, for example, brewers first discovered how to systematically brew with lager yeast, which requires a longer brewing time and more storage capacity (*lager* means to store in German), but also results in a product that takes longer to spoil.[12] Other technological innovations also helped expand geographic markets for commercial beer brewers around the turn of the 20th century, such as pasteurization, cheaper glass bottles, ice houses, and refrigeration, as well as faster forms of transportation such as railroads and automobiles.[13] While these technological improvements also benefited smaller brewing companies, they served as key strategic advantages in Big Beer's pursuit of profitability, mass-production, and market expansion.

Another strategy that Big Beer uses to optimize access to raw materials is to purchase ingredient suppliers outright, or at least secure large, long-term contracts for their products. Doing this helps Big Beer achieve greater control over the supply chain from ingredients all the way through the production process. This is why Coors owns large hop farms and malting facilities in Colorado that exclusively supply its Golden, Colorado flagship facility. It is also why AB-InBev has for years sought to stockpile large supplies of hops, far exceeding their immediate production needs.[14] For example, beer writer Stan Hieronymus noted that in 2008, Anheuser-Busch contracted ahead of time approximately 75% of all hops grown in the famous hop-growing region of Willamette Valley, Oregon. Doing so limits the extent to which craft breweries (or any other competing business) can access these resources.[15] By controlling the ingredients necessary for the production of beer, large breweries can bring down the cost of their products while also making it harder for their competitors to obtain these products.

Big Beer also seeks to produce beer more cheaply by using less expensive ingredients in their flagship recipes. For one, the pale lagers produced by Big Beer, particularly in the United States, do not call for premium-priced ingredients, such as the roasted malts in a dry stout or the extra pounds of hops per barrel in a dry-hopped India Pale Ale from your local brewery. Instead, many of their products incorporate inexpensive adjuncts into the malt bill, such as corn, rice, and sugar.[16] For instance, Miller's flagship lagers are brewed with corn; Budweiser's popular lagers use rice as a proportion of their grain bill. These companies argue that they use adjuncts in their beers not solely to reduce costs but also to intentionally adjust flavor and lighten the body of their beers to their customers' liking. Even if this were true, the end result is still, conveniently, a beer that is cheaper to make in large quantities and less vulnerable to fluctuations in the supply of barley. For Big Beer, managing key ingredients in their beer with an eye trained on cost-benefit analysis is simply smart business.

By comparison, many craft breweries take a different approach to think about what it takes to make their beers. Rather than competing by lowering ingredient costs—a race to the bottom for which small brewers will not win—they seek to compete on the quality of what they put in their beers and the integrity of how they make them. As the aforementioned use of premium ingredients implies, craft beer is rarely the cheapest option to either make or buy; nor is it intended to be. Some craft breweries choose to strategically partner with ingredient suppliers who they feel align with their artisanal principles. Ron Silberstein, the co-owner of Admiral Maltings in Alameda, California, explains that his company offers locally grown, locally kilned malts with distinctive flavors to breweries and distillers throughout the region. Admiral Maltings, which started production in 2017, is tiny compared to industrial malt suppliers such as BSG and Country Malt Group (which also retail leading malt brands such as Weyermann and Briess). Silberstein knows he cannot compete on the price of his malt alone: in order to turn a modest profit, Admiral Maltings' products cost substantially more per pound to buy than the malt produced by their large competitors. This translates into more expensive beers to make for small brewers. However, Silberstein says that the California-based breweries and distilleries that he partners with—which now number in the hundreds and include breweries like Seismic Brewing in Santa Rosa, Standard Deviant in San Francisco, and Humble Sea in Santa Cruz— believe in the added value of using locally grown barley and freshly kilned malt made from a traditional "floor malting" technique in their products regardless of cost. Sticking to these principles helps render the craft products coming from these small producers distinct from their corporate counterparts.

Mergers, Sellouts, and Collectives

The strategies that Big Beer companies use to interact with their market competitors are much like those depicted in the popular HBO drama, *Game of Thrones*, in which a small number of powerful families try to overwhelm other families (or sometimes join together with them) in order to increase their control over the kingdom. Multinational beer firms such as AB-InBev, MolsonCoors, and Kirin Holdings use a variety of strategies in an attempt to increase their business advantages over competitors. This includes brokering mergers and pursuing acquisitions of other companies. These strategies are done for one simple reason: combining resources together while simultaneously eliminating threatening competition puts the new company in a position to be more dominant within the industry.

A prime example of Big Beer's competitive playbook is the creation of AB-InBev, which was born out of a 2008 merger between Anheuser-Busch (AB), the largest brewery in the United States, and InBev, a Belgium-Brazilian brewer. Prior to the merger, AB had a long list of other brands within its portfolio which were the result of its prior acquisitions and controlling interest purchases from prior decades. However, facing flattened profits domestically and the need to continue expanding into overseas markets, in 2008, the 150-year-old family-led company made a decision that shocked the beer world: AB agreed to sell a majority of their stake to a foreign beer conglomerate: InBev. The purchasing company itself was born of a similar merger/acquisition: InBev was created out of a 2004 merger between Belgium-based Interbrew and the Brazilian brewer AmBev. AB-InBev immediately became by far the largest brewer in the world, a behemoth multinational company built to dominate the global beer industry. Less than a decade later, AB-InBev agreed to purchase their chief rival and the world's second-largest beer conglomerate, SABMiller.

Craft breweries were not a target of the mergers and acquisitions strategies of Big Beer until relatively recently because they were not viewed as an appreciable market threat by the latter (recall the idea of "resource partitioning"—a market split into dominant and specialized segments). As beer writer Tom Acitelli notes, Big Beer initially missed the signs that craft beer was on the rise and would siphon of a growing share of customers from Big Beer. Even by the late 1980s, the "microbrewery" trend still appeared to be a mild curiosity, a small group of upstart brewers and their DIY operations that together amounted to less than 1% of the total beer market. But as craft beer continued to enjoy double-digit growth into the 1990s, Big Beer began to respond. Their first strategy involved imitation. AB created knock-off brands that appeared to be made by small and independent breweries, such as "Pacific Ridge" (an imitation of Sierra Nevada Pale Ale) and "Ziegenbock" (an imitation of Shiner Bock). However, by the late 1990s, it was clear that the majority of these mass-produced faux products—what we might call "crafty" beers today—did not catch on (with several notable exceptions, such as Blue Moon, which was first produced by MillerCoors in 1995). Instead, for Big Beer, acquiring promising craft brands or purchasing a controlling interest in them offered an attractive alternative. It was a strategy that leveraged their vast advantages of resources and power within the industry. This process started slowly. In the mid-1990s, AB purchased a 25% stake in Independent Ale Co (1994), which owned Redhook Ales, followed by a 27%

stake in Widmer Brothers (1997). Other larger brewing conglomerates would go on to purchase stakes in smaller breweries in the years that followed (see Figure 4.1). To many observers, AB-InBev's purchase of Chicago-based Goose Island Brewing Company in 2012 for an undisclosed amount represented the pinnacle of this business strategy.[17]

Why would a small brewery ever be inclined to "sell out" to Big Beer, their ruthless competitors and industry nemeses? This question has surely gone through many people's heads after the sales of popular craft breweries such as Goose Island, Ten Barrel, Lagunitas, and Elysian, all within a few years from each other during the 2010s.[18] The simple reason is that selling out to a major corporate company gives a smaller company access to resources that they would otherwise have no way of acquiring on their own, such as national distribution channels and up-front capital needed to expand their facility.[19] Counterintuitively, agreeing to let Big Beer acquire a stake in your company—as Tony Magee, the founder of Lagunitas Brewing Company, did—can look like a good strategy to help build your brewery's brand. In a Tumblr letter following the sale of his company to Heineken, Magee explained that this move, "will help us go farther more quickly than we could have on our own." He dismissed criticism that he had "sold out" by reframing his decision as "buying in" to the advantages of being acquired by Big Beer.[20]

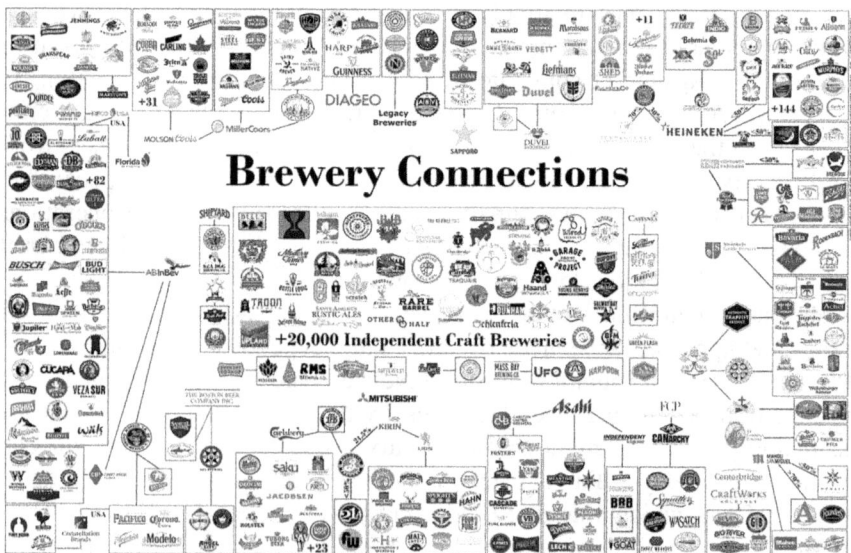

Figure 4.1 A Composite Image of Beer Companies and Their Ownership Status as of 2020. The inner rectangle represents small, independent breweries. The companies outside this box are larger corporate entities, as well as the Catholic Church, with connections to other beer brands (outermost ring). *Source:* Courtesy of Michael Tonsmeire.

Another reason why a buyout can be an attractive option for craft breweries is that it doesn't seem like a buyout at all. At least not initially. Several veteran craft brewery owners such as John Hall (Goose Island) to Dick Cantwell (Elysian) have stated that they felt their original deals with AB-InBev represented "strategic partnerships" rather than buyouts, where key personnel would be allowed to retain creative control of their brewhouse while their company is able to leverage the vast resources of a corporate business partner. Indeed, as beer writer Josh Noel notes, this characterized the circumstance of Goose Island Brewing's sale to AB-InBev in 2011, in which it appeared that no recipes were going to be altered, and the pet projects of the brewery, such as the brewery's popular Bourbon County Stout barrel-aged series, were not only continued but also expanded. After Goose Island's sale to AB-InBev, Goose Island IPA quickly went from being a popular Chicago offering to the number-one selling IPA nationwide, offered in many sports stadiums and large chain supermarkets.[21]

Buyouts bring craft breweries into a tenuous relationship with their much larger and more powerful competitors. While buyouts threaten to compromise core aspects of the former's craft business ethos, some brewery owners see a silver lining. In 2019, Fort Collins-based New Belgium Brewing Company became the first *employee-owned* craft brewery to agree to an acquisition (by Australia-based company Lion Little World Beverages, makers of Kirin beer). The buyout needed to be approved by all employee stakeholders at New Belgium in order to go through, as they would be relinquishing their stakes in the company. On this point, New Belgium's cofounder and CEO, Kim Jordan, commented in an open letter:

> We will no longer be employee owned and it would be easy to see that as a drawback. But here's another way to look at it. More than 300 employees are receiving over $100,000 of retirement money with some receiving significantly greater amounts. Over the life of our ESOP (employee stock ownership plan), including this transaction, the total amount paid to current and former employees will be nearly $190 million. We will have helped a significant number of people realize the upside of having equity in something, being a part of the American Dream![22]

What goes unacknowledged in Kim Jordan's statement is that the beer industry in 2019 was not the same as the one that existed ten years ago—when craft beer was enjoying significant growth, and profitable craft companies like New Belgium were showing the beer world a more progressive of employment through employee ownership.[23] New Belgium's sale epitomizes the pressure that craft breweries are under as they attempt to use the strategies available to them in a competitive market while simultaneously trying to retain their independence and integrity. For craft producers, buyouts come with powerful allure: *you can continue making the fantastic stuff you've always made, only in larger quantities and using improved equipment. You'll just be doing it for us now.*

As an alternative, some craft producers have attempted to team up to form collaborative business ventures born out of similar interests. Numerous partnerships have flourished in the craft beer world over the past two decades. These include collaborations between breweries, collaborations with other craft businesses such as coffee roasters (to make coffee stouts) and local farmers (to make seasonal, fruit-infused beers), and collaborations with local nonprofit organizations and creative personalities. While there are a variety of reasons why companies may seek to engage in these short-term collaborations, doing so allows them to build ties and pool resources with other companies, all while continuing to highlight their craft identity.

Brewery "collectives" represent more formal attempts to team up with like-minded producers in a mutually advantageous way. An early example of this was the Craft Brewers Alliance (CBA), which was originally a partnership formed in 2008 between two of the original craft breweries in the Pacific Northeast: Portland-based Widmer Brothers Brewery and Seattle-based Redhook Brewery. In the years following its formation, CBA added Kona Brewing Company, Hawaii's largest craft brewery at the time, and went public by offering shares to investors. CBA established a regional powerhouse that at the time was among the largest craft brewing companies in the United States. Their independence, however, was short-lived: in a multistep deal finalized in early 2020, CBA agreed to a buyout by AB-InBev. Another example is a craft brewery group that goes by the name of the CANarchy. CANarchy was originally composed of Oskar Blues in Colorado and Cigar City Brewing Company in Florida, before adding several more breweries such as Three Weavers in Los Angeles and Squatters in Utah. CANarchy's philosophy follows a familiar tune: share resources to reduce costs and sell more products in multiple beer markets. However, CANarchy has a hidden weapon at its disposal: the group is backed by a private equity firm. While CANarchy has not "sold out" in the sense of agreeing to business terms with a corporate beer competitor, the nature and intentions of its financial partnership remain a gray area. Craft breweries, particularly established regional ones, are continually trying to adjust to growing competition "from below" (among local breweries) while also fending off the incursion of Big Beer "from above." Today, craft producers no longer fly under the radar of market competition. They must fight to remain in place, balancing their business needs and aspirations for growth with their desire to adhere to core craft values, including that of independence and authenticity.

Controlling the Middle

Because of the three-tier system in the beer industry, most commercial beer that consumers see on retail shelves or coming out of a tap has to go through distribution in order to arrive there. As classic "middleman" businesses within an industry, distribution companies specialize in moving products from brewers to retail accounts, taking a small cut of profits in exchange. Ideally, this is to the benefit of all parties: consumers get more choices available to them; breweries can focus on making beer without having to worry about the logistics of shipping it out; and retailers benefit from having full shelves or tap handles stocked with a variety of offerings instead of having to go to each of these vendors in order to buy their beers. But distribution rarely works out in this ideal form. Instead, the way beer is distributed works to the benefit of companies that are able to use their power and resources to give them unfair advantages over others, especially smaller craft producers. Eli describes the moment when the power of Big Beer in distribution became clear to him. Ironically, it was during a visit to a regional beer distributor in the southwest in which he was there to meet the company's craft beer specialist, a White man named Tyler:

> Tyler's office was decorated with rare bottles of beer from around the world; a small beer fridge filled with the latest craft beer samples sat next to his desk. Tyler described his love of trying new beers and visiting new breweries in the area, some of which he signed on to be distributed by his company.
>
> We walked to the main warehouse where products awaited delivery to local retail stores, restaurants, and bars. The warehouse was huge, the size of a Costco superstore with men driving forklifts carrying pallets of products stacked 30 feet high on steel shelves.
>
> "Craft beer is doing even better than I thought!" I exclaimed, looking around in awe.
>
> "Yes, sales are definitely going strong," Tyler said. "But our craft beer section is just this aisle." He pointed down an aisle off towards the rear of the warehouse. There, many familiar craft beer brand logos were crammed together. Adjacent to the craft beer aisle were entire walls of Big Beer products, each adorned in a half dozen different forms of packaging. Another aisle down, I gazed at hard ciders and seltzers of every flavor under the rainbow. Here on the grounds of a distribution warehouse ready to supply the region with beer, Big Beer's presence was everywhere.

Large regional distributors, like the one Eli visited, have specialized teams of employees whose job is to draw up a design of a given retailer's shelf space and fill it with products in a way that is advantageous to their company. They present "set designs" to their retail clients as a way to help that client manage their beer inventory. One distributor employee, a White man who works as a "Set Captain," compared his job to a game of "adult Tetris," in which the goal is to slot products with different sizes into the shelf space that he is given by the retail account. "You have to know how to balance your brands with *some* of your competition's brands in order to keep the client [the retailer] happy," he explained. If a brand isn't selling, it is also his responsibility as a set captain to convey this information to the client, and quickly pull the product off of the set in the next rotation.

Beer distributors and the set captains they employ have tremendous power within the industry as gatekeepers. They take an active interest in building their portfolio and expanding the presence of their brands on retail shelves and tap handles. For this reason, powerful beer companies use a variety of strategies to gain influence over distributors. Big Beer has for years attempted to curry favor from distributors by using strategies of suspect legality. Josh Noel, author of *Barrel-Aged Stout and Selling Out*, notes that in the mid-1990s, Anheuser-Busch rolled out an incentive program for distributors that offered them substantial monetary rewards in exchange for prioritizing the sale of AB products. Called the "100% Share of Mind" campaign, AB incentivized distributors to sell AB portfolio products and rewarded them based on different tiers of success.[24] To complement this strategy, Big Beer manufactures a wide variety of products to sell. For example, AB-InBev's popular brand Bud Light now includes an ever-growing line of related products in the United States, such as Bud Light Ice, Bud Light Platinum, Bud Light Chelada, and Bud Light Lime. More recently, Bud Light's Seltzer lineup launched with a half dozen flavors.[25] Many of these brands also come packaged in a dizzying variety of formats (e.g., six packs, twelve packs, cans, bottles). As programs such as the 100% Share of Mind campaign are designed to achieve, many large distributors are motivated to prioritize Big Beer products in ways that can box out craft breweries or at least limit their growth. For example, a craft brewery owner in New Mexico named Marlene says she was doing a "ride-along" with a sales representative from her distributor when the owner of a liquor store asked the sales rep to recommend a new, lighter beer option for his store. The sales rep jumped on the opportunity to hype up a Big Beer brand that had just released a new "SKU" (brand product). Marlene was shocked: her brewery's flagship beer was also a light beer that should have been the perfect product to recommend in this situation. But unlike the Big Beer brand, Marlene's product didn't come with a free trip to Hawai'i to whoever sold the most cases of this new beer over the fiscal quarter.

A former distributor sales representative named Matt explains how behind-the-scenes incentives work for sales "reps":

Most sales reps are not *sales* reps, they are just order takers. They go into bars or retail establishments and say, "okay what do you need? How many of this and this? Okay bye!" *Unless someone is paying them to sell something.* Then, they will be like, "oh hey, I have this." And if they have a relationship with the person at the bar they'll be like, "listen, if you put this on tap I'm making some money, so can you run a keg [for free] . . ." and it'll get done.

The game of distribution is designed to favor companies that can use their power and resources to shift the game in their favor. As Matt notes, behind the scenes, Big Beer orchestrates "pay to play" incentives for sales reps who can choose to favor selling one product over another. They provide similar under-the-table incentives for retailers themselves. Stories abound of large breweries offering bars and restaurants everything from wall décor and out-door banners to new draft systems and cooler boxes—all for favoring their products on shelves and in draft lines. While several lawsuits have been filed to curb such practices over the years, some of them resulting in million-plus dollar penalties for beer companies, "pay to play" schemes have been notoriously difficult to prove and even harder to eradicate in practice from the industry.[26]

Big Beer has long had a presence in the business of distribution in order to increase their influence over the supply chain. In recent years, however, companies such as Anheuser-Busch have ramped up these efforts as a way of strategically complementing their acquisitions of key regional craft breweries like Goose Island, Golden Road, and Lagunitas.[27] Big Beer also continues to lobby for changes to distributor ownership laws at the state level that would further compress the three-tier system and expand their control over the industry. Big Beer need not own distribution companies outright in order to exert powerful influence over the latter's actions. For example, in beer markets where sales of AB products are still robust, the threat of withholding access to Bud and Bud Light is too risky for distributors and retailers to resist. AB is able to get their wishes—for access, for prime placement, for distribution priority—by being the biggest and most important player in the beer industry. Yet by doing so, AB threatens to compromise the independence of independently owned distributors (remember the three-tier system is designed to not let any one company dominate all three tiers).[28] Josh Noel points out that many AB regional distributors signal their allegiance prominently by naming their company in ways that suggest both AB brand themes and their top position in the industry: Regal, Ace, Premiere. All of these efforts continue to make it very hard for craft breweries to compete for consumer dollars outside of their taprooms and local retail channels.

For small breweries, partnering with a distributor, despite the risks, can be one of the most important decisions they make in their efforts to expand their business. This is because distributors can also help small breweries expand their brands beyond what they could do themselves. As one craft brewery sales rep named Paul explains:

What is your relationship with [your distributor] like?

Paul: To describe it, I would say it's pivotal. Our relationship with [the distributor] is the most important component of our sales endeavors. It's so much more so than our relationships with retailers or consumers. They are the warehouse. They are the distribution. They decide what they sell. Our job is more so than me convincing these retail purchasers to buy our products. It's them that sell our products. And, it's a career of different ways of doing that. And understanding how their business works and applying it to our products and creating the right kind of business outlook and agenda that yields the highest number of sales. So much of it is supply to distributor.

Paul explains that some distributors specialize in the art of selling and delivering products in a way that many small breweries benefit tremendously from. They benefit from the relationships that distributors have with existing accounts, and without a doubt, the most important of those relationships is with chain retail stores that do the bulk of all beer sales by volume nationwide.[29] However, for craft breweries producing limited volumes of beer, distribution can be very expensive. Distributors typically take a 25–30% cut of the profits of every beer sale and, as a result, the only way craft breweries can turn a profit through partnering with a distributor is by selling a *lot* of beer.

This has led many small breweries opting for self-distribution in the states where this is allowed. By cutting out the middle business, breweries can save on costs. But they may also lack the in-house resources to deliver products to retail accounts quickly and effectively. Jeff Erway, the owner of Albuquerque-based La Cumbre Brewing Company, explains the challenges of expanding the business beyond the brewery taproom and into distribution channels:

Jeff: If your goal is to make a multimillion dollar a year production brewery, good luck. It's a very tough market to do that in.

Eli: Why is that?

Jeff: Well how long you got? (laughs). Shelf space. Shelf space, tap space. And who controls it.

Eli: Are you talking about distribution?

Jeff: Yeah, I mean you're up against enormous companies that are throwing a lot of money around both legally and illegally to make sure that they maintain as much of the shelf spacings and the taps space as possible. You're talking about multi-billion dollar corporations that you're going up against.

Jeff's own brewery has continued to self-distribute in its home market, the metropolitan area of Albuquerque, New Mexico. This allows the brewery to increase profits while keeping more of business dealings under house control. Beyond this region, however, Jeff's decision represents the give and take that many other small breweries face with distribution: he decided to partner with a distributor because it didn't make sense to send employees to drive for hours away from the brewery to make deliveries.

Keeping It Local?

For craft breweries, an alternative way to deal with the double-edged sword of distribution is to favor independence over growth by committing to remaining small and local. An example of this business strategy is Indie Brewing Company in Los Angeles. Back when the business plans for Indie Brewing were being drawn up, co-owner Morgan Keller says that their ambition was to become a regional player in the Southern California market. However, that goal changed over the couple of years it took to open the brewery's doors: Morgan and his co-owners quickly learned of the challenges of distribution, especially in an increasingly crowded beer market. They chose to scale back their ambitions:

> Now we are sort of flying under the radar. And the bigger [craft breweries] do kind of get pushed back down [by the corporate players]. But, there is the war of the trenches too, fighting tap handle to tap handle with Big Beer all the time. And products that are pretending to be craft beer when they are not. The Golden Roads of the world that are brewed at the Budweiser plant in the same tanks as the bud light. And then it is marketed as the craft beer of Los Angeles. That seems disingenuous to me.

Morgan has decided not to compete head-to-head with large corporate breweries and their cutthroat business practices. Yet "flying under the radar" and concentrating on his local market has not meant that Indie Brewing has stagnated. Recently, Indie Brewing partnered with a "craft" distributor that serves Southern California and represents roughly a dozen craft breweries in the region. The upside, says Morgan, is the greater care that this distributor shows his brand; they are partners in craft philosophy as well as partners in business.

Other craft breweries have opted to sell their beer directly from their brewpub or tasting room only. On the one hand, the idea of a "neighborhood brewery" can be an attractive model for brewery owners who value staying local and serving their clientele with a personal touch. This is the case with Anne O'Neil and her husband Jim, owners of Sidetrack Brewing in Albuquerque. Opening Sidetrack Brewing represented "second careers" for the two of them, a transition away from nine to five professional jobs to something more creative and in line with their passions.[30] Running a neighborhood brewery or brewpub—with deliberately scaled-back business ambitions—comes with another important plus: it allows craft brewers to avoid competing directly with Big Beer on turf where the latter has an unfair advantage (such as distribution and retail price point). Operating a neighborhood brewery that serves a local clientele is one way to remain independent and authentic in their commitment to craft beer—albeit in ways that leave the dominant position of Big Beer unchallenged.

Marketing Beer and Creating Brands

Why do people who can't stand Budweiser beer still know about their Clydesdales? Why do your friends who enjoy beer know that Coors is supposedly cold-fermented at the lowest temperatures, that the beer is ice cold because the mountains on the can have turned blue? Companies in all industries use branding strategies to frame their identity and value to consumers in strategic ways. Because many consumers buy what they know and what feels familiar—often based on unconscious "front of mind" intuition and positive associations—branding can provide important cues to guide their purchasing decisions. Big Beer has known this for years; their marketing budgets always exceed that of research and development. Branding is not, of course, a business strategy used exclusively by Big Beer. Many craft breweries use branding to help construct their image as the local, "handcrafted," and "authentic" option.[31] This has grown increasingly challenging in the last decade, as craft breweries must find ways to not only differentiate themselves from thousands of other craft brands but also contend with the appropriation of "craft" and "heritage" branding by Big Beer.

Branding is the driving engine for *creating consumer desires* rather than merely reflecting them. Branding steers consumption choices toward products that a company makes or represents. Big Beer spends millions of dollars each year to ensure that their products remain at the forefront of public awareness. The power of branding is clearly evident in the seltzer craze that swept through the United States starting in 2019. Brewers—and we suspect industry marketers, too—will tell you there isn't anything particularly new or technically challenging about creating a fizzy alcoholic product with a touch of fruit flavor. Instead, leading seltzer makers like Truly (owned by Boston Beer Company) and White Claw (owned by the makers of Mike's Hard Lemonade, Mark Anthony Brewing) have rolled out advertisement campaigns on popular social media sites that portray seltzer as an alcoholic drink associated with a healthy lifestyle, delicious fruit flavor, and a fun-loving social environment. What you are consuming when you buy seltzer, according to its corporate makers, is bottled entertainment. Branding was one of the main factors that contributed to sales of hard seltzer growing 300% in the spring of 2020. This spurred Big Beer to launch new hard seltzer brands based on variations of their own iconic products such as Corona Seltzer and Bud Light Seltzer, marketed to both men and women.[32]

Big Beer companies emphasize that their iconic beer brands are about having laid-back fun, socializing with friends, and engaging in many of life's most enjoyable pastimes with their product by your side. There are subtle differences to these brands by design, which point to working-class comforts, sex appeal (especially featuring the hyper-sexualization of women), or an edgy, youth-centered lifestyle. "Let's grab a beer," state the various workers in plainspeak in a recent Budweiser commercial; "That's the fine life, baby," coos Snoop Dogg while relaxing in a beach chair holding a Corona. In a new ad series by Heineken, young, attractive people at a swank party pass around Heineken's iconic green bottle without ever uttering a word to each other. The most effectively branded brands hardly need an introduction.

In recent years, some corporate breweries have expanded their branding efforts to pitch the heritage of their company. They play up generations-old recipes and tradition-bound brewing methods uniquely theirs. By doing so, they assert authenticity in brand despite mass-production in the process. One example of this would be Budweiser's "aged on beechwood" slogan and corresponding advertisements. According to the company, every Budweiser beer goes through a fermentation process that involves contact with beechwood. Whether or not this method results in any perceptible difference in sensory experience for consumers is unclear, but the story adds just enough air of uniqueness to their brewing process that complements Bud's marketing message that plays up the heritage of the brand. Similarly, branding for Coors' Banquet Beer includes a dedicated website designed to evoke the heritage of this product and, by extension, Coors itself. Despite Coors Banquet Beer being mass-produced and widely distributed, the company plays up its idiosyncratic history: "Coors Banquet is the result of tradition. One that can be traced back for generations. While there may be a simpler method, we stand by our techniques. After all, there's no sense in changing what works so well."[33] Big Beer thus attempts to use "heritage" branding to depict the artisanal qualities of their products.

Craft breweries today also use branding strategies to help them stand out. Craft breweries emphasize their authenticity, independent ethos, and local roots, which have particular appeal to more affluent consumers today with high levels of cultural knowledge (see chapter 2).[34] Sociologists Amanda Koontz and Nate Chapman note that craft breweries actively construct an image of authenticity through their founding stories, as depicted on company websites and beer labels. These stories portray the opening of a brewery as a "quest" or "journey" by someone who is a hard-working beer enthusiast. Consider Sam Adams's marketing campaigns. In select TV and print ads, Jim Koch, the founder and co-owner of Boston Beer Company, leads the audience through a brewhouse in which brewers sample beer pulled fresh from the tank and based on an original, time-honored, recipe of Jim's. It is an inventive piece of marketing idealizing an artisanal brewing process and signaling the values that purchasing a Sam Adams product, particularly Boston Lager, represents.

Of course, few craft breweries can pay for expensive national TV advertisements that Boston Beer Company can. Instead, they use their distinctive labels and other aspects of their operation to convey their brand. One prominent branding strategy of craft breweries is to convey their image as the *opposite* of what Big Beer stands for. This can range in meaning and imagery from anti-corporate to not-bland to not-mass-produced.[35] For example, several brewers we interviewed mentioned that the brand that stuck with them when they first got interested in craft beer was Stone Brewing Company's gargoyle imagery and general attitude of arrogance. "You're Not Worthy," reads the label of Stone's iconic Arrogant Bastard Ale. "This Beer is *Not* for You." Stone's message is as arrogant as it is unforgettable, influencing a whole general of young brewers, particularly men.[36]

One of those brewers was Justin Collins, co-owner of Warcloud Brewing Company in Temecula, California. The branding of his brewery, which features artist-renditions of warriors and military leaders, reflects a love for military lore from around the world which he and his brewery co-owners share (see Figure 4.2). Justin, who is African American, explains the decision to incorporate this imagery in Warcloud's brand:

> [The imagery] comes from the Army Special Forces, and Shaka Zulu, who was a military mastermind in Africa. This ties everything in for us because at first, all the [co-owners] in Warcloud, we were fighting for something different. We were fighting for territory. We were fighting for who-knows-who, who knows what. We were able to channel that energy into a business.

As Justin illustrates, emphasizing the authenticity of one's craft operation can take many different forms. Craft beer brands today represent a wide range of themes, ranging from cultural sophistication (The Bruery's ornate beer labels and Reserve Society membership), to pride of place (Maui Brewing's labels and beer names all have distinct Hawaii-based themes), to specific hobbies and interests (Warcloud's military imagery).

While craft breweries continue to attempt to portray themselves as unique and artisanal through their branding, they face growing pressure to stand out amidst a sea of other breweries that include corporate-owned brands and "faux craft" breweries. One organized effort to support craft breweries

Figure 4.2   Members of the Warcloud Brewing Company in 2019. *Source:* Courtesy of Justin Collins.

has been the creation of "Independent Craft Brewer" seal, by the Brewers Association (BA), a large trade group of brewers. "What the seal provides is a clear message to the beer drinker that this beer comes from a small and independent craft brewer," says Paul Gatza, senior vice president of the professional brewing division at the BA.[37] The seal is intended as a complement to a brewery's craft branding. Only breweries that fit the BA's definition of a craft brewer are allowed to display this symbol on their products and brewery spaces.

Finally, beer consumers also play an outsized role in helping craft breweries spread word about their products on a grassroots level. By displaying brewery insignia organically, through social media feeds as well as bumper stickers, keychains, logoed hats, and logo'd t-shirts, fans embody the appeal of these small operations and spread that message to others. As a result, even as Big Beer strategizes brand campaigns that appropriate the symbols and slogans of craft (e.g., "handcrafted" processes or ingredients of "only the highest quality"), the way consumers themselves interact with these brands become an important way in which craft breweries continue to differentiate their businesses in the larger market.[38]

Imagine a world in which beer enthusiasts rise up, vote with their dollars, and tip the scales against Big Beer in favor of locally owned, craft operations. To some extent, this is already happening in the United States, where there are now more breweries than any period in this country's history. Yet despite the steady rise of craft beer, we are still far from a moment in which Big Beer has lost its grip over the industry in business terms, as evident in annual sales, production volume, and profit. It is telling that the largest brewing company in the world, AB-InBev, is also the largest company in human existence. Meanwhile, by the end of the 2010s, the number of small brewery openings had slowed while craft beer production declined faster than the market as a whole.[39]

This chapter had highlighted the strategies that Big Beer uses to maintain its advantages, and those that craft breweries use to shore up their own position in a competitive business landscape. Big Beer has money and global influence; they control vast supplies of the ingredients used to make beer and have demonstrated a willingness to merge with their competitors in order to shore up their bottom line. Companies like AB-InBev and Heineken International do not just produce beer—they control the distribution of beer and have key retail "partners" that help ensure that their corporate brands are prominently displayed to consumers and priced lower than any craft brewery's offerings. Big Beer has embedded itself within the very infrastructure of the beer industry such that the industry's growth becomes intricately tied to their own profit. The importance of understanding these strategies goes beyond beer. It is about understanding the inner workings of the capitalist enterprise itself.

Today the clearly demarcated lines between Big Beer and craft beer have blurred. For the first three decades of the craft beer revolution, brewing beer with flavors other than "light" was done exclusively by craft breweries (with the exception of a handful of European brands, such as Guinness and Bass). Big Beer now understands that today's consumers are willing to pay a premium for specialty beer styles and unique flavors; they are not designed to give up on this growing segment of consumers. Corporate buyouts of craft breweries have been a major part of this strategy to eat away at the business of small businesses. Goose Island IPA is made in the same facility that makes Bud Light,[40] and AB-InBev alone owns several brands that once represented the crown jewel of their local craft beer scenes, such as Ten Barrel in Portland, Oregon, and Elysian Brewery in Seattle, Washington. What this means is that Big Beer has the potential to threaten the craft beer segment and cut deep into the profits of top craft brands—especially if the only thing that sets craft beer apart is flavor. It is now harder than ever for small breweries to grow beyond their literal and figurative neighborhood corner. In their attempts to do so, some craft breweries have been forced to adopt Big Beer-like business strategies. However, it is important to keep in mind that Big Beer can never be a truly local or "handcrafted" option for knowledgeable consumers, where a dollar spent on beer goes back to a small business that cares deeply about brewing and building local community. Therein lies the enduring distinction between Big Beer and craft beer, the source of the dual segments within the market that are at once distinct and in perpetual competition, especially today.

We have established that the beer industry is made up of a web of Big Beer and craft breweries, workers and consumers, and many other actors in between. All of these relationships are fundamentally mediated by the rules of the playing field of beer itself, by which we mean the laws and regulations that structure the world of beer. In the next chapter, we detail how these rules are a source of both constraint and opportunity for beer companies. They also affect how we as consumers drink beer in ways that you may not expect.

NOTES

1. Borer (2019: 12) notes that the distinction between craft and mass-produced has become a key distinction in many cultural fields, not just beer.

2. While craft breweries have been found to have positive impacts on neighborhood revitalization, they have also raised concerns about gentrification. See Barajas, Jesus M., Geoff Boeing, and Julie Wartell. 2017. "Neighborhood change, one pint at a time: The impact of local characteristics on craft breweries." In N. G. Chapman, J. S. Lellock, and C. D. Lippard (Eds.), *Untapped: Exploring the cultural dimensions of craft beer*. Morgantown: West Virginia University Press; Borer 2019; Florida, Richard. 2004. *The rise of the creative class and how it's transforming work, leisure, community and everyday life*. New York: Basic Books; Wallace 2019.

3. Acitelli 2013; Carroll 1985; Carroll and Swaminathan 2000.

4. Carroll and Swaminathan 2000. We also borrow insights from the "production of culture" perspective, as theorized by sociologist Richard Peterson and colleagues (see Peterson 1990; Peterson and Anand 2004).

5. Based on Brewers Association data in 2020. Craft beer's market share decreased slightly in 2020, during the pandemic. See https://www.brewersassociation .org/statistics-and-data/national-beer-stats/.

6. The relative proportion of craft beer sales is higher in some regional markets known to be hotbeds for craft beer, such as San Diego, California, Asheville, North Carolina, and Portland, Oregon.

7. Nugent, A. 2005. *The global beer market: A world of two halves*. London, UK: Euromonitor International. Accessed 8/1/20 (http://blog.euromonitor.com/2005/02/ the-global-beer-market-a-world- of-two-halves.html).

8. In the United States, the two companies agreed to divest interest and sell off SAB Miller's North American holdings to Canadian brewers Molson Brewing Company. See also Ascher, Bernard. 2012. *Global beer: The road to monopoly*. Washington, DC: American Anti-trust Institute.

9. Hess, Alexander. 2014. "Companies that control the world's food." *USA Today*, August 16, 2014. Accessed 2/21/2021 (https://www.usatoday.com/story/money/business/2014/08/16/companies-that-control-the-worlds-food/14056133/).

10. Ogle 2007; Van Munching, P. 1997. *Beer blast: The inside story of the brewing industry's bizarre battles for your money.* New York: Random House.

11. Friedmann, Harriet. 1992. "Distance and durability: Shaky foundations of the world food economy." *Third World Quarterly, 13*(2): 371–383.

12. Van Munching 1997.

13. Ascher 2012; Ogle 2007.

14. In 2017, part of AB-InBev's deal to purchase SABMille included the acquisition of a series of hop farms in South Africa that SABMille created and invested in scientific research in order to bring hop farming to the region. See Notte, Jason. "Opinion: Anheuser-Busch InBev shuts out craft beer brewers by hoarding hops." *MarketWatch.* May 12, 2017. Accessed 2/15/2021 (https://www.marketwatch.com/story/anheuser-busch-inbev-shuts-out-craft-beer-brewers-by-hoarding-hops-2017-05-11).

15. Hieronymus, Stan. 2012. *For the love of hops: The practical guide to aroma, bitterness and the culture of hops.* Boulder, CO: Brewers Publications.

16. Different brewing traditions around the world technically use "adjuncts" in the brewing of beer, such as candied sugar and honey. That said, these traditions differ from the practices of corporate beer production in that the former are not deployed with the primary aim of reducing the cost of commercial beer production.

17. Noel, Josh. 2018. *Barrel-aged stout and selling out: Goose island, anheuser-busch, and how craft beer became big business.* Chicago, IL: Chicago Review Press; Vinepair. "The Definitive Timeline of Craft Beer Acquisitions." Accessed 2/15/21 (https://vinepair.com/craft-beer-sales/).

18. These buyouts respectively occurred in 2011 (by AB-InBev), 2014 (by AB-InBev), 2015 (AB-InBev), and 2017 (by Heineken International).

19. Noel 2015.

20. Tuttle, Brad. 2017. "Here's why craft beer pioneer lagunitas says it sold itself to Heineken." *Money.com.* May 5, 2017. Accessed 2/15/21: (https://money.com/craft-beer-lagunitas-heineken).

21. Noel 2015.

22. Hefty, J. 2019. "New Belgium founder: Sale 'not the last chapter' for Fort Collins Brewer." *Coloradoan*, November 19, 2019. Accessed 2/21/21: (https://www.coloradoan.com/story/money/2019/11/19/new-belgium-brewing-company-founder-kim-jordan-letter-fort-collins-beer/4238705002/).

23. During this period, New Belgium Brewing Company was successful enough that its owners planned to expand to a second brewery location in Asheville, North Carolina.

24. Noel 2015: 80–85.

25. Hannaford, Steve. 2007. *Market domination!: The impact of industry consolidation on competition, innovation, and consumer choice.* Westport, CT: Praeger; Howard, Philip H. 2014. "Too big to ale? Globalization and consolidation in the beer industry." In *The geography of beer* (pp. 155–165). Springer, Dordrecht.

26. Examples of "pay to play" abound in the industry and have been extensively covered elsewhere, see Borer 2019: Chapter 2; Nurin, Tara. "The pay-to-play scandal in the beer biz: How far it goes nobody knows." *Forbes*. March 16, 2016. Accessed 2/15/2021: (https://www.forbes.com/sites/taranurin/2016/03/31/the-pay-to-play-scandal-in-the-beer-biz-how-far-it-goes-nobody-knows/?sh=307b5363b0d5).

27. Bennet, Sarah. 2016. "Wholesale wars: The battle for the future of beer distribution." *Beer Advocate*. Accessed 7/1/21 (https://www.beeradvocate.com/articles/13526/wholesale-wars-the-battle-for-the-future-of-beer-distribution/).

28. Lynn, Barry. 2012. "Big beer, a moral market, and innovation." December 26, 2012. *Harvard Business Review*. Accessed 2/28/21 (https://hbr.org/2012/12/big-beer-a-moral-market-and-in).

29. According to one distribution manager in New Mexico, more than three out of every four beers sold in the state are sold in chain retail stores such as Walmart, Costco, and Vons.

30. Whereas Jim retired from his architecture firm in order to focus on the brewery, Anne has retained her full-time profession at a nearby university.

31. Koontz and Chapman, 2019.

32. Pellechia, Thomas. "Off-Premise Alcohol Sales are Up, With Hard Seltzer Especially a Boom." *Forbes*. Accessed 2/21/21: (https://www.forbes.com/sites/thomaspellechia/2020/06/03/nielsen-cga-alcohol-dollar-sales-report-is-good-with-conditions/#3770ebd51729).

33. Coors Brewing Company (https://www.coors.com).

34. Currid-Halkett, Elizabeth. 2017. *The sum of small things: A theory of the aspirational class*. Princeton, NJ: Princeton University Press; Gatrell, Jay, Neil Reid, and Thomas Steiger. 2017. "Branding spaces: Place, region, sustainability and the american craft beer industry." *Applied Geography,* 90: 360–370; Koontz and Chapman 2019; Maguire, Jennifer. 2019. "Wine, the authenticity taste regime, and rendering craft." In E. Bell, G. Mangia, S. Taylor, and M. L. Toraldo (Eds.), *The organization of craft work: Identities, meanings, and materiality*. New York: Routledge.

35. For examples of branding boutique wine, see Beverland 2005. Anthropologist Sherry Ortner (2012) has argued that independent film occupies a similar relationship to Hollywood, in which the cleavage between the two is not only economic but also about distinctions of culture and ethos.

36. Interestingly, Stone brewing pivoted their main branding away from the kind of in-your-face arrogance that defined their labels, artwork, and marketing of the 2000s and early 2010s. They created a separate brand for "Arrogant Ales," while the Stone Brewing beers moved to more conventional content.

37. According to the BA, this seal can be used by any brewery that is (1) sl (less than six million barrels produced per year) and (2) independent (less than 25% corporate owned). The quote from Paul Gatza is from Craftbeer.com. "Seek the SealTM." Accessed 7/1/21: (https://www.craftbeer.com/breweries/independent-craft-brewer-seal).

38. For a good overview of the contested nature of "craft" representation today see Bell, Emma, Gianluigi Mangia, Scott Taylor, and Maria L. Toraldo (Eds.). 2018.

The Organization of craft work: Identities, meanings, and materiality. New York: Routledge.

39. Brewers Association, "National Beer Sales and Production Data."
40. Noel 2015.

Chapter 5

Laws and Regulation Are Everything

In 1999, at the urging of two small brewery owners, Tim O'Leary and Brian Smith, Montana's state government passed a law that allowed small breweries to sell their own beer on premise for the first time since Prohibition. "We had people that just wanted to come in and drink a beer," says O'Leary, who owns Kettlehouse Brewing, which operated as a brew-on-premise operation for homebrewers before the change in legislation.

> We'd say, "Well, we can give you [space] and you can brew your own and when you bottle it you can sample your own bottle." But people wanted brew pubs in this state, and when your customers are asking for something, if you're a smart business person you give it to them.[1]

For Montana-based craft breweries, the change in legislation directly was huge. It directly contributed to a sudden upswing in the number of brewery taproom and "brewpub" openings in the state. Within one decade, Montana went from less than ten breweries to nearly one hundred, almost all of them being small, craft brewery operations.

That's when the pushback started. According to the Montana Tavern Association, small breweries are being given an unfair advantage over bars and taverns, which are required to purchase a liquor license that can cost up to $100,000 in order to sell beer on premise. While the Montana Tavern Association has tried unsuccessfully to require breweries to purchase a liquor license for taprooms and brewpubs, they have managed to stymie efforts led by the Montana Brewer's Association to get additional laws amended that would extend taproom hours and expand the current cap on brewery size for breweries eligible to sell beer on premise (currently at 12,000).[2]

The timing of Montana's 1999 "brewpub" legislation is also noteworthy. It arrived nearly *seventeen years* after the first United States approved such a bill. As a result, until very recently, Montana had some of the fewest breweries in the country per capita, whereas states that were early adopters of laws allowing small breweries to sell beer on premise have become home to the most prominent craft beer scenes in the country, such as in San Diego, California (law passed in 1982), Portland, Oregon (law passed in 1985), and Denver, Colorado (law passed in 1988). It was key changes in legislation that, in the words of one journalist, "made the craft brew revolution possible" in these locales.[3]

The story of Montana's brewpub law may seem idiosyncratic but it illustrates a broader and more far-reaching point: that laws *do* really important things in the world of beer—just as they do in the rest of society. National and state governments establish laws and regulations that everyone must operate by, which in turn influences how beer is produced, distributed, sold, and consumed.[4] Yet because laws are drafted using particular language and subject to revisions and alterations, they are also the site of contestation: organized groups such as the Montana Tavern Association and the Montana Brewers Association continue to attempt to influence key regulations in their state in ways that align with the interests of their constituents. In other words, laws are socially produced, negotiated, and embedded within society, which is known as the *socio-legal perspective*.[5]

Previously, we observed how large companies (Big Beer) secure their dominant position in industry through competitive business strategies and how smaller craft companies attempt to shore up their specialized niche within the market (chapter 4). In this chapter, we lay out how laws and regulations fundamentally impact the business of beer as well as the consumption of it. Laws and regulations: (1) *establish the playing field* for producing, distributing, and selling beer; (2) alter how local industries *develop over time*; and (3) influence the *strategies and opportunities* that companies seek to take advantage of. While we draw mainly on examples from the U.S. beer industry and specific state-level legislation to illustrate our points, it is important to keep in mind that different arrangements of legal policies surrounding beer vary significantly across time and place; the uneven landscape of beer has much to do with the legal playing field on which it sits.

Because laws and regulations reflect societal values and institutions, it should come as no surprise that the official rules of the land uphold existing arrangements of power. As critical legal scholars note, the historical exclusion of women and BIPOC from owning land, starting businesses, and entering certain professions in the United States has locked in socioeconomic disadvantages for members of these groups. Even with many of these discriminatory restrictions formally lifted—for instance, the Fair Housing Act of 1968 makes overt discrimination during the sale or renting of housing based on race, color, national origin, religion, sex, familial status, or disability illegal—the legacies of these policies remain with us. This is as true in the world of beer as it is elsewhere. As sociologists Nathaniel Chapman and Dave Brunsma note, African Americans were systematically denied access to loans that could have helped them gain a foothold in the beer industry through entrepreneurship. In the Jim Crow South, Blacks were barred entry to many of the saloons that were the site of daily sociality, particularly for working-class White men.[6] If we are to understand how "beer became White," argue Chapman and Brunsma, we need to look seriously at the role that laws played in undergirding systemic racism in the United States.

Picture a game of Monopoly with many players participating at the same time and competing to own more of the board. Breweries and other beer businesses are the individual players in the game; each player attempts to make calculated decisions in order to gain a leg up based on a blend of strategy, resources, and knowledge of the game. The board itself, the way it is arranged, and the rules of gameplay represent governing laws that all participants must follow at any given time. Some of these laws are pertinent to business in that industry (such as copyrights and labor protections), whereas others regulate consumer behavior as well as how businesses interact with consumers (such as restrictions on hours of operation for alcohol establishments). But unlike the game of Monopoly, the rules of the game themselves can be altered. This in turn becomes a strategy that savvy and powerful players can use to gain an edge over their competitors. This is why brewery owners and other industry stakeholders take beer laws and regulations very seriously. It is also why many players have turned a blind eye in the past when the rules of the game have oppressed or outright excluded other players or groups that they are competing against.

THE REGULATORY LANDSCAPE OF
BEER AND ITS CONSEQUENCES

Alcoholic beverages remain one of the most highly restricted substances on the planet. Every government maintains legal restrictions over how commercial alcoholic beverages such as beer can be produced, distributed, and sold to the public. How these laws have been historically formulated, revised, and retooled are not only relevant to the development of that region's beer industry but also reflect deeply held social norms, moral beliefs, and cultural values.

The Prohibition Era

In the United States, the years of Prohibition have become an indelible part of the country's culture and history. The years 1920 and 1933 represent the years that bookended the period in which a federal ban on the production and sale of alcohol stood in place.[7] Prohibition was, for obvious reasons, a dramatically different legal playing field for the nation's beer producers and consumers. It was also not unique to the United States during this period: Canada, Iceland, Norway, Finland, and the Soviet Union were among the other countries that enacted national Prohibition policies in the early 20th century that lasted at least one year.

The push for Prohibition had been years in the making. When legislation calling for the restriction of alcohol first began to circulate in the United States, prominent organized groups, such as the Anti-Saloon League, were vocal about the fact that drinking alcohol was a widespread social ill that needed to be curbed.[8] Facing growing political pressure, the government's unprecedented decision to shut down the domestic alcohol industry through the passing of the 18th Amendment left a profound impact on the country's beer industry and public drinking culture for decades to come. Prohibition immediately shuttered the nation's thousand-plus commercial breweries, hundreds of which would never reopen.[9] While Prohibition didn't exactly curb the public's thirst for alcohol, it drove demand underground, to be met through a black market for beer, wine, and spirits. Within this new extralegal landscape of beer, new business players rose to prominence such as "boot-leggers" (someone who makes or sells alcohol illegally) and "speakeasy" establishments (a place that sells alcohol illegally).

Prohibition continued to reshape the beer industry landscape even after it was repealed thirteen years later. For one, the 21st Amendment that repealed Prohibition, known as the Cullen Harrison Act, came with heavy restrictions on how beer could be made as well as when and where it could be sold. Further regulation of the beer industry was left up to individual states and their governing bodies.[10] It was during this era that Big Beer saw its control over the national beer market increase dramatically. This is because large, well-established breweries such as Anheuser-Busch and Pabst were better able to adjust their business practices to the new, restricted playing field than smaller companies who were hanging on by a thread even after Prohibition was repealed.[11]

The "Three-Tier" System

Following the repeal of Prohibition, what would prove to be one of the most consequential regulations of the beer industry was the "three-tier" system.

The three tiers of the beer industry legally separate producers (brewers), distributors, and retailers, whereby a company located in one tier is not allowed to have simultaneous dealings in the other two. Lawmakers originally designed this rule to prevent any one company from dominating too much of the industry supply chain and having an unfair advantage in the market.[12] The three-tier rule was also designed to encourage greater transparency in business dealings within the industry by eliminating the problem of "tied houses," in which pubs or taverns would agree to offer a single brewery's beer(s) exclusively in exchange for special benefits. Three-tier laws were intended to produce a more even marketplace for the beer industry, one that was also easier for bar owners who would only need to deal with one or two distributors supplying a wide variety of beer brands rather than dozens of individual producers. The implications of these laws on the industry, however, was another matter.

In the 1970s, at the urging of distributors, the government amended distribution laws to support distributors in their contractual dealings with increasingly large and powerful corporate breweries.[13] These changes made it very difficult for commercial breweries to leave their contracts with distributors. Today, distribution laws cause many craft breweries a huge headache as they seek to have their beer delivered by a distributor. "Buy a small brewer a beer, and pretty soon he or she will be regaling you with war stories about fights with distributors," writes Steve Hindy, cofounder of Brooklyn Brewery in New York.[14] According to Hindy, the contracts that brewers enter into with a distributor are very difficult to get out of. This leaves the former with little recourse should they feel their distributor is not doing a good job with their brand. Ironically, at the time these distribution laws were passed, they were designed to protect distributors in their dealings with Big Beer companies: having Budweiser threaten to sever a distribution contract could be catastrophic for a small distributor reliant on moving Bud products.

Yet the distribution rules now set in place have had the opposite effect for the craft beer industry. "Distribution contracts are like a marriage," explained Tyler, the craft beer specialist working for a distributor introduced in the previous chapter. "Once you enter into it, you have to find a way to make it work together." The binding nature of distribution contracts means that small breweries have an incredibly difficult time renegotiating or nullifying their distribution contracts. If distribution contracts are like marriage, the option of a divorce if it doesn't work out the way you hoped is limited, especially if you are a small brewery. Several larger craft breweries, such as Dogfish Head and Boston Beer Company, have engaged in prolonged and expensive legal battles with their distributors as they seek to get out of their contracts. While legislation seeking to amend these laws has gained traction in some states, the legal binds of distribution promise to remain an issue for craft brewers for years to come. Argues Hindy, "The success or failure of a beer should depend on whether consumers like it—not on whether archaic distribution laws prevent them from finding it in the first place."[15]

The Legal Definition of Beer

How governing bodies decide to define beer in legal terms can have lasting effects on the development of their respective brewing industries and beer cultures. Beer's changing definition matters because it is integral to how products are marketed, sold, and regulated in that region. A prime example of this comes to us from Germany, in the form of the *Reinheitsgebot* law of brewing "purity." First passed in 1516, the purity law mandates that beer produced in Bavaria must consist only of malted barley, hops, and water (yeast, which was discovered later, was incorporated into this law as a legal ingredient of beer in 1906). During the time, there were growing concerns about brewers using questionable ingredients to make "beer," such as wood shavings and poisonous fungi. The purity law was originally put in place by officials looking to regulate the beer produced in the region by improving both its safety and consistency for consumers.[16]

The effects of Reinheitsgebot on the German beer industry—and more specifically Bavaria—have resonated for centuries. Some beer scholars argue that the purity law helped improve German breweries' innovation by forcing them to refine their brewing technologies while using only four main ingredients. Others say that the purity law continues to stunt the development of the German beer industry at a time in which brewers outside of the country, free of such legal restrictions to their beer making, are able to experiment with a wider range of ingredients and export these products internationally. As legal scholar Tammy Lam points out, France and Italy, two wine-making countries with no such "purity" rule for brewing, have seen the opening of hundreds of innovative small breweries at a time when the German beer industry remains stagnant.[17]

Back in the United States, the Brewers Association (BA) has for years sought to define and subsequently restrict the usage of the term "craft beer" and "American craft brewer." The BA's definition of an American craft brewer currently specifies commercial breweries that are (1) small, meaning under six million barrels produced annually, and (2) independent, meaning less than 25% corporate owned. These definitions, and how they have come about, are the subject of controversy. For instance, in 2018, the BA removed third criteria for the definition of a craft brewer, which stated that a craft brewery must also be "traditional," based on the standard of having an "all-malt flagship" beer. Many industry observers quickly noted this definition change was done to accommodate Boston Beer Company—the maker of Sam

Adams and a major donor to the BA over the years—which was moving away from beer production at the time and risked losing its "craft brewer" status.[18] As the official definition of craft beer continues to change, the direction of this change represents vested interests.

License to Brew

The government's role in issuing business licenses and setting rules for the beer industry may seem like unremarkable and overly bureaucratic red tape to the average beer drinker. In reality, business licenses for breweries, distributors, and retailers legitimize these businesses while rendering others illegitimate. That is, government-issued licenses tell us who else has the right to be on the playing field competing in the first place; they protect the rights of licensed businesses just as much as they restrict others, which including unlicensed businesses and, albeit more informally, women and BIPOC who have historically faced sexism and racism within the business licensing process.[19]

For licensed businesses, regulatory protections can become a part of a brewery's business strategy, not merely a legal hurdle to be passed and forgotten. Copyright protections are a good example of this. Holding a trademark to a name of a beer or brewery can be a fundamental business strategy, a way to stand out in an increasingly crowded market. Several high-profile copyright lawsuits in the beer industry have been filed over the past two decades that illustrate just how important these copyrights are to breweries. Many copyright violations, to be sure, are unintentional and get settled out of court following a Cease and Desist letter and a suitable response from the company allegedly in violation of copyright rules.[20] For example, a recent name copyright dispute between two Texas breweries, Gambrinus and New Braunfels, surrounded the use of the word "Wicked" in the latter's coffee stout ("Wicked Fuel"). Gambrinus, one of Texas' biggest breweries and the maker of Shiner Bock, bought a company called Pete's Wicked Ale back in 1998. With this purchase came the exclusive right to use the word "Wicked" in branding. Kelly Meyer, the owner of New Braunfels, disagrees with how Gambrinus handled the order for his company to immediately stop using the term. He took to Twitter to air his grievances over what he described as a "stupid" issue. The companies later settled out of court by drafting an agreement for when and how New Braunfels could use the name "Wicked" for its seasonal beer.

Other copyright infringements escalate into formal disputes between companies that each lay claim to a name, image, or slogan. For example, at the time of this writing, Escondido, California-based Stone Brewing Company, is in the midst of a three-year court battle with MillerCoors, the makers of Keystone beer. Stone Brewing Company originally filed a lawsuit against

MillerCoors over the latter's prominent use of the word "Stone" on their newly rebranded cans of Keystone beer. Stone alleges this is an instance of a large and powerful beer company deliberately attempting to steal market share from a small brewer by confusing consumers through their labeling.[21] While the fate of this lawsuit is still pending at the time of this writing, it points to the way in which formal regulations regarding business copyrights are a key dimension of the legal playing field by which companies do business.

Legalizing Homebrewing

When Fritz Maytag first purchased Anchor Brewing Company in 1965, it was a felony in the United States for someone to brew beer in their own home. This was still the case eleven years later when Jim McAuliffe founded New Albion Brewing Company, the country's first microbrewery built from scratch since the repeal of Prohibition. (This almost certainly made McAuliffe a law breaker—how else was he supposed to learn to brew before opening his brewery?) Finally, in 1978, President Jimmy Carter signed Bill HR 1337 into law, making homebrewing legal at the federal level for the first time since Prohibition. Scholars regard the legalization of homebrewing as a key step that helped lead to a broader cultural shift eventually culminating in the U.S. microbrewing boom of the 1980s.[22] In the wake of the legalization of homebrewing, stores selling amateur brewing equipment began popping up around the country. The same year that HR 1337 passed, the American Homebrewers Association (AHA) was founded, followed soon after by a homebrewing magazine called *Zymurgy* and a sanctioned homebrewing festival originally called "Springfest." Many of AHA's founding members, including Charlie Papazian, were highly influential in advocating for the legalization of homebrewing. A change in beer's federal regulation laid the groundwork for the takeoff of craft beer in the United States.[23]

If certain laws catalyze industry growth, others can stunt it. In comparison to the United States, homebrewing alcoholic beverages remains illegal in many countries around the world. This continues to impact the development of their respective beer industries in profound ways. For example, in Japan, it remains illegal to homebrew beer higher than 1% alcohol. Many industry observers argue that the restriction on homebrewing in Japan, coupled with the high tax rate on commercial beer production, has directly contributed to the small number of craft breweries in operation in the country. Only 200 breweries are currently in operation in Japan, the equivalent of one brewery for every 630,000 people in the country. Compare this to the 8,000-plus breweries in the United States, one brewery for every 41,000 people. Because of homebrewing restrictions, Japan also lacks a critical training ground for amateurs to "learn by doing" by developing the necessary tools and engendering interest in brewing beer on a small scale.[24] Japan's craft brewery scene continues to lag behind its Western counterparts in the number of breweries opened by former homebrewers: a handful of brewers in Japanese craft breweries are expats originally from the United States and Britain rather than Japanese-born brewers.

Remarkably, while the passage of HR 1337 remains a landmark occasion for homebrewing and craft beer in the United States, only nine states initially followed suit by legalizing homebrewing at the time. It took another *thirty-five years* for all fifty states to legalize homebrewing and repeal state-level restrictions. Those that were the first to allow homebrewing became early centers for the craft beer revolution, such as California, Colorado, and Oregon. By contrast, more socially and culturally conservative-leaning states tended to be among the last to legalize homebrewing. For example, Utah, home of the Mormon church and its powerful lobbying arm, did not legalize homebrewing until 2009; Mississippi and Alabama were the last to legalize homebrewing in 2013. Each of these states has among the least craft breweries per capita in the country today, which points to the long-term significance of local and state regulations on the beer world, which we turn to next.

LOCAL REGULATIONS, LOCALIZED DEVELOPMENTS

As college seniors attending school in Connecticut, my friends and I used to engage in an elaborate game of state-hopping just to buy beer. If we wanted to buy beer on Sundays, or after 9 p.m., we knew we'd have to drive an hour north to cross the state line into Massachusetts to find a liquor store that was open. If we wanted Yuengling beer, which wasn't available in Connecticut or Massachusetts at the time, a different course of action was required. We would drive an hour and a half south, entering New York just to buy that coveted 12-pack of amber lager (and a few more for our friends who had placed orders with us). None of us had any idea why we were forced to take these extreme actions; rules were rules. We just knew we wanted beer.—Eli

Many alcohol-related laws in the United States are handled at the state level rather than the federal level. As a result, local beer industries develop in strikingly different ways based on their respective regulatory environments.[25] State lines mark changes in legal policies that can alter everything from the cost of doing business there to the places where beer can be sold to the brands found on retail shelves. We as consumers experience the impact of these state-level regulations, too (though not all of us are as zealous about seeking out their favorite beers when they want them as Eli and his friends were in college!).

Let's start by illustrating the impact of local regulations by looking at how beer is taxed. In addition to federal excise taxes, each state sets and collects its own excise taxes on beer which breweries factor into the overhead of making and retailing beer. These taxes are far from insignificant: by the time beer hits the retail shelves, some researchers estimate that 40% of the sticker price of that beer ends up going toward various state and federal taxes.[26] However, these taxes vary dramatically by state. According to the Distilled Spirits Council of the United States, state excise taxes on beer range from a low of $.02 per gallon in Wyoming to a high of $1.29 per gallon in Tennessee.

Not surprisingly, states with lower taxes on commercial beer production make it easier for small breweries to do business and turn a profit.[27] Some states also allow smaller breweries to pay less in taxes per barrel than large breweries through a tiered tax system. In all, sixteen U.S. states have beer excise tax rates that are not uniform across the board and instead vary based on the alcohol content of the beer, place of production, size of package container, and place the beer is purchased (on premise or off premise).[28]

States also control the days and hours that breweries and other beer retailers are allowed to remain open selling beer. Many states maintain "blue laws," sometimes known as "Sunday laws," that restrict the sale of alcohol at certain times of the week for religious reasons (this is why Eli and his friends had to leave Connecticut in order to buy beer on Sundays). Blue laws embody moral and religious beliefs about the ills of alcohol and how these ills should be publicly managed. The roots of these legal restrictions run deep—some date well before Prohibition—and have been amended or removed entirely over the years. Blue laws today thus reflect their sociocultural contexts: alcohol laws in socially conservative states tend to be more restrictive than in socially liberal states. For example, in Utah, home of the Mormon church which also serves as a powerful lobbying group, draft beer cannot be over 4% alcohol (although bottled beers may be higher), and the sale of liquor is controlled entirely by state-run stores. In North Carolina and Arkansas, as well as a handful of other states, beer cannot legally be brewed above 6% alcohol by volume. Dry counties—by far the most restrictive local measures where you cannot buy alcohol at all—are still scattered around the country, clustered mainly in the south.

Other kinds of local restrictions help explain the spatial landscape of beer. Have you ever wondered why breweries seem to be clustered in certain areas of your city as opposed to others? These decisions aren't simply about which places have the cheapest rent or the coolest industrial-chic aesthetic. As with other kinds of businesses, the location of breweries within certain neighborhoods reflects specific zoning regulations negotiated by city planners, businesses, and local residents. Zoning laws dictate where breweries, which are designated as light industrial manufacturers, are allowed to open. The most straightforward way for an aspiring brewery owner to find a location for her brewery is to do so in an area that is already zoned for this function (rather than trying to petition the city for a change or exception to existing zoning regulations). This is why many breweries are clustered in industrial manufacturing warehouses nearby other breweries, and in spaces that have previously been used by other types of manufacturing companies.[29]

Once someone locates a correctly zoned area to put a brewery, obtaining the legal licenses to sell alcohol can face stiff challenges from other stakeholders in that area. Neighborhood boards often put up a fight to prevent a new brewery from opening in their area, fearing negative repercussions on their community. To skeptical neighborhood boards, a craft brewery can represent an unwanted alcohol establishment as well as a sign of gentrification. This is what Morgan, the cofounder of Indie Brewing Company, said he and his cofounders initially faced when standing in front of local neighborhood meetings in Boyle Heights, Los Angeles, trying to garner approval for their upcoming brewery. He says that many residents, most of whom were from working-class immigrant Latinx families, did not understand what a craft brewery was and therefore were wary of he and his co-owners intentions, all of whom are class-privileged White men:

> The residents associated what we were doing with seedy liquor stores and bars, I think. We were like, *no*—that is not what this is going to be like. But as the months went on and we kept facing resistance at these neighborhood meetings, we felt like no one wanted us. And that was tough, because we knew what we wanted to do, and we were putting our heart and soul into the operation.[30]

As Morgan indicates, neighborhood opposition to the opening of a new brewery can create significant barriers for brewery owners. Much of this is understandable given that craft breweries typically involve race and class-privileged owners attempting to set up shop in areas of the city where rents are cheap. Yet once one brewery opens in an area, things begin to shift. Navigating the legal hurdles to opening a brewery often get easier, such as the time it takes to get a brewery license approved and regulatory inspections passed.[31] Morgan has seen several other breweries open in and around the Boyle Heights area where Indie Brewing had been launched; according to him, all have experienced less red tape.

Many other local rules and regulations affect the development of the local beer industry in unique ways. For example, in several states, such as Massachusetts, a "brewpub" license alone does not authorize the sale of beer on premise, which requires an additional "pouring" license—and the latter can be very difficult and costly to obtain. In New Mexico, state regulations stipulate that a commercial brewing license allows the owner of that brewery to open not only a brewery facility but also three "satellite" taprooms. Local brewers can also apply for a winegrowers license if they make hard apple cider, which can give them the right to open an additional three taproom locations to sell their beer and cider. These policies have been a major reason why a number of leading New Mexican breweries, such as Santa Fe Brewing Company, Bosque Brewing Company, and Tractor Brewing Company, have more than one establishment scattered throughout the state. Breweries must choose to adjust their businesses to fit existing regulations or agitate to change these regulations—many do both simultaneously.

LEGAL STRATEGIES, BARRIERS, AND OPPORTUNITIES

In Monopoly, the players who strategize innovative, even ruthless, ways of managing their resources do better than their competitors who sit back and let the roll of the dice dictate their fate. Rules and regulations don't just structure the game, they dictate which moves will be to one's greatest advantage. However, the ability to access these moves favors those with power, resources, and insider knowledge.

Jeremy and Daniel, two White men in their mid-thirties, are already strategizing second and third locations for their upcoming brewpub in Los Angeles, which has yet to open. Having both worked around the industry for years, including as head brewers of small breweries, their combined knowledge of local regulations as well as the industry landscape led to their decision to obtain a brewing license that will allow them to quickly open additional taproom locations. By taking on "silent" financial investors for their brewery, they have the capital to do so. Jeremy explains his thinking below:

So let's fast forward a year. Which brewery in LA do you hope to resemble?
Jeremy: It would be *Sunshine Brewery*, because they were really smart. The way
   that the licensing works, once you have your Type 23 brewer's license you are
   entitled to 6 duplicate locations, and some of those are allowed to serve food.
   [The owners of Sunshine Brewery] were smart because that is the highest margin place for your beer to go into and get the full retail margin for each pint.

Jeremy sees planning ahead for brewing licenses and what they allow his company to do as a key part of his business strategy. Whereas a standard "production" brewing license would have allowed him to operate just a single-site brewhouse, other types of licensing can cover multiple locations and accelerate his business growth plans. It helps that he and Daniel have a number of other friends and acquaintances in the industry on speed-dial.

Similarly, Patrick, a White man who co-owns Ale Republic in Albuquerque, New Mexico, explains how he and his business partner have changed their brewery's business strategy upon learning about what an additional type of alcohol license, called a "public celebration" license, would allow them to do:

> We're really exploring the limits of what our beer license can do right now, in the sense that as of this week I've been calling the city and talking to the city attorneys about it. Right now we're in the space of public celebration permits, in which you can apply to have your license cover a separate property for an event. It's like being able to serve beer at a pop-up festival, or you can actually do a private event like a wedding.

As enabled by his new business license, Patrick envisions his brewery functioning as a mobile taproom that could be stationed at various local events, art shows, and private parties to legally serve beer. Patrick feels he is in a position to leverage this rule as a unique business opportunity for his company that many other breweries may not even know is available. Yet it is also important to recognize that Patrick's social and cultural capital as a college-educated White man with previous entrepreneurial experience lubricated this opportunity in subtle yet important ways. Patrick knew who to call to find out more information about the license; his ties to the local cultural scene allowed him to connect with potential business partners outside the beer world. While local laws and regulations facing brewery owners may be the same on paper, their relative levels of privilege—in the form of social ties, financial resources, and cultural capital—affect how they are able to leverage these same rules.

These same advantages also hold true when it comes to the brewery licensing and approval process. Small brewery owners want to see their operations get up and running sooner rather than get mired in a drawn-out arbitration process. Andrew Kalemba, the owner of High & Dry Brewing in Albuquerque, says he took preemptive steps to build goodwill with local residents and the neighborhood board prior to breaking ground on his brewery. He met with his local neighborhood board, introduced himself, and invited board members out to inspect his brewery's buildout process. Kalemba's strategic efforts to build and deploy social capital paid off handsomely—first in the form of minimal resistance to his building permit application from city inspectors, according to Kalemba, and later in the form of tremendous support of his brewery from local residents. "This neighborhood has always been the heart and soul of the brewery," says Andrew. "I want them to think of this as their brewery, a place for the community to gather."

Those who have been historically oppressed by the legal playing field do not have the same access to these business strategies. Research shows that while Black and Brown entrepreneurs are more likely to need external funding in order to launch their business, they are less likely to receive this funding as a result of a complicated entanglement of racial inequalities in credit and discriminatory perceptions of creditworthiness.[32] Even once members of minoritized groups obtain funding, their lack of knowledge of how to successfully navigate a regulatory system of permits, approvals, and licenses can lead to costly delays. In the beer world, these structural disparities contribute to the fact that less than 1% of all U.S. breweries are Black owned. Justin Collins, the co-owner of Warcloud Brewing Company, notes that it has been an uphill battle for him and his co-owners to open their brick-and-mortar brewery:

We have to get good at what we're doing. Because honestly, it's not meant for us.
   The whole entire brewing industry isn't meant for us.
Eli: But when you say, "Not made for us," are you saying for... Who's us?
Justin: Us, people of color. We're multicultural. We have White, Black, Brown, Pacific Islander. It's a 10-man team, but everyone's mixed with something, except for me and my brother and another set of brothers. We kind of don't care for color lines or racial issues. The only thing we know is that cards are stacked against us, because we are who we are.

For Justin, his experience trying to launch a small brewery has been fraught with unanticipated challenges that he has struggled to find a way. While he is not one to make excuses, Justin acknowledges that many of these challenges stem from the color of his skin or his lack of resources. Most likely, both.

The resources that some small brewery owners can deploy to navigate business regulations are also available to bigger and wealthier breweries. Well-established firms can put themselves at a competitive advantage by leveraging industry laws and regulations to suit their needs. Consider the actions that Oregon hop growers took during Prohibition. According to historian Peter Kopp, the hop producer association in the Willamette valley was able to pull from collective resources to negotiate the sale of Oregon-grown hops to European and Mexican breweries. By swiftly recalculating at the moment, hop growers were ultimately able to pivot and sell their hops in other beer markets that remained open during this time, such as in Great Britain, Germany, and Mexico. Against all odds, many Oregon hop growers were able to increase their hop sales despite the nationwide legal shutdown of the beer industry around them.

Then there are strategic workarounds that take advantage of legal gray areas surrounding beer. By law, breweries cannot meddle in the independence of beer retailers, which would be a violation of the three-tier law mentioned earlier. One way in which Big Beer, corporate distributors, and even regional craft breweries like Boston Beer and Sierra Nevada can throw around their weight without technically violating any rules is through providing indirect material support of retailers and distributors. Tim Obert, CEO of Seven Stills in San Francisco, explains his frustration with how corporate breweries and distributors get around "tied house" laws, which are supposed to restrict the undue influence of any one producer on retailers:

> The tied house laws do not say anything about a marketing company providing something of value to a retailer, therefore the work around macro breweries have is to literally start or purchase a marketing company and pay that marketing company to advertise for them and/or go out and pay retailers to carry the company's product or host events "on behalf of their client" where they give away promotional materials that the macro brewery legally cannot give away on their own.[33]

Obert's comments came on the heels of his own distillery and brewery being hit with "tied house" violations by the California Department of Alcohol and Beverage Control (ABC). However, it also echoes the sentiment of many in the industry who say that Big Beer and their affiliated distributors use "gifts" and perks to steer more sales in their direction. These gifts, ranging from new window decorations to new beer refrigerators worth thousands of dollars, can be difficult to resist, especially for a cash-strapped, bar or retail store owner. While laws may deter these types of flagrant violations, they do not prevent Big Beer—or any other company for that matter—from trying to massage the rules to get their way in terms of what consumers see on shelves and in tap lines.

Changing the Rules

One of the most direct ways that any business can engage with industry rules and regulations is by trying to change them outright. Succeeding in doing is less simple. Brewery guilds and national associations represent member-led organizations in the beer industry that advocate for legal changes on behalf of its members. The changes they seek, such as reduced taxes or amended distribution rules, amount to long-lasting changes that benefit their constituents. This is the primary purpose of many brewery guilds, as Leah Black, the executive director of the New Mexico Brewers Guild, explains. Leah describes her organization's role within the local industry:

> We have 81 members currently out of roughly 90 breweries in the state. You don't have to be a member of the Brewers Guild or even the Brewers Association to join, but we have definitely done a lot to help them. Take

growlers. You didn't use to be able to fill growlers or take them away [in New Mexico]. This was something that the Guild helped get passed this year with our Senate bill 413 that passed, and that the governor signed into law. There were so many other amazing things rolled into that bill, too. Now, at 11:00 AM on Sundays, New Mexico tap rooms can serve their product and sell it to go. And that was not allowed before July 1st of this year.

State brewer's guilds like the one that Leah Black runs can be valuable ways in which members advocate for rules and regulations to help them increase business through more favorable laws and regulations, such as lower tax rates for small producers and the removal of alcohol caps for beers in certain states. However, the proposed changes that craft brewer guilds push for face stiff opposition from other groups with divergent interests.

Think back to the example that led off this chapter. By the time the Montana Brewers Association began pushing for further laws favorable to craft breweries in Montana, they encountered strong resistance. The Montana Tavern Association argued that small breweries were being given an unfair advantage over bars and taverns, the latter of which are required to

Figure 5.1   New Mexico Brewers Guild (NMBG) Social Event in June 2021 at Boxing Bear Brewing Co.'s Newest Taproom in Albuquerque, New Mexico. *Source:* Courtesy of Leah Black

purchase a liquor license that can cost up to $100,000. While the Montana Tavern Association tried unsuccessfully (thus far) to require breweries to purchase a liquor license in order to sell beer on premise, they have managed to stymie efforts led by the Montana Brewers Association to get additional laws amended that would extend taproom hours and expand the current cap on brewery size for breweries eligible to sell beer on premise (currently at 12,000).[34]

Large lobby groups representing Big Beer and other powerful corporate interests in the industry also seek to protect legislation that helps secure or expand their dominant market share—much to the chagrin of craft brewers. AB InBev and SAB Miller spend a reported $5 million annually on lobbying efforts. They are not alone. The National Beer Wholesalers Association (NBWA), representing distributors, is currently the third-largest political action committee in the United States. It is not in the NBWA's interest to give up the power that distributors currently wield over their contracted breweries; the NBWA has consistently fought efforts to amend the current way beer distribution contracts are legally structured. Therefore, while it is true that some proposed changes to industry laws and regulations would benefit the beer industry as a whole relative to wine or spirits, many other proposed law changes led by powerful lobby groups are catered to specific segments of the beer market. Legally speaking, to paraphrase an old saying, if you aren't attending to the ground below your feet, it can shift before your eyes.

As any professional brewer or brewery owner knows firsthand, understanding how to navigate the regulatory environment of the industry is vital to one's success. It also goes far beyond that. As this chapter has illustrated, the world of beer, its companies, its players, and its culture are fundamentally shaped by the rules of the playing field itself. These rules depend on social and cultural contexts. They differ based on the particular socio-legal histories of nations and their local jurisdictions. Beer laws play a key role in explaining why German breweries, adhering to the centuries-old *Reinheitsgebot*, are famous for their technical brewing prowess but less so for their creativity; they explain why microbreweries continue to flourish in areas of the country where making and drinking alcohol are less subject to morally and ethically tinged legal strictures.

Changes to laws and regulations in beer reflect active and organized interests. Doing so successfully is a game better played by those with power, both economically and socially. Right now, there are currently proposals from craft brewers' guilds in each U.S. state that advocate for changes to beer regulations that would support small operators who produce only a modest amount of beer per year, or have just a few employees instead of a few thousand. Industry advocates such as Steve Hindy remain optimistic that the beer industry can address its thorny distribution problem, but not without sustained effort and outreach. Some states have already changed distribution laws to make it easier for small breweries to get out of contracts that no longer suit their interests; others are looking into legislation that would raise the production cap for small breweries who wish to self-distribute (circumventing the need for a distributor).[35] Other advocacy groups seek to repeal antiquated Blue Laws to allow local breweries more flexibility to conduct business as they see fit. Each of these examples illustrates that laws and regulations are dynamic processes.

Today the positive reputation of craft beer among many consumers and city officials has made it easier to persuade policymakers to favor laws and regulations that support small brewery growth rather than inhibit it. Even then, state-by-state variations in the legal playing field of beer can make it easier for craft beer to flourish, or for Big Beer to tighten its grip over the industry. The dual rise of craft beer and Big Beer raises questions about how the culture of beer continues to be formed and reformed—and how issues of power, authority, and tradition play into this global story.

NOTES

1. Quote from O'Leary is from: Sarkissian, Alex. "Missoula and beer: A history." *Missoula Independent*, April 29, 2010. Accessed: 7/1/21.

2. Healy, Jack. 2013 "A Montana loophole leaves a bitter taste with bar owners." *The New York Times,* April 20, 2013. Accessed 2/22/21 (https://www.nytimes.com /2013/04/21/us/montana-loophole-leaves-bitter-taste-among-bar-owners.html).

3. Homstrom, Peter. 2016. "The law that changed Oregon's beer culture forever." *Portland Monthly*, July 2015. Accessed 2/22/21 (https://www.pdxmonthly .com/eat-and-drink/2016/03/the-law-that-changed-oregons-beer-culture-forever-june -2015#:~:text=In%20early%201985%2C%20the%20House,Brewpub%20Bill%2C %E2%80%9D%20HB%202284).

4. Beer laws also vary significantly across countries. For a comparison between U.S. and E.U. beer laws, see Lam, Tammy. 2014. "Brew free or die: Comparative analysis of U.S. and E.U. craft beer regulations. *Cardozo Journal of International and Comparative Law*, 23(1): 197–xviii.

5. For more on the "relationality" of law and culture, see Yazdiha, Hajar. 2017. "The Relationality of Law and Culture: Dominant Approaches and Ne Directions for Cultural Sociologists." *Sociology Compass*. DOI: https://doi.org/10.1111/soc4 .12545

6. Chapman and Brunsma 2020. For more on saloon life around the turn of the 20th century, see Powers 1998.

7. The 18th Amendment, known as the Volstead Act, was first passed on January 16, 1919.

8. Calls for prohibition in the United States actually go back to the first half of the 19th century, see Hieronymous 2015. For a discussion of the temperance movement in the 19th century, see Michael Young's *Bearing Witness against Sin* (2006).

9. Many U.S. states had already passed state-level bans on the sale and production of alcohol prior to the passing of the Volstead Act in 1919. For more information about the run-up to federal prohibition, see Ogle 2007: Chapter 4.

10. For instance, as beer was legally phased back into production during this era, the maximum alcohol content that it could contain was 3.2%. See Gately, Iain. 2008. *Drink: A cultural history of alcohol.* Penguin.

11. Ogle 2007.

12. Other countries vary in their degree of centralized government control over the beer industry. For instance, in Finland, following its period of prohibition of alcohol (1919–1932), a single government-run company called Alko maintained a monopoly on the production, distribution, and retail of beer throughout the country until 1994.

13. This discussion draws heavily from *Good Beer Hunting*'s three-part series on beer distribution and regulation. See Roth, Bryan. "Distress in delivery." *Good Beer Hunting*, March 7, 2018. Accessed 9/1/20 (https://www.goodbeerhunting.com/sightlines/2018/3/7/distress-in-delivery-pt-1-why-distributors-need-to-adapt).

14. Hindy, Steve. "Free craft beer!" New York times opinion section, March 30, 2014. Accessed 9/15/20 (https://www.nytimes.com/2014/03/30/opinion/sunday/free-craft-beer.html).

15. Hindy 2014.

16. Handwerk, Brian. "Celebrating 500 years of German's beer purity law." *Smithsonian Magazine*, April 22, 2016. Accessed 7/1/21 (https://www.smithsonianmag.com/history/celebrating-500-years-germans-beer-purity-law-180958878/).

17. Lam 2014.

18. Allworth, Jeffrey. "'Craft Beer' means . . . anything boston beer wants it to?" *Beervana*. October 31, 2018. Accessed 7/1/21: (https://www.beervanablog.com/beervana/2018/10/31/craft-beer-is-basically-anything).

19. see Chapman and Brunsma 2020: Chapter 3.

20. Sexton, Josie. 2015.

21. See Stone Brewing's 2018 instagram post: https://www.instagram.com/p/B8eg6rtplKe/?igshid=b2yj2nfxemvn.

22. Elzinga, Tremblay, Tremblay 2015; McCullough, Michael, Joshua Berning, and Jason L. Hanson. 2019. "Learning by brewing: Homebrewing legalization and the brewing industry." *Contemporary Economic Policy*, 37(1): 25–39.

23. Elzinga, Tremblay, Tremblay 2015.

24. McCullough, Berning, Hanson 2018.

25. Williams, Alistair. 2017. "Exploring the impact of legislation on the development of craft beer." *Beverages 3*(18). doi:10.3390/beverages3020018.

26. See Craft Beverage Modernization and Tax Reform Act. Accessed 9/15/20: (https://www.beerinstitute.org/wp-content/uploads/2016/11/S.-1562-Craft-Beverage-Modernization-and-Tax-Reform-Act-of-2015-One-Pager.pdf).

27. Gohmann, Stephan F. 2016. "Why are there so few breweries in the South?" *Entrepreneurial Theory Practice 40*: 1071–1092; Williams 2017.

28. These states are: Alaska, Iowa, Kentucky, Michigan, Minnesota, Montana, New Mexico, New York, Ohio, Pennsylvania, Rhode Island, Texas, Washington, Wisconsin, and Wyoming. See Elzinga, Tremblay, Tremblay 2015.

29. To be sure, there are other business reasons for companies to cluster together in a designated area, as this allows them to benefit from a "spillover effect" of knowledge, personnel, and resources.

30. Morgan is very aware of the critique that what he and his cofounders, who are all college-educated white men, are doing by opening a brewery in a working-class, majority Latino neighborhood is a form of gentrification. In light of this, Morgan has made a concerted effort to give back to the local neighborhood and create events that are more inclusive of the broader community. We revisit the growing movement for social inclusivity in the beer industry in the final chapter.

31. See McCullough, Berning, Hanson 2018.

32. Federal Reserve Banks. "Small business credit survey 2020." Accessed 2/26/21 (https://www.fedsmallbusiness.org/medialibrary/FedSmallBusiness/files /2020/2020-sbcs-employer-firms-report).

33. Excerpt from Obert's email released to customers, as reported by: Alcademics. Temporary Page. Accessed 2/1/20: (https://www.alcademics.com/).

34. Healy 2013.

35. Lam 2014.

Chapter 6

Brewing Cultures

Growing up in Japan, I rarely had opportunities to take road trips because trains took us places much faster and more comfortably than cars. I enjoyed riding bullet trains and watching the scenery changing rapidly, but I always felt like I was missing out by not experiencing the fresh air on the other side of the hermetically sealed windows. Because of this, I had long held a romantic notion of road trips with open windows and my hair blowing in the wind under the vast sky of backcountry—a kind of trip I only saw in films. When I moved to the United States as a first-year student in college, one of the very first things I did was take a road trip through rural Vermont. I saw brilliant blue skies between green deciduous leaves, the sun rays peeking through the forest, and the shadows whizzing by on the winding roads. "This is so much better than I ever imagined!" I said to my roommate and road trip companion. I rolled down the window to savor the moment, inhaling deeply. I closed my eyes.

That's when I was suddenly hit by a very powerful odor. Caught completely off guard and coughing uncontrollably, I turned to my roommate and said, "There must have been a car accident nearby." I began to look around for evidence but all I could see was the pavement stretching before us. My eyes began to water and my nose plugged up from the odor. I quickly rolled up the window.

"A car accident? Why?" she said and turned to me briefly with a puzzled look. Now I was confused.

"Wait, don't you smell that?" I felt the odor lingering in the car even after all the windows were closed. I explained to her that I thought there was a car accident because I smelled burning rubber.

"Oh, honey." She raised her eyebrows and shook her head. "That's not burning rubber—that's a skunk!"

That was my introduction to the term "skunkiness." It was not only a new smell for me but also a new way to talk about that smell. Growing up in Japan, where there are no skunks, I could only equate what I smelled that day with burning rubber. This triggered other expectations for me: I was looking for the smoldering car wreck nearby where the smell must have originated. My roommate, on the other hand, was unfazed by it because she was accustomed to smelling the scent of skunks on the open road. Even though I'm now familiar with skunkiness and have trained myself to use it as a descriptor for a specific off-flavor in beer, I still associate the smell with burning rubber. I'm often reminded of that day whenever I think about how our cultural upbringing influences our expectations and experiences, and how our expectations and experiences frame our relationships to the world around us.—Asa

From the way we experience the world to the way we talk about our experiences, we are each products of our social and cultural surroundings. These memories leave imprints that we carry with us and use to make sense of new surroundings. As the title of this chapter suggests, more than one culture of beer exists today. Though these cultures overlap and influence each other in important ways, they are also distinctive "webs of significance" for people intimately familiar with them. Culture, in this sense, functions as a set of personal reference points, as Asa's enduring relationship to skunkiness illustrates.[1]

The verb "brewing" in the title is instructive. Culture, like brewing, is an active process continually made and remade in the world of beer.[2] In other words, culture is "brewed up" by people rather than simply "discovered"; it is *socially produced* instead of naturally occurring. In this chapter, we examine who is doing this brewing, and for what purpose. We illustrate that how culture is produced and used has important stakes for everyone involved.

At a basic level, culture is a way of encoding the world around us. Culture is what transforms raw stimuli into things that have meaning within everyday social life. Let us use the idea of "skunkiness" in beer to illustrate this point. The way beer is transformed by exposure to light rays—"lightstruck" beer, for short—is an objectively definable phenomenon. This process transforms beer at a molecular level, as isomerized alpha acids from hops come in contact with ultraviolet light from the sun (or other light sources); this reaction produces 3-methyl-2-butene-1-thiol, which gives off a distinct odor. But the way we interpret lightstruck beer and file it away in our memory banks is related to our cultural background. Lightstruck beer is known as skunked beer in the United States, but in other regions of the world, especially those where skunks do not live, people describe this same compound as burnt rubber or freshly brewed coffee (we've even heard it described as "that cheap tourist weed in the Red Light District"). In this way, how we relate to beer is sourced not only from our physical interaction with the chemical compounds of beer but also from our surrounding social and cultural environment.

The more we learn about beer, or just about any other specific good or practice, the more vocabulary we develop to help us communicate its specific qualities to others. This vocabulary is culturally dependent in that it is embedded within cultures with their own histories, traditions, and hierarchies of knowledge. In what follows, we examine three specific areas where culture imprints the modern beer world: (1) the cultural relativity of beer, (2) the cultural production of beer knowledge, and (3) the cultural heritage of beer. To be sure, these are not the only ways that culture manifests in the world of beer—think of the social identities of beer drinkers we explored in chapter 2 or the gendered and racialized patterns of employment in breweries we covered in chapter 3. Here we emphasize specific aspects of culture that pattern interpersonal differences, as well as how distinct beer cultures come to be produced, understood, preserved, and sometimes changed.

CULTURAL RELATIVITY AND THE
MYTH OF UNIVERSAL EXPERIENCES

The first time I stepped foot into an izakaya (traditional Japanese bar) was in Sendai, Japan, well after I had stopped living in Japan myself. As soon as we were seated, each of us received carefully plated little appetizers along with a glass of water and an oshibori (hot towel). The server used a word I've never heard in Japanese as she served us, so I asked one of my companions about it. "Did she say—'otoshi'? What's that?" My companion pointed at the small plates of food in front of us.

"These. They come with the table. Everyone gets one automatically."
I was delighted by the little complimentary dishes of assorted braised vegetables, noting how well they paired with a glass of Japanese lager.

When the bill came a couple of hours later, I was confused. "It looks like they made a mistake. There are more items here on the check than what we ordered." We looked at the bill closely.

"It says otoshi is 500 yen per person," said one of my companions.
"But wait, wasn't otoshi free? Why are they charging us?" I replied. My Japanese friends looked puzzled by my confusion.

"Of course you pay for otoshi. It's common sense! . . . Stupid gaijin (foreigner)!" one said playfully.

"Wait, aren't you Japanese? Why don't you know this?" said
another of my companions.

Even though I grew up in Japan, my years of living in the United
States led me to believe that otoshi was the Japanese equivalent of free
peanuts or popcorn at American bars.

I paused so long that everyone moved on. I, on the other hand,
kept thinking about "common sense" and how it relates to culture—
including my own.—Asa

Culture is often described as a set of beliefs, values, traditions, and norms that are shared and practiced by a group of people. Culture has a material dimension, evident in specific kinds of clothing, foods, and drinks, and an immaterial dimension, evident in the unspoken rules that those intimately familiar with that culture understand. In both these forms, we observe culture in action based on how members of a given group interact with and make sense of each other.[3] In short, culture imprints what we understand to be common sense. It can also complicate it.

As Asa's experience above illustrates, even though people raised in one culture may be familiar with a general cultural practice or principle (*otoshi*), they may not be cognizant of how these practices work in local settings (Japanese *izakayas*). This is particularly true for those who have spent extended time in more than one cultural environment or were raised in an immigrant family growing up hearing stories about "home" in a faraway place. In other words, cultural "common sense" is not as commonly shared as people tend to assume, even among people from a similar cultural background.

We can observe snapshots of culture and cultural differences all throughout the world of beer. Take how we toast. As rituals of collective celebration, many societies feature the tradition of toasting that involves both linguistic and behavioral norms (see Figure 6.1). Let's consider the former. In many romance languages, like Spanish (*Salud*) and French (*Santé*), people toast to their health. This is the case in Russian (*Na Zdorovie*) as well. Yet the German word "*Prost*," which originates from the Latin word for "be well" (*prosit*), has a unique history: according to some accounts, German university students in the 18th century began using "*Prost*" as a toast to their school mates during feasts they would put on for their professors held before their exams. The goal would be to get their professors inebriated so that they would grade student exams more leniently.[4]

Distinct cultural practices of toasting around the world go beyond the words we exchange to involve unspoken group rituals. Toasting norms, for instance, convey our relationship with others present in that setting. Across different societies, however, how one toasts, and with (or toward) whom, signals a person's standing within the group. In China, people lower their glasses

Figure 6.1 Many Countries Maintain a Cultural Tradition of "Cheers," Though the Practice Varies Considerably across Locations. *Source:* Photo by Fred Moon, courtesy of Unsplash.

as they clink them together to show respect toward the other person. In large group settings, they also tap their glass on the table in lieu of clinking glasses with those sitting far away. By contrast, in parts of the United States, tapping your glass on the bar top or table signifies a toast to the house. Other aspects of toasting bring different meanings around the world. In countries like France, Germany, and Spain, many people believe that breaking eye contact while toasting is a bad omen that brings seven years of bad sex. Whereas in Japan, no one expects you to make eye contact at all while toasting. Instead, a sign of respect for your companion involves holding a bottled beer with both hands while pouring it into a glass with the label clearly shown to the person receiving the drink. Each of these unique traditions involving beer has developed over time and is sustained through person-to-person exchanges among those familiar with these traditions.

Culture shapes how we experience specific aspects of beer itself through exposure to certain foods starting at an early age. We begin to develop our perceptions of certain aromas and tastes well before we are born. For example, research shows that our first exposure to food is through amniotic fluid in our birth parent's umbilical cord. This exposes us to our birth parent's food culture, which in turn lays the groundwork for our own food preferences.[5] Similarly, breastfeeding has been shown to increase a child's willingness to explore new foods, especially when a nursing person consumes healthy foods during lactation.[6] While our food preferences may later evolve to reflect our diversified sociocultural experiences in adulthood (including exposure to different food cultures), culture plays an important role in laying the foundation for how we approach food, drink, and many other kinds of preferences.

Because of how deep our personal relationship to our own culture can be, encountering interpersonal cultural differences can feel jarring and unexpected. Asa recounts another vivid example of this from their own experience:

> *It began with a disappointing look from my dear friend from New Zealand. He was visiting me in Albuquerque, New Mexico, so a few of us got together at one of my favorite local breweries to catch up. "I ordered a pint of beer, and this ain't one!" he said, shaking his head once the first round of beer arrived.*
>
> *But nothing seemed off to me. "That's a proper pour," I said.*
>
> *Not to him. Unable to shake his disappointment, he explained that he was accustomed to being served imperial pints (20 oz) instead of what he received: a 16oz American pint poured with two fingers worth of foam. For my friend, it was hardly aesthetically pleasing or emotionally satisfying to have his beer served this way, which in turn affected his experience of it.*

We suspect that there was nothing Asa could say or do to convince their friend about what a pint of beer "should" be. The nature of their disagreement was rooted in divergent cultural frames surrounding beer rather than a lack of knowledge about it. The way people from a similar cultural background perceive practices such as the serving of beer as common sense leads people to feel strongly about them. In England, Mark Tranter, head brewer and founder of Burning Sky Brewery in East Sussex, England, explains, "You get a lot of these CAMRA (The Campaign for Real Ale) stalwart types who just want a complete pint and, if part of their pint is foam, they get annoyed about it."[7] According to Mark, serving some British people a draft beer with "too much" foam will cause a knee-jerk reaction in which they feel they aren't getting their money's worth.

Yet for many craft brewers in the United States, serving draft beer with a frothy head is an integral part of the beer serving process and one closely linked to ideas about the correct way to experience beer. "Pouring a beer with a proper head is only proper," says Dan Suarez, owner and brewer of Suarez Family Brewery in Hudson, New York.

> What I tell people is that it's not a gimmick. It's something super special. It enhances the experience. When you knock out some of that CO_2 from the solution, the body is more supple. [It] volatizes the aromatic compounds, and that provides a pop in the nose.[8]

To Suarez, serving beer with a proper head is a key component of how he and his staff strive to provide the best possible drinking experience to customers at his brewery.

Another controversial cultural practice surrounding serving beer is the use of frosted glass. Fans of frosted glasses—typically a pre-frozen pint glass—describe it as "that sexy, icy beer mug" and advocate for its advantages in keeping beer cold and refreshing, especially on a hot day.[9] Yet according to beer experts, frosted or frozen glasses are detrimental to the optimal beer experience. The Draught Beer Quality Manual, a leading resource for the proper pouring of draft beers, published by Brewers Association (BA), reads:

> Chilled glasses are preferred for domestic lager beer, but they should be [dry] before chilling. Wet glassware should not be placed in a freezer or cooler as it may create a sheet of ice inside the glass. Frozen glasses will create foaming due to a sheet of ice being formed when the beer is introduced to the glass. Extremely cold glass surfaces will cause beer to foam due to a rapid release of CO_2 from the product.[10]

On the one hand, the physical sciences tell us that our beer experience objectively improves by serving beer at a specific temperature into a specific glass with a specific pour rate to release more aromatic compounds. On the other hand, our cultural understandings about beer deeply influence our expectations about the "right" way to drink it. For this reason, one seasoned beer expert that we know says he understands the logic against chilled glassware for beer but still chooses to have a few frosted glasses in their freezer at all times for those who prefer it.

Other cultural differences in drinking rituals within the world of beer abound. Yet what all these examples illustrate is that our respective relationships to beer are patterned by our cultural backgrounds. By examining distinct norms, values, and practices across beer cultures—evident in *otoshi* norms in Japan or the "proper" amount of foam atop a freshly poured beer in England—we see that what is common sense to us can be anything but commonsensical to others.

CULTURAL KNOWLEDGE AND
THE PRODUCTION OF EXPERTISE

When I lived in Den Haague in the Netherlands, I visited Brasserie Cantillon in Brussels, one of the most recognized producers of Lambic in the world, and had the good fortune of getting to know Jean Van Roy, the head brewer and blender of Cantillon. Jean walked me through his brewery to taste barrel samples that would be blended into his new batch of Nath, a two-year-old Lambic with rhubarb added. He explained that he blends his Lambic based on intuition. He first tastes a variety of Lambic from different barrels and imagines how they will evolve with rhubarb added in the barrel: "this one has a lot of character. Very aromatic . . . and this one. A good level of sweetness. Nice and soft. Not too acidic." While we talked about different barrel characteristics and how they might interact with the rhubarb, I couldn't help but notice how abstract and artful Jean's descriptors were. It was as if each Lambic had a unique personality that words could only loosely capture.—Asa

Given how evocatively Jean Van Roy, a luminary in the world of Lambic production, described his beers to Asa, we might expect that other beer enthusiasts knowledgeable about Lambic would describe them similarly. Yet none of Jean's descriptors make it into a review of *Nath* by the reference website Lambic.Info. The review reads:

[*Nath*] opens with a slight pop and pours with a pillow head that sticks around for a bit. Many have mentioned a sulphury note, but this bottle had nothing of the sort. Full bouquet of rhubarb with hints of apricot, lemon, grass, and mineral dryness dominate the taste while the nose is somewhat funky/cheesy and brightly acidic.

The stark contrast between how two leading experts of Lambic—one a Lambic producer, the other an experienced beer writer—describe the same beer is striking. This begs the question: Is there a "right" way to taste and describe Lambic, or any other beer for that matter? If so, who determines this standard? Based on what criteria? While Jean's descriptions of his Lambic reflect an intimate knowledge of Lambic as a master brewer and blender with knowledge passed down in his family for generations, his impressions of these beers are not the only ones that get disseminated and treated as credible in the world of beer. In fact, Jean's descriptions of Nath do not follow the strict guidelines that beer judges and beer sommeliers use to describe Lambic. It reviews like the one on Lambic.Info that more closely adhere to how beer experts are trained to talk about beer. This tension points to how we come to understand "good" quality in beer—including what it looks like and tastes like. Ideas about quality and standards point to the broader system of cultural classification that exists within a given society.

Professional beer knowledge is formed and subsequently disseminated by dominant institutions and "expert" authorities within the world of beer. This is because rendering the value of a cultural object is an iterative process performed by multiple people and organizations; just because *you* say something is valuable, right, or important does not make it so.[11] While the process of expert knowledge production about beer often incorporates the perspective of the people who make the stuff (such as Jean Van Roy), it also involves a variety of other *cultural intermediaries* who engage with these products and impart new kinds of meaning and value onto them.

In the world of beer, a number of organizations claim to be formal authorities of beer knowledge. These organizations offer classes, certifications, and professional titles to those who wish to signal their expertise in beer to a wider audience. They also strive to professionalize beer itself, which has not always been seen as worthy of the same elite cultural treatment given to wine or scotch. One of the leading certification programs for beer professionals in the United States is the Cicerone® Certification Program based in Chicago, IL, and founded in 2007. Cicerone's founder, Ray Daniels, explains why he believed that there needed to be a centralized program that could certify beer professionals:

> Anyone can call themselves an expert on beer. But when consumers want great beer they need help from a server who really knows beer flavors, styles, and service. They also want to buy beer from a place that understands proper storage and serving so the beer they drink will taste the way it should. Too often great beer is harmed by improper handling and service practices. In the wine world, the word "sommelier" designates those with proven expertise in selecting, acquiring and serving fine wine.[12]

Taking cues from the wine world and its sommelier system, the Cicerone® Certification Program strives to establish the recognizable authority of one's beer expertise. It has strategically positioned itself as a key source of claims-making for people who wish to convey "expert" knowledge on beer culture.[13] As a result, the qualifications that Cicerone bestows on people who pass its tests—Cicerone currently offers four levels of certification: certified beer server, Certified Cicerone®, Advanced Cicerone®, and Master Cicerone®—are proudly displayed on personal resumes or on the back walls of breweries and beer bars to signal their staff's level of beer knowledge.

While organizations such as Cicerone® systematize cultural knowledge about beer in ways that they see as beneficial to the people who obtain these certifications, these organizations also run the risk of marginalizing other forms of knowledge about beer. Notably, in valorizing European brewing traditions (e.g., the technical efficiency of German brewing, or the creativity and lore surrounding Trappist brewing), many dominant organizations in the beer world have inadvertently contributed to the systematic erasure of a wider and more socially-diverse brewing history—one that goes beyond White, Euro-American men and their brewing companies. Few professional texts about brewing history note that prior to the industrial era of beer, it was women who headed up household brewing operations, or that beer "occupied a central role in pre-colonial West African religion and social life—and still does."[14] Further, as Smithsonian historian Theresa McCulla explains, "we know that enslaved Africans and African Caribbeans were brewing beer or were cultivating hops or other grains that would have been used in the brewing process."[15] In Monticello, home of Thomas Jefferson, an enslaved man Peter Hemings was known to be a master brewer who supplied fresh beer to the large household and its guests.

What these examples illustrate is that the production of dominant forms of beer knowledge is about power. And the power to shape cultural discourse lies with dominant societies and social groups. In privileging some narratives about beer over others—whether to describe the specific lineage of a famous beer style or characterize existing "professional" standards of beer brewing—alternative forms of beer cultures and traditions must be cast aside.

Widely accepted cultural standards about beer also contain assumptions about who is consuming the stuff. This can make it challenging for people who don't fit or possess these assumed traits to relate to beer. We can see this in standardized beer flavor descriptors, which are widely circulated by leading organizations of expert beer knowledge. For instance, the aroma associated with oxidized hop resins, a byproduct of Brettanomyces called isovaleric acid, is often described as "cheesy." Yet for those who are lactose intolerant or vegan, it can be difficult to understand what people mean by this term. The same applies for longtime vegetarians who are taught to use the term "meaty" to describe the aroma given off by autolysis (self-destruction of yeast). The list goes on (how about "gym socks" for people who've never been to a Western-style gym?). Though these terms may seem unusual descriptors for beer, all are used by industry professionals to convey specific kinds of knowledge about beer—and to evaluate others' level of knowledge.

We brought this up to Jen Blair, one of the only beer professionals to hold the titles of Advanced Cicerone® and National Beer Judging Certification Program (BJCP) Judge. Blair advocates for more inclusive beer and food pairings that are less reliant on descriptors that only make sense to a proportion of the population. Blair, who is a lifelong vegetarian, offered her perspectives on the use of the term "meaty" to describe autolysis:

I typically equate "meaty" with umami . . . but obviously it is more than that. I can agree with your assessment now that I'm thinking about it for a couple reasons. First, I comprehended on a certain level what sherry notes in an aged beer meant but it wasn't until I actually tasted sherry that I fully comprehended what it meant and how I was detecting it in aged beers. I'm not going to try meat to fully comprehend "meaty" as a descriptor, so the description does exclude me from fully grasping the explanation. Second, "meaty" as a descriptor also seems a little lazy and not specific. I don't use descriptors like "malty" and "fruity" because they are too vague and don't convey an accurate picture. I put "meaty" in that same category-what kind of meat? What kind of preparation? If you can break that down into specifics that more accurately convey the flavor, then you can likely move away from exclusionary language to more inclusive language.

As Jen notes, many of the beer descriptors that are commonly used by beer experts and beer certification programs assume that the person drinking beer, or studying to be a beer "expert," will be immediately familiar with these referents. However, for the approximately 5% of adults in the United States who are vegetarian, a descriptor such as "meaty" becomes a challenge to try and understand about a given flavor and aroma, much less used to describe this aspect of the beer. The same goes for the term "cheesy," used to describe an aroma found in some beers. Because a disproportionate percentage of BIPOC are lactose intolerant—research suggests that up to 80% of the Black and Latinx population and a majority of Native and Asian Americans are lactose intolerant—"cheesy" can be difficult for members of these groups to understand let alone use with confidence to describe beer.[16]

Other terms synonymous with beer "expertise" in the United States are shaped by access to knowledge about, and experience with, distinct aromas and flavors. For example, "West Coast" style IPAs are commonly described as having citrus and piney notes, while many New England IPAs and Hazy/ Juicy IPAs are said to feature tropical notes. Some beer connoisseurs break down these descriptors even further, referencing specific types of fruit (orange, lemon, lime), components of fruit (pith, peel, rind, juice), and preparations of fruit (ripe, zested, freshly squeezed, candied, etc.). Yet if someone has not tasted fresh guava, mango, or passion fruit, they wouldn't be able to distinguish them or their components. Thus, describing beer in the way preferred by dominant cultural authorities is most conducive to those who have developed a broad and cosmopolitan palate—or what we described in chapter 2 as "omnivorous" cultural capital. Cultivating this kind of cultural knowledge is closely associated with social privilege in the sense that acquiring and performing beer knowledge using exotic descriptors favors those who have first-hand experience traveling—and eating—in many different cultures.

To be sure, language is always a signifier, a way of referring to human experiences by proxy and in ways that will never be experienced by everyone (who has ever looked for a "needle in a haystack" or "pulled themselves up by their own bootstraps"?). But people such as Jen remind us that dominant cultural forms of beer knowledge speak most directly to the interests and experiences of a sliver of the population, and especially those that are privileged. This impedes others from acquiring the language and tools necessary to be recognized as beer authorities. Even if one does learn to use the "proper" terms for beer, this doesn't guarantee that person will be treated with the same level of professional credibility. Who we perceive as "experts" in society is shaped by our gendered, racialized, and classed assumptions about expertise.[17] Men, particularly White men, are more often seen as experts and authorities than women, stemming from the former's access to social power and superior positions within the structure of Western society.[18] This fact is highly problematic for women, BIPOC, and LGBTQIA+ people who seek to advance within professional careers of all kinds.

In the world of beer, one way that some individuals seek to gain professional respect is by leaning on formal credentials. In an interview for the podcast *Good Beer Hunting*, Ray Daniels notes that women, BIPOC, and LGBTQIA+ people seem to be drawn to the Cicerone® certification process as a way to help establish their authority in the industry:

> Anecdotally, absolutely, women, [and] minorities frequently come to us and say, "thank you. You know, you allow me to get in the industry. People weren't taking me seriously or I was coming from outside the industry and I had no way to break in. I walked in with certified Cicerone under my, under my belt, and now all of a sudden, like, people are paying attention to what I have to say." So that's, you know, that's very gratifying and that's, that's a lot of fun. And it does, it does help people get past some of those barriers that they would otherwise face.[19]

While the Cicerone® program does not currently collect demographic data about its participants, interviews posted to its website with those who have achieved the level of Certified Cicerone (level 2) reveal a distinct pattern as to why they were motivated to get their certification.

> I think it helps validate my knowledge with other people, and it proves how serious I am about the work that I do. Sometimes being a woman in beer, I think people don't take me as seriously.—Loy Maierhauser (pronoun: she/her)[20]

> I pursued my certification in 2013 when there weren't many Certified Cicerones yet in Canada. I realized timing and opportunity were on my side to make a difference in the beer community and contribute a unique perspective as a woman and beverage professional. But I knew in order to do that, I needed the knowledge and credibility that only a professional certification could provide.— Michelle Tham (pronoun: she/her)[21]

> As a Black member of the LGBTQ+ community, I'm not afforded the benefit of the doubt when it comes to my beer knowledge, so getting the certification has given me some footing when comes to presenting myself as a professional member of the beer community.—Toni Boyce (pronoun: they/them)[22]

Women, BIPOC, and LGBTQIA+ people in the beer industry such as Loy, Michele, and Toni describe that using credentials to signal their status within the industry is an important way that they are able to shore up their credibility relative to their peers who are men. Few of them believe they are afforded the same assumptions about their level of cultural knowledge and skills as their cishet White man counterparts. This trend is not unique to beer. Research shows that women are more likely to invest in credentials to signal their expertise than men because women are not afforded the same assumption of expertise.[23] Yet because of persistent forms of racism, sexism, heterosexism, and gender binarism within the industry, even those who achieve higher levels of certifications such as Advanced Cicerone® and Master Cicerone® say they continue to face skepticism and trivialization of their credibility from both consumers and industry peers. Even when credentials lead to assumptions of expertise, women, BIPOC, and LGBTQIA+ people are often tokenized and pigeonholed into a predetermined deficit narrative based on their identity expressions. Natasha Peiskar, a professional brewer and a cofounder of Pink Boots Society (PBS) Canada, points out such issues.

> We are much more than the sum of labels. Yes, I am a brewer, woman, and a PBS member. But to appreciate the multi-faceted nature of people, it's impor-tant to know that we are more than those labels. And your interactions with me need to be mindful of that. Pigeonholing me as a "female" brewer and asking me about the challenges I overcame as a woman or tokenizing me as though I speak for all women in the industry is such a loss of opportunity to learn about me, my passion, my strengths, and my unique experiences. So, the next time you approach someone, whether it be for an event, talk, panel, or educational ses-sion, don't pigeonhole us. Instead, let each of us create our own narrative—you are the amplifier.[24]

While "expert" credentials in beer are intended to convey authority to others within this field, the way this knowledge gets interpreted and used by others reflects simultaneous narratives about gender, race, sexual orientation, class, and other social categories.[25] Dominant forms of beer knowledge are unequally wielded by different members of a society—just as these forms of beer knowledge are unequally produced in the first place.

INTANGIBLE CULTURAL HERITAGE

We have thus described the constructed nature of culture, but can culture also have a true essence? If that essence can be identified, can it also be preserved? In 2016, the United Nations Educational, Scientific and Cultural

Organization (UNESCO) declared the "Beer culture in Belgium" to be an Intangible Cultural Heritage.[26] The international organization bestows this designation on a "practice, representation, expression, knowledge, or skill considered by UNESCO to be part of a place's cultural heritage, which comprises nonphysical intellectual property, such as folklore, customs, beliefs, traditions, knowledge, and language." UNESCO also takes into consideration the historical distinctiveness of the cultural practice in order to promote a "mutual respect for other ways of life." In honoring Belgium's beer culture, UNESCO explained:

> Making and appreciating beer is part of the living heritage of a range of communities throughout Belgium. It plays a role in daily life, as well as festive occasions. Almost 1,500 types of beer are produced in the country using different fermentation methods. Since the 80s, craft beer has become especially popular. There are certain regions, which are known for their particular varieties while some Trappist communities have also been involved in beer production giving profits to charity. In addition, beer is used for cooking including in the creation of products like beer-washed cheese and, as in the case of wine, can be paired with foods to compliment flavors. Several organizations of brewers exist who work with communities on a broad level to advocate responsible beer consumption. Sustainable practice has also become part of the culture with recyclable packaging encouraged and new technologies to reduce water usage in production processes. Besides being transmitted in the home and social circles, knowledge and skills are also passed down by master brewers who run classes in breweries, specialized university courses that target those involved in the field and hospitality in general, public training programmes for entrepreneurs and small test breweries for amateur brewers.[27]

The Intangible Cultural Heritage recognition attempts to record and ultimately preserve what UNESCO's governing body believes makes certain cultures and cultural elements unique. This is, at best, a moving target. In a world that is globalized and modernized, cultures constantly blur and borrow, as cultural anthropologists such as Anna Tsing and Arjun Appadurai have long argued.[28] Our cultural backgrounds may pattern our individual experiences, but cultures writ large are hardly discrete entities that lend themselves to cataloging.

Still, UNESCO is not alone in its attempts to consecrate distinctive cultural elements within the world of beer. These organized efforts have both material and symbolic stakes for those involved. One such case is Kölsch from the Köln region of Germany. The term Kölsch became a Protected Geographical Indication (PGI) by European Union in 1997. Since achieving this official designation, Kölsch must be made within 50 km (30 miles) of Köln using the brewing method in accordance with the Kölsch Konvention as defined by Kölner Brauerei-Verband (Köln Brewery Association). Protecting Kölsch has helped secure its place within a larger cultural context that is constantly borrowing, blending, and changing beer styles and recipes. These kinds of designations serve as powerful ways for breweries in the region to signal the distinctiveness of place ("essence") and authenticity of the beers they make. More pragmatically stated, the goal is to give consumers confidence that beers with this label will have a family resemblance to one another.

However, few beer styles enjoy the same level of national, regional, or international protection that Kölsch does. One example is of this is Lambic beer, which is produced in the Pajottenland of Belgium. Unlike Kölsch, Lambic received a Traditional Specialty Guaranteed (TSG) nomenclature by the European Union in 1997. The difference between TSG and PGI is that the former only applies to ingredients and brewing processes and not to any specific geographic location. In other words, anyone around the world can use the word "Lambic" to brand their products regardless of the geographical location where it is made. This vexes many Lambic producers, who, in addition to the prospect of lost sales to foreign producers marketing their products as Lambic, spend years perfecting their craft using recipes handed down for generations. Beer writer Matthew Curtis tells a story of conflict and reconciliation between HORAL (Hoge Raad voor Ambachtelijke Lambikbieren, or High Council for Traditional Lambic Beers) and an Austin, Texas-based brewery called Jester King:

> In 2017, Jester King came under fire from the consortium for the use of the term "Méthode Gueuze" in relation to Spon, a spontaneously fermented beer produced in a similar fashion to the Belgian style. The Texas farmhouse brewery had the backing of Cantillon's Jean-Pierre Van Roy—who isn't a HORAL member—in the creation of the term. Initial tensions made it seem like the situation could have generated long standing issues between the U.S. and Belgian producers.
>
> Instead, Jester King co-founder Jeffrey Stuffings traveled to meet with Boon [the president of HORAL] and HORAL to talk things through. The outcome of that meeting saw Stuffings change the descriptor of Spon to "Méthode Traditionelle." Around the same time, Stuffings and a group of likeminded beer makers formed the Sour and Wild Ales Guild, a HORAL-like group intended to help establish and guide the future of sour and wild beer in the United States. Despite the beers that HORAL's members produce not technically having any kind of legally-enforceable security outside of the European Union, the respect given to HORAL, along with Lambic and Gueuze in general, appears to have a continent-spanning reach. Stuffings' travel and willingness to compromise is just one way to see this.

"As a group of producers we have more impact than individually," Pierre Tilquin, himself a HORAL member, says, reflecting on the situation. "We will most likely need to be very vigilant and monitor the use of the words 'Gueuze' and 'Lambic,' as many brewers are willing to start spontaneous fermentation. But the recent agreement we found with Jester King might help us to avoid this."[29]

In the business of beer, many different producers, such as Jester King, see it in their interest to evoke terms that they think will add prestige and authenticity to their products. Yet to traditional producers of the cultural objects in question, such as Lambic makers in Pajottenland, these things embody the essence of the area, its people, a way of life, and generations-old traditions (not to mention a key way these producers brand their own products). Allowing others to use the term Lambic, or Kölsch, simply to sell more beer made on the other side of the world, they claim, is an example of *cultural appropriation*, or the adoption of an element of one culture by someone not of that culture for personal gain and without respect for its meaning to people of that group.[30]

Cultural appropriation can occur in many different contexts and has a considerable gray area. The most blatant cases of cultural appropriation involve people or companies from privileged socioeconomic positions or societies adopting something closely associated with those from more disadvantaged positions. An example of this would be Westerners wearing Indian *Sari* as a fashion accessory devoid of cultural meaning, or worse yet, selling it as their own.

While instances of clear-cut cultural appropriation may be rare in the modern beer world, there are numerous cases of beer makers "borrowing" styles and terms that have a distinct place of origin. Take the recent controversy surrounding a new style of beer in the United States known for its cloudy appearance and "juicy" aromas and flavors. Following the growing popularity of these beers, two of the leading organizations responsible for establishing beer styles, the BJCP and the BA, independently responded by coining new styles of beer. The BJCP called this style "New England IPA," to focus on the geographic origins of the style, whereas the BA called it Hazy/Juicy IPA, to focus on the visual and flavor characteristics of the style. Pat Fahey, Master Cicerone® and the content director of the Cicerone® Certification Program, describes the origins of the disputed beer style as follows:

Hazy/Juicy IPA is a style that has sort of exploded onto the scene in recent years, but you know its history goes back a little bit further than I think a lot of people know. So, the beer that most people consider to be the first New England IPA or the first example of this style is a beer called Heady Topper from the Alchemists in Vermont. This style has become really popular within the last maybe two three four years. The first time that Alchemists brewed Heady Topper was nearly twenty years ago, 2003. When they first made that beer, it was just a one-off. It wasn't necessarily intended to explode or become extremely popular, but their customers liked it a lot. Over time, they brewed it more and more often and eventually in 2011, they opened up a production facility primarily just to get this beer out to the world. The beer was tremendously popular, and over time, in the early 2010's, some other breweries in the area like Hill Farmstead [and] Maine Beer Company started emulating this type of beer around 2015-2016. We saw it explode into popularity across the nation, and now we see people all over the US and really all over the world making this style of beer.[31]

A given product may start at a specific geographical location and grow to become internationally popular in time, one made by companies that have little relation or even knowledge of the original product and those who made it. Juicy/Hazy IPAs are a prime example of this, as Fahey describes. However, controversy has followed. In 2017, Berkeley, California-based Fieldwork Brewing Company released a one-off beer called "The Meadows," in a style they labeled as Vermont Farmhouse Ale.[32] This led to Shaun Hill, the owner of Vermont-based Hill Farmstead Brewery, to contact the *Burlington Free Press* and State Representative Samuel Young stating that this label, used by a brewer in California, was in violation of the "Representation of Vermont Origin Rule."[33] When Young subsequently tweeted, "It might be time to change the name" to Fieldwork Brewing Co. with the link to the Burlington Free Press article, a Twitter feud broke out over who has the authority to claim ownership over a style of beer.

The issue covered in this section illustrates the complex entanglement of cultural heritage, appropriation, and adaptation today. A thin line separates the use of someone else's product or practice in a way that others view as respectful or inappropriate—even exploitative. Such issues often boil down to matters of communication between parties. This is evident in Jester King's amicable resolution with HORAL just as it is in the spiraling, social media-fueled dispute between Fieldworks and Hill Farmstead. What remains true is that efforts to preserve the essence of what is culturally "ours" run deep. These efforts transcend mere business to involve matters of the heart, and of legacy.

We started this chapter by acknowledging that there is no such thing as universal common sense when it comes to beer—or of any other aspect of culture for that matter. The way we experience beer, talk about it, and value it reflects our cultural backgrounds as well as the constructed nature of culture itself. One practical way to think about this is by recognizing the relativity of culture—there is no one "right" way to enjoy beer. The behaviors, preferences, and rituals that people display toward beer are a window into who they are and where they are from. Appreciating cultural differences involves not only the products associated with that culture but also the distinct social practices surrounding those products.

At the same time, not all forms of knowledge about a given cultural product are treated as equal. In beer, what we value as "quality" and "expertise" speaks to dominant forms of knowledge production of which leading organizations play an outsized role in producing, disseminating, and institutionalizing. The way we talk about beer, particularly among those who occupy positions of authority in the industry, reflect the "taste regimes" within dominant beer cultures in the United States and Western Europe. This is precisely why some beer professionals such as Jen Blair have started to use their platform to advocate for greater social and cultural inclusion within the world of beer. If beer is to resonate with a wider range of audiences and succeed at bringing new voices into the fold, it needs to first be able to speak its language.

Efforts to change the culture of beer find their counterpart in efforts to preserve its cultural heritage. As we've described, culture is deeply personal, experienced as an intangible connection to distinctive groups, places, products, and activities of the past. Many of these elements of culture are imperfectly constituted, resting on the exclusion of certain groups and the erasure of other histories, as has been the case with stories of the rich connection that women and BIPOC have historically had to brewing and beer cultures. That said, efforts to change or preserve beer cultures do not necessarily have to be antagonistic; there is room for multiple voices just as there are multiple cultures.

A promising trend within the world of beer is thus the expansion of inclusivity—finding ways to invite more people in rather to participate than excluding them at the door. These efforts are being spearheaded from "below" (through social media) more than from "above" (through leading institutions). They signal the potential for cultural change by amplifying the voices of the oppressed and their experiences in the industry. There is a growing chorus of new voices that are working to build a more equitable, inclusive, and just beer community today. They are doing so on both a local and global scale, adapting existing beer cultures—and reviving elements of nondominant ones nearly lost to history—in ways that mirror our changing society. What is brewing next has the potential to draw from a new recipe book.

NOTES

1. Understanding culture as meaningful "webs of significance" in a society comes from Geertz, Clifford. 1973. *The interpretation of cultures.* New York: Basic Books.

2. Berger, Peter L., and Thomas Luckmann. 1967. *The social construction of reality: A treatise in the sociology of knowledge.* Garden City, NY: Doubleday.

3. Durkheim, Emile. 1915. *The elementary forms of the religious life.* New York: Free Press; Geertz 1973.

4. Personal correspondence with Iris Eickert, a professional beer sommelier from Germany.

5. De Cosmi, Valentina, Silvia Scaglioni, and Carlo Agostoni. 2017. "Early taste experiences and later food choices." *Nutrients, 9*(2): 107.

6. Ventura Alison K. and John Worobey. 2013. "Early influences on the development of food preferences." *Current Biology, 23*: R401–R408. doi: 10.1016/j. cub.2013.02.037

7. CAMRA is an independent consumer organization headquartered in St Albans, England, which promotes real ale, real cider, real perry, and traditional British pubs and clubs. See Drinks Maven. "The iceman pour." Accessed 2/23/21: (https://drinks-maven.com/2017/03/the-iceman/).

8. Holl, John. 2019. "Patience for a pint: The art and science of the slow pour." July 16, 2019. *Beer & Brewing.* Accessed 2/23/21 (https://beerandbrewing.com/patience-for-a-pint-the-art-and-science-of-the-slow-pour/).

9. Bell, Emily. "Why good bars don't serve your beer in a frosted glass." *Vinepair.* Accessed 7/1/21 (https://vinepair.com/wine-blog/why-good-bars-dont-serve-your-beer-in-a-frosted-glass/).

10. Brewers Association. 2019. Draught Beer Quality Manual, 4th Edition. *Brewers Association.*

11. Maguire 2018; Maguire, Jennifer S., Jessica Bain, Andrea Davies, and Maria Touri. 2015. "Storytelling and Market Formation: An Exploration of Microbrewers in the UK." In N. G. Chapman, J. S. Lellock and C. D. Lippard (Eds.), *Untapped: Exploring the cultural dimensions of craft beer* (pp. 236–260). Morgantown: West Viriginia University Press.

12. Cicerone® Certification Program. "About Cicerone." Accessed 7/1/21 (https://cicerone.org/us-en/about-cicerone-0).

13. See Brady (2018) on a similar process among dietitians.

14. Bennett II, J. 2021. "We're reclaiming beer because it's ours." *Eater* February 23, 2021. Accessed 2/23/21 (https://www.eater.com/22262702/beer-culture-in-america-black-brewers-history).

15. Quoted in Bennett II 2021.

16. By contrast, roughly 15% of people of Northern European descent are lactose intolerant. Swagerty Jr., Daniel L., Ann D. Walling, and Robert M. Klein. 2002. "Lactose intolerance." *American family physician, 65*(9): 1845–1850.

17. See Brady 2018; Witz, Anne. 1992. *Professions and patriarchy.* London: Routledge.

18. As sociologist Christine Williams has shown, even when men work "women's" jobs, such as nursing, they are granted more authority than their women colleagues. Williams, Christine. 1991. *Gender differences at work: Women and men in non-traditional occupations.* Berkeley: University of California Press.

19. Good Beer Hunting. 2020. "EP-255 Ray Daniels, Founder, Cicerone." Accessed 2/23/21 (https://www.goodbeerhunting.com/gbh-podcast/2020/2/6/ep-255 -ray-daniels-founder-of-the-cicerone-program).

20. Solarte, Shana. "My road to Cicerone®: Loy Maierhauser of MAP brewing company." Cicerone Certification Program. Accessed 7/1/21: (https://www.cicerone .org/us-en/blog/my-road-to-cicerone-loy-maierhauser-of-map-brewing-company).

21. Solarte, Shana. "My road to Cicerone®: Michelle Tham of Labatt brewing company." Cicerone® Certification Program. Accessed 7/1/21: (https://www.cicerone .org/us-en/blog/my-road-to-cicerone-michelle-tham-of-labatt-brewing-company).

22. "My Road to Cicerone®: Toni Boyce of Beer Kulture." Cicerone® Certification Program. Accessed 7/1/21 (https://www.cicerone.org/us-en/blog/my-road-to-cice-rone-toni-boyce-of-beer-kulture).

23. Risse, Lenora. 2018. "The gender qualification gap: Women 'over-invest' in work-place capabilities." *The Conversation*. Accessed 4/26/21: (https://theconversation.com/ the-gender-qualification-gap-women-over-invest-in-workplace-capabilities-105385).

24. Peiskar, Natasha. Brewers Lectures. Spring session, March 2021.

25. Brady 2018.

26. United Nations Educational, Scientific, and Cultural Organization. "Beer culture in Belgium." Accessed 7/1/21 (https://ich.unesco.org/en/RL/beer-culture-in -belgium-01062).

27. UNESCO ibid.

28. We borrow this from Anna Tsing's notion of cultural "friction," which captures messy interactions between cultures. Tsing, Anna. 2011. *Friction: An ethnography of global connection*. Princeton, NJ: Princeton University Press. See also: Appadurai, Arjun. 1990. "Disjuncture and difference in the global cultural economy." *Theory, Culture & Society*, 7(2–3): 295–310.

29. Curtis, Matthew. "The emperor's new Gueuze: A wild revival in a post-appellation age." *Good Beer Hunting*, May 16, 2018. Accessed 7/1/21 (https://www .goodbeerhunting.com/blog/2018/5/12/the-emperors-new-gueuze-a-wild-revival-in-a -post-appellation-age).

30. For prominent Lambic producers to take steps to limit the use of the term Lambic could also be construed as a market protection mechanism, that is, a business strategy to protect a category of product and thereby raise its value. However, owing to the fact that many Lambic producers appear fiercely protective of the tradition of Lambic making more than merely trying to increase their profits, we choose to frame the issue described in this passage as cultural appropriation.

31. Cicerone Certification ProgramCicerone Certification Program. "Tasting Toget : NEIPA with Master Cicerone Pat Fahey." *Youtube*. Accessed 7/21/21 (https:// www.youtube.com/watch?v=2s_tSkx5Hpo).

32. Fieldwork Brewing Company. "The Meadows." Accessed 7/1/21: (https:// fieldworkbrewing.com/beers/the-meadows/).

33. Baker, Jeff. 2017. "Flattery or unfair? 'Vermont' beer pops up out of state." 3/17/17. *Burlington Free Press*. Accessed 2/23/21 (https://www.burlingtonfreepress .com/story/life/food/2017/03/17/flattery-foul-play-vermont-beer-pops-up-out-state /99252424/).

Conclusion

Toward a Deeper Appreciation of Beer and Society

It could never be just about beer.
—Ken Carson, owner of Nexus Brewery
in Albuquerque, New Mexico.

Change, as the old adage goes, is the only constant. Yet some changes come on faster than others. Their effects cause a visceral and unexpected shock to the system. In the early months of 2020, breweries braced for impact as the novel coronavirus known as COVID-19 swept across the globe. The pandemic prompted governments around the world to enact mandatory stay-at-home orders, lock down public facilities, and mandate temporary closures of businesses. By January, the first known cases of COVID-19 reached U.S. shores, and despite a tepid federal response from the Trump administration, many state- and city-level governments decided to shut down all businesses deemed "nonessential" in an effort to curb the spread of the virus. The closures brought on-premise business at breweries, restaurants, and bars to a halt—a necessary but unprecedented blow to the beer industry and its roughly two million domestic workers. Many small brewery owners were initially supportive of these closures. Some even embraced what they thought would be a short-term pause in daily operations as a chance to clean the house, tighten training protocols, and brew more beer in anticipation of a busy summer season. But as months passed with taprooms closed and keg sales to restaurants and bars flatlined, breweries began the painful process of laying off employees. By the end of 2020, the list of small breweries, beer taprooms, and bars that had been forced to close their doors grew longer.

Yet amid the backdrop of the pandemic, other prominent storylines have emerged within the world of beer with the potential to change our relationship with beer for the next few decades. Many of these storylines parallel

141

broader social and cultural trends in society. Widespread movements for social justice, particularly those related to racial and gender equity, have forced Americans to grapple with the lack of diversity and economic opportunity within many workplaces and other key institutions. In beer, these same movements have exposed uncomfortable truths about the way members of marginalized groups have been excluded from the industry or rendered invisible within their workplaces. This moment marks a time when owners, workers, and consumers alike are reevaluating business as usual within the world of beer. The old results no longer seem acceptable.

In this concluding chapter, we showcase two contemporary trends in the world of beer that have the potential to shape its future and legacy: the rise of social justice initiatives in beer and the struggle for power and control in the industry. Both mirror larger issues sweeping through our society. Before diving into these topics, let us begin by summarizing the overall perspective of this book and its key arguments. Throughout these pages, we have shown how beer is embedded within the social and cultural fabric of society, structured in ways that reflect existing institutions, social hierarchies, and cultural arrangements. Our own relationship with this larger world of beer are also deeply personal, which is where we began our journey. Using the framework of "beer psychology," we examined how our conscious and unconscious perceptions affect our relationship to beer. While we drink beer, our brain's interaction with external stimuli shapes our moods, our memories, and our attention—just as our moods, memories, and attention profoundly shape our experiences with beer itself.

What we *"taste"* in beer is a social process. As we explained in chapter 2, taste preferences encompass not only the physiological aspects of imbibing beer but also the values, social identities, and group memberships that come packaged with these tastes. While preferring one type of beer over another is not inherently "good" or "bad," it does have significant social implications. This is because expressing specific tastes—Big Beer-produced pale lagers or specialty stouts from your local brewery—translate into forms of cultural capital that communicate our social location within groups with unequal standing in society.

Moving from consuming beer to producing beer, chapter 3 examined beer as a context of employment, one where specific jobs are associated with social categories such as race, gender, class, and sexual orientation. We explained how social networks, socioeconomic resources, and cultural capital pattern not only access to industry jobs but also *job segregation within the industry.* These forces together have allowed "bearded White guys," who enjoy privileged positions within the existing power structure, to occupy higher-ranked jobs such as brewery owner and head brewer in the industry.[1] Meanwhile, women and BIPOC remain overconcentrated in feminized service jobs and racialized low-level distribution jobs, respectively.[2]

To better understand the market context that structures the world of beer, we then turned our attention to the business of beer. Drawing on organizational perspectives as well as theories about the production of culture, chapter 4 examined the distinct competitive strategies of Big Beer and craft breweries that allow both to maintain their position, albeit unequally, within the industry. Big Beer uses a strategic business game plan that leverages their superior resources and market position to dominate the industry. Meanwhile, small, craft breweries cultivate an image of authenticity and craftsmanship in order to preserve their niche in the market. This is precisely what has come under increased threat as Big Beer mimics and acquires crafty brands of their own. All of these business strategies are fundamentally embedded within the existing playing field of laws and regulations in the beer industry, as chapter 5 showcased. Yet because laws and regulations are constructed and reconstructed within specific sociocultural contexts, we illustrate that competing industry groups go to great lengths to attempt to change these laws in their favor.

Different configurations of laws, businesses, and consumer norms also mean that beer cultures manifest differently across time and place. These cultures pattern our distinct relationships with beer in the process. Yet as we show in chapter 6, beer cultures today cannot be understood without interrogating issues of power as well as the social construction of knowledge and "expertise." Both flow from dominant organizations in the beer world. Beer cultures also involve contested issues of *heritage* and *appropriation*, as groups try to preserve the essence of what makes their culture unique amid an increasingly globalized, market-driven landscape.

DIVERSITY ON TAP?

In 2019, BA acknowledged that craft beer has a diversity problem. This was based on the findings of the first industry report to collect demographic information on the race and gender of craft brewery workers.[3] Roughly a year later, another survey led by journalist Holly Regan found similar results with regard to the lack of LGBTQIA+ inclusivity in beer. Together, these surveys painted a sobering picture: as one of Regan's survey respondents put it, "the craft beer industry can feel like a frat party gone wrong" for those who are not cishet White men.[4] In this sense, despite its community-focused branding and counter-cultural ethos, the craft beer industry is little better than corporate America in terms of *social* inclusivity. For many in craft beer, these surveys served as a wake-up call, hard proof of the problematic social homogeneity in the industry that has been hiding in plain view all along.[5]

The response has been swift. Industry advocates and consumers alike have launched new efforts to address diversity, equity, and inclusion (DEI) within the world of beer. These initiatives within the industry parallel larger social movements centered on improving racial justice and gender equity in society at large, such as Black Lives Matter and the beer industry's reckoning with gender-based violence. Today, breweries all across the country are signaling that they care about these issues, that they need to do better. Yet in an industry that remains predominantly White and men, what is less clear is *how*.

Changing beer will require addressing both its material organization as well as its symbolic dimensions. Over the last few years, there has been a growing number of organizations, consumer groups, and media collectives that wish to see the oppressive Whiteness and maleness of craft beer dislodged from its place as industry norm and *de facto* ideal. Efforts to promote inclusivity in the world of beer come with great promise, but also plenty of pitfalls. As sociologist Sarah Mayorga-Gallo notes, the efforts of well-intentioned organizations and their leaders to "diversify" their ranks often come up short of their goals. Mayorga argues this is because diversity efforts rarely address the structural issues and power imbalances that underlie inequitable outcomes.[6] Without addressing these issues, diversity rings hollow. Breweries may say they want to welcome in more people, but even well-meaning breweries have struggled to make their spaces inclusive of all people by making them *feel* welcomed. Patrice Palmer, a diversity specialist at New Belgium Brewing Company who was also named one of *Hop Culture*'s "Most Important Voices in Craft Beer in 2020," explained that today's organizations need to actively *invite* diversity into their workplaces not just signal their openness to it. Palmer, who identifies as Black and queer, explains: "if I don't see someone like myself there, the place doesn't seem welcoming."[7] Similarly, Holly Regan argues that the terms "inclusive" and "diverse" cannot and should not be separated. Regan writes, "The counterfactual to the industry's claims of inclusivity is the homogeneity of its ranks."[8]

Addressing inclusivity at a symbolic level means taking seriously beer's existing image and the gendered and racialized values and identities that come packaged with it. This is what underlies recent efforts in the beer world to make sexist and racist beer labels a thing of the past. In 2019, the BA declared that any blatantly sexist beer name would not be acknowledged on stage if it were to win a medal in either of the two national competitions that the BA organizes: the World Beer Cup and the Great American Beer Festival.[9] The BA hopes this rule will dissuade breweries from adopting offensive labels. Some feel that this policy alone does not go far enough. For instance, as of this writing, the BA still allows offensively labeled beers to be entered into the medal competition, just as breweries that make these beers are still allowed to be members of the association.

Perhaps a more sweeping form of pressure to eradicate sexist and racist symbolism in the industry comes by way of the court of public perception. Several breweries have apologized for insensitive beer labels after having been "called out" on social media by fans and industry peers. Others have decided to change or discontinue beers with offensive labels for similar reasons (e.g., Saugatuck Brewing's "Hop on a Blonde"). These changes have often been accompanied by considerable reluctance on the part of brewery owners, particularly White men. Take the controversy in 2020 around Reckless Brewing's "Sultry Black" beer. Sultry Black featured the punchline "black lagers matter"—a tone-deaf reference to the ongoing Black Lives Matter movement for racial justice. According to the online publication *VinePair*, the owner of Reckless Brewing, Dave Hyndman, initially defended the beer's branding through a series of tweets. After facing continued social media scrutiny, Hyndman later apologized, citing a joke gone wrong.[10] This is hardly an isolated incident: other breweries have remained indignant about their right to free speech with regards to labeling and branding. Further, the public outrage against beer labels perceived as inappropriate or offensive has not found the same success in the court system. Maryland-based Flying Dog Brewery recently won a five-year lawsuit against the Michigan Liquor Control Commission, which sought to bar distribution of the brewery's "Raging Bitch" beer on the grounds that it perpetuated harmful stereotypes of women. Flying Dog has continued to defend its beer names and labels as a form of artistic expression and free speech.[11] To some observers, however, the reluctance to take a unified stance against the racist, sexist, and homophobic imagery and representations in the industry illustrates that the problematic "White bro" culture of craft beer is still alive and well.

As these incidents illustrate, efforts to render the industry more inclusive on a symbolic level have achieved real gains in spite of pushback. These efforts alone will not be enough to supplant structural barriers that women, BIPOC, and LGBTQIA+ people face within the industry. Fortunately, a growing number of U.S. breweries, industry organizations, and consumer-led groups are committing material resources to initiatives promoting DEI. While their methods differ—as, inevitably, will their degrees of success in achieving their goals—these initiatives strive to help members of marginalized groups cultivate social networks, access information, meet expenses, and develop professional skills. All of these are resources that are readily available to their privileged White men counterparts in the industry.

At the industry level, the Brewers Association has launched a series of equity and inclusion initiatives in the form of professional workshops and trainings, online resources for breweries, and the hiring of a "diversity ambassador" to champion these issues. Dr. J. Nikol Beckham, who was the first person to serve in this role, has also started several nonprofit programs of her own (Craft X EDU, Crafted for All) that feature an array of scholarships and grants, opportunity fairs, and other resources aimed at promoting "inclusion, equity, and justice" in the craft brewing community.[12] Other industry-wide organizations devoted to supporting under-represented members of the beer industry are gaining in numbers and prominence. The Pink Boots Society (PBS), founded in 2007, has become an international organization in support of women in the beer industry and related alcohol industries. PBS, which now counts over 2,000 members, provides a space to share information, access resources (the organization offers scholarships every year in support of women furthering their education and career development within the industry), and build comradery for women members. Recently, PBS has sought to expand partnerships with other organizations that focus on other issues of diversity in the industry, especially those related to intersectional inequalities. One such program is called the "Road to 100 Initiative," launched by Eugenia Brown (aka @blackbeerchick) with support from the Cicerone Program. The Road to 100 Initiative seeks to mentor women professionals, specifically women of color, in the industry by supporting their efforts to obtain professional credentials in the form of a Cicerone Beer Server certification. Brown, who herself is a Black woman, sees this as a practical step to promoting equity in the industry:

> Guys, in particular, can show up to a brewery, volunteer on brew days, and make connections. They don't always need the Cicerone certification. I hate to say it, but I almost feel like [women of Color] need to come to the table with that something extra. We don't have families who own breweries, we don't grow up going to breweries. We need this other way in.[13]

Creating more "ways in" to the industry, as Brown calls it, is the aim of another new organization called the Michael Jackson Foundation. Founded in 2020 by Garrett Oliver, the brewmaster of Brooklyn Brewery and one of the few Black brewers in the United States, Oliver envisions his Foundation providing financial scholarships to people of color and Indigenous people who are seeking to launch careers in the beer industry. During an interview featured on the podcast *Beervana*, Oliver explained that in the past he wasn't doing enough to promote African Americans in the industry, even in his own brewery. "In 30 years, I haven't had any Black people apply for a brewing job," he says. "If anyone had come to me asking for help, I would have helped them. But no one did." Oliver recognized that it wasn't enough for him or anyone else in a prominent industry position to simply not contribute to the problem further. Through his new foundation, Oliver seeks to create structured opportunities so that people of color can gain the credentials needed to enter the brewhouse and launch gainful careers in beer, not just access low-level, dead-end jobs. "Being anti-racist takes work," he says. "And usually money."

A growing number of individual breweries have also spearheaded company DEI programs of their own. Many of these programs strive to make a difference in their workplaces and local communities. In 2020, for example, New Belgium Brewing Company launched a new campaign called "Beer for All," with accompanying equity and inclusion of standing committee within the brewery comprised of employees themselves. Dozens of other breweries, such as Albuquerque-based Bosque Brewing Company, UK-based Cloudwater Brewing, and Los Angeles-based Crown & Hops, have also launched innovative efforts in support of employees (or aspiring employees) from marginalized groups both within the beer industry and in local communities. To be sure, these businesses must weigh DEI goals alongside practical business concerns; they capitalize on a moment to rethink their company culture during a time when consumers actively support these efforts. But to be successful in the long run, they will need to find ways to institutionalize DEI in the form of sustained support and stable funding, and ultimately, greater representation of women, BIPOC, and LGBTQIA+ people in positions of leadership.

Beer consumers both inside and outside the industry are also playing an important role in social movements for change within the world of beer. Several annual beer festivals founded in the past few years have championed beer culture within communities that have historically been left out of the dominant craft beer culture. These include FreshFest (founded by Day Bracey with the intention of bringing together African American culture and craft beer), ColdXella (founded by Ray Rivera to help bring craft beer to the Latinx community in East Los Angeles), and Beers Without Beards (founded by Grace Weitz in support of greater gender inclusivity in craft beer). These events have drawn thousands of attendees, helping to normalize craft beer for new audiences.

Nowhere is the resonance of a new generation of craft beer voices more evident than on social media. Beer influencers on sites like Instagram and TikTok embody new relationships with craft beer through their words, imagery, and actions; some also provide a platform for others to do the same. In turn, their success is more homegrown than manufactured—a message resonating with an audience, often unexpectedly. For example, Edgar Preciado, aka @beerthuglife, who we first introduced in chapter 2, never thought he would reach the point of having thousands of followers on Instagram. As a Mexican American man and former gang member living in South Central Los Angeles, Edgar's relationship to craft beer bears little resemblance to the typical craft beer enthusiast. Edgar explains how he got his start unexpectedly (see Figure 7.1):

> What I did was, I was able to acquire some highly-valued beers. And just to piss beer geeks off, I'll say okay, here's your $1000 bottle, man. Here you go, boom! I fucking chug it and people are like, "What the fuck?" "What's up? What's up motherfuckers? I'm Edgar," and all this and I fucking pound it, and all of a sudden the next day, dude, I had like 3000 views. I've never ever seen so many views in my life or on my page. So it started just to piss people off. Because at the end of the day, dude, it's just beer.

By shedding the social exclusivity of craft beer, and deviating from craft beer's elitist practices, beer influencers like Edgar are engaging with beer in ways that make it approachable, democratic, and—dare we say—fun.

Others are using social media to foster solidarity across the world of beer in ways previously not possible. In March of 2021, the Instagram handle of a brewer named Brienne Allen (@ratmagnet) became a lightning rod for sharing stories of sexism and sexual harassment in the craft beer industry. In her original post, Brienne posed a simple question to her followers: "what sexist comments have you experienced?" Hundreds of replies followed, many of them detailing vivid accounts by women of violence, abuse, and predatory

Figure 7.1 Edgar Preciado, aka "Beer Thug," in South Central Los Angeles, California.
Source: Courtesy of Edgar Preciado.

behavior going back years in the industry. In the immediate aftermath of this reckoning—the beer industry's equivalent of the Me Too movement—several prominent men in the industry stepped down, having been mentioned on the social media thread.[14] While there may be nothing new about these marginalizing experiences for women, BIPOC, and LGBTQIA+ people in craft beer settings, what is noteworthy is how the conversation about them are now able to spread from the ground up on social media, reaching even the highest ranks of the industry.

Messaging Beyond Beer

As we have described earlier, cultural objects such as beer have always come with implicit messages. For years, marketers portrayed beer brands in ways that complemented the lifestyles, preferences, and ideals of Whiteness, maleness, middle-classness, and heteronormativity.[15] Beer companies shied away from associating with other lifestyles and social groups that might tarnish this image. However, today a growing number of breweries, particularly craft breweries, are asserting clear social and political messages on issues ranging from gay rights, racial justice, and anti-sexism. Rather than leaving politics at the door, they invite them in. Ken Carson, the owner of Nexus Brewery in Albuquerque, New Mexico, is explicit in how he supports the African American community through his brewery and two other taproom locations. According to Ken,

> One of the things that we do is offer [the brewery's] dining room as a meeting place and stuff like that. Any community organization that wants to have a meeting here, they can have it. I don't charge them anything. The Black community has figured it out, and they have a lot of meetings here. We had scholarships and fundraisers. We are very open to try to help with scholarships and fundraisers. I do what I can to help community organizations as much as I can.

These changes start with representation and imagery. People need to be able to see people like themselves engaging positively with beer and within brewery spaces (as Ken does by hosting community meetings and fundraisers), as opposed to being made invisible or worse, demeaned through racist and sexist beer labels. Breweries have also sought to go beyond the beer world to collaborate with people and organizations that they support or align with. As Ting Su, cofounder of Eagle Rock Brewery in Los Angeles, notes, "Rather than collaborating with another brewery, consider creating an event or series of events in collaboration with music industry friends, or knitting groups, or baking groups, or running groups, or a wide range of other organizations."[16] Su promotes what she calls "cross-collaboration" and community building through joint ventures that recognize something that we have explored in this book: that beer is embedded within larger cultural worlds that are also clustered with other activities. If beer always comes with certain symbols and messages, collaborating with other companies can be a way that breweries can signal their values and their greater sense of community (see Figure 7.2).

A related version of joint partnerships outside the beer world is *collaborations for a cause*, meaning partnerships with a social justice mission and affiliated organizations. These types of collaborations take a number of different forms, such as charity nights at the brewery, festival partnerships, and joint sponsorships. Perhaps the most innovative effort has been the rise of collaboration beers made either with a social advocacy group or for a social cause. There was a time not too-long ago when the majority of beer "collaborations" only meant brewers getting together with their industry friends to make a beer together and jointly release it to the public. While there is nothing wrong with this as a form of creative expression, *collaborations for a cause* represent more purpose-driven partnerships. One example of this was the collaboration known as "Black is Beautiful," which was launched in the spring of 2020 by Texas-based Weathered Souls Brewery. Hundreds of breweries across the country signed on to brew a version of the same beer, an imperial stout, in support of the Black Lives Matter movement. A

Figure 7.2 Jess Griego of Bosque Brewing Company, Shelby Chant of Steel Bender Brewyard, and Swarupa Watlington, Formerly with Storehouse, at a charity event in Albuquerque, New Mexico. Ms. Griego and Ms. Chant have been strong advocates for equity and inclusion initiatives and other charity-focused partnerships through their respective breweries. Source: Courtesy of Jess Griego and Shelby Chant.

portion of the proceeds from the sale of Black is Beautiful beers was to be donated to a local organization that supports racial justice. The project was widely successful, with some breweries reportedly selling out of their cans in mere weeks. While the Black is Beautiful project did also receive some pushback (mostly centered on accusations of armchair activism by White brewers and a lack of accountability regarding donations), its commercial success insures that it not be the last of these collaborations for a cause beer releases.

Some of the strongest pushes to get companies to package beer with a social message of diversity, equity, and inclusion may not be producers of beer at all. Samantha, a woman who works for a Los Angeles-based craft beer distributor, says she has seen an increasing number of calls and emails from her clients looking to support social causes with the beer they buy:

> [I think] we are heading in a more inclusive direction, greater diversity in gender, in race. People are starting to use beer as a message, as a political message. Their labels can be very intentional. Especially now with what is happening in the world. I think beer might be becoming more political, people might be expressing more of their beliefs on the forefront. And I don't know, it is possible that people might only support breweries that are aligned with their beliefs, like, I am not buying from this brewery because they are racist, or something. I feel like that is already started to happen. Which I love. Also, consumers are starting to demand it. I had someone email me the other day saying, "hey do you have any Black owned breweries?" And I had to say no, unfortunately I don't, but I'd want to carry some, not for tokenism, but for the right brewery.

Samantha continues to push for her boss to actively support brands led by people from marginalized groups. To be sure, one could read these moves as superficial, window dressing for businesses done in order to fit a moment in history where certain social issues are "trending" in public consciousness and a business opportunity exists.[17] But the level of interconnectedness between mission-driven branding, collaborations for a cause, and deliberate efforts to support ongoing social movements suggests that social messages can now belong inside beer—or at least paired alongside it.

THE SHIFTING LANDSCAPE OF BUSINESS AND EMPLOYMENT IN BEER

The rising social and cultural impact of craft breweries has rightfully garnered an incredible amount of media attention over the past decade. But these trends must be assessed alongside other important economic undercurrents that continue to affect the business of beer and the quality of employment that workers experience within the industry.

The story that preoccupied beer news for much of the 2010s was Big Beer's relentless efforts to increase their domination of the industry. As we detailed in chapter 4, what was at stake was not only *control* over the industry but also the legitimacy of craft beer itself at a time when Big Beer was appropriating its branding ("authenticity") and buying up leading brands (Goose Island, Elysian, Ten Barrel). Big Beer had finally found a way to beat back the rise of craft beer—or at least hold it at bay. Yet, by the end of the decade, Big Beer's assault strategies of corporate mergers, craft beer acquisitions, and the (mass) production of faux-craft beer were in flux. In January 2020, MillerCoors announced the closing of one of its largest production plants, located in Los Angeles county. A year earlier, Constellation brands sold off its high-profile purchase of San Diego-based Ballast Point Brewing Company at a reported loss of millions. The rate of craft brewery acquisitions has slowed.

Meanwhile, the number of small- and mid-size breweries in the United States continues to skyrocket despite slowed sales growth. This trend has exposed rifts between smaller and larger craft breweries as they jockey for shelf space. Regional craft breweries in particular have struggled to continue expanding their operations. In the last five years, Lagunitas, New Belgium, and Stone have had to scale back ambitious attempts to open or operate multiple production facilities outside of their home regions (e.g., Stone sold their Berlin-based brewery in 2019 to Brewdog). Meanwhile, more smaller brewers are opting for "neighborhood" operations focused on an intimate taproom-based experience. In order to differentiate themselves, these breweries emphasize their *hyper*-locality—catering to residents of specific neighborhood blocks within larger cities. To be sure, for some owners of neighborhood breweries this aligns with their vision of an ideal brewery operation: a corner operation that remains both humble in ambition and human in scale. However, from another perspective, the rise of neighborhood breweries is a mixed signal for the industry and its workforce. For aspiring brewery owners, it may be the only viable option left—one with capped business potential. A Los Angeles-based brewer explains these business terms:

> You have to understand that the need to distribute in the craft beer world is gone because nowadays there are *so* many breweries. Competing on the shelf is a *bad* idea. Because, why compete for pennies when you can just sell to your neighborhood for more dollars?[18]

While this brewer remains in favor of neighborhood breweries, he also alludes to the fierce competition *between* craft breweries for business. An increasing number of small producers today are competing for a slice of the beer industry pie that is not growing any larger.

The realities of industry competition are testing the solidarity between craft breweries. Things have grown testy behind the scenes. In addition to jockeying for retail shelf space and draft handles, breweries have begun lobbying for legislation that would benefit only the smallest of craft breweries (rather than them all). For example, a new law in Massachusetts now defines a small brewery as one producing less than 250,000 barrels for the purposes of taxes and other rules and regulations. This leaves larger craft breweries like Boston Beer Company paying higher taxes on their beer than their smaller craft peers. Up until now, the communal culture within the industry has been undergirded by decades of economic growth. As the rifts within craft beer indicate, small producers will need to find creative ways to chip away at corporate control over the industry—by far the largest piece of the pie—if they want to retain craft beer's momentum as well as the social and cultural changes packaged along with it.

Making a Living While Making Beer

In 2018, the media outlet *Good Beer Hunting* produced a four-part series titled "Will Work for Beer" focused on the labor conditions and business economics of craft beer.[19] Among their conclusions: in a feel-good industry full of mostly cishet White men "doing what they love" by brewing and drinking beer, the wages paid to workers leave a lot to be desired. In other words, the line between pursuing one's passion and being exploited for too-long labor hours and too-low wages remains uncomfortably thin. Beer may not be the industry you want to enter to get rich, but shouldn't it offer jobs that allow you to support a family?

Those who love beer often see deliberately engaging in hard work for little pay as a sign of their true devotion to their jobs.[20] As a thirty-five-year-old head brewer named Will explains:

I think there is something to be said for paying your dues in any career. [. . .] I think it is important to come into an industry young and hungry and willing to show people what you are capable of and what you want to do. That you are there to kick ass and take names. What needs to happen? I'll brew this beer and then afterwards I'll scrub the toilets. Then I'll be your bartender, you know? Yeah, I think that that is a necessary part of this career or any career for that matter. But do I think that someone in this industry should be pumped for getting a dollar raise, where they are finally making ten dollars an hour? That's insane. That disgusts me.

Will describes the high degree of personal motivation expected of those who pursue a career in brewing ("come into an industry young and hungry and willing to show people what you are capable of . . ."). Unfortunately, these expectations of workers are often out of step with industry norms of compensation. Another former brewery worker, a White man with a degree in chemical engineering named Chance, echoes this sentiment. Chance describes his reason for leaving the beer industry after five years:

> Even the brewers at the big craft breweries, the ones making a ton of beer, none of them are making over $65, 70k a year. [. . .] So I never wanted to go down the brewer path because I knew I would get hooked on it because I love brewing beer and I have that passion, but I wouldn't want to get stuck on that job where I don't make enough money to justify my passion, if that makes sense.

As both Will and Chance articulate, if jobs in beer are viewed more as passion projects than gainful employment, companies have little incentive to pay their workers more. The average wage of a brewer in the United States ranges from $12 to $20 an hour with limited employer-paid benefits.[21] While this may sound fine to some, it can cause others, particularly those trying to support a family, to leave this industry or seek a job in Big Beer for more pay. To be sure, owners of small breweries contend that the business margins they face are exceedingly thin. Many also provide their employees with other kinds of perks, such as shift beers and flexible schedules. But as one brewery owner admitted, "let's just say this is not an industry you want to get into in order to make money." Another brewer, recognizing the considerable financial hurdles that opening a small brewery entails, told us half-jokingly, "The best way to make a small fortune is to start with a large one and open a brewery."

Some workers have sought to organize in order to improve the economic prospects for those employed in beer. Several recent labor unionization efforts in breweries have made national news. In January of 2020, for instance, the sixty-two employees at Anchor Brewery (which is now owned by the parent company of the Japanese brewery Sapporo) successfully unionized. Through collective bargaining, management agreed to raise wages, offer paid lunch breaks, and extend paid time off (PTO) to part-time employees.[22] Months later, employees of Fair State Brewery, located in Minneapolis, also followed suit, becoming one of the first craft breweries to do so.

It remains to be seen whether these scattered efforts will spawn a larger movement toward unionization or other forms of labor advocacy in the industry. It is worth noting that rates of unionization across all U.S. industries have steadily fallen for the last sixty years: private industry unionization rates are now under 10%—less than one worker out of ten—having dropped from a high water mark of 35% in 1955. In contrast to social movements like Black Lives Matter and the beer industry's reckoning with gender-based violence, brewery ownership has been far more reluctant to embrace labor movements among its worker ranks. Some have actively opposed such efforts. In the fall of 2020, Surly Brewing Company made headlines for announcing the closure of its large Minneapolis-based brewpub—just days after employees informed management of their intention to unionize (Surly management released a statement denying their decision to close the brewpub had anything to do with the unionization effort). Improving the material quality of employment for workers within breweries remains a subject with high stakes for the future of the industry but little sustained national conversation. We find this short-sighted. Achieving quality employment for workers is a crucial task that should be in lock-step with other parallel movements to support positive change in the industry. After all, what good are diversity, equity, and inclusion efforts in an industry that offers jobs with little possibility of earning a living wage or advancing in one's career?

THE FUTURE OF BEER AND SOCIETY

While the struggles over social inclusion and economic power in the world of beer rage on, the battle for its "soul"—to paraphrase U.S. president Joe Biden's 2020 campaign slogan—has the potential to reshape the culture of beer for generations to come. What goes on within beer will reflect changes in society and possibly signal more to come. But will any of these impassioned efforts for change stick? History has shown us that change is an uphill battle—one tilted in favor of those with existing power and access to institutional resources.[23] In the world of beer, change efforts must contend with large, corporate businesses that control the majority of the industry and set its economic terms. It must also contend with the norms and ideals of Whiteness and heteronormative masculinity that have dictated beer's dominant culture for decades.

What is clear is that visions of change in the world of beer, be it racial justice or economic advocacy, need to be supported by as broad and sustained a base of interlinked individuals, groups, and organizations as possible. Change initiatives need to be reflected in cultural shifts, such as the use of inclusive symbols and imagery that represent beer's diversity and inclusiveness. They need to find footing in structural contexts in order to sustain real gains, such as through organized efforts for better employment conditions or expanded programs that allow people from under-represented groups to develop skills, receive mentorship, and gain access to pathways into power and influence in the industry. There is no one magic solution, only slippery footholds along a long climb upwards.

We echo the calls of groups focused on issues of equity and inclusion within the world of beer. Finding space within the world of beer as consumers, workers, or brewery owners should be something everyone is able to enjoy. None of these goals are unique to beer, for the forces that structure the world of beer are the same that pattern our everyday experiences, our identities, our institutions, our cultures. We began this journey by asking you to attend to your own relationship with a beer that evokes a strong memory or emotion for you. We hope that it's clear now that this was just the first sip. We close by encouraging you to look beyond beer and back at our ever-evolving society, which will leave a much longer aftertaste. Cheers to that.

NOTES

1. Chapman and Brunsma 2020; Withers 2017.
2. Understanding these social patterns within the industry requires that data be collected and made available. Yet as of the writing of this book, little data exists on LGBTQIA+ representations in the industry.
3. This 2019 survey by the BA was called the "Brewery Operations Benchmarking Survey."
4. This quote is taken from one of Holly Regan's (2020) survey respondents. Regan, Holly. 2020. "All in the (Chosen) family, part one—How queer erasure plagues craft beer." *Good Beer Hunting*. November 24, 2020. Accessed 2/28/21 (https://www.goodbeerhunting.com/blog/2020/11/23/all-in-the-chosen-family-part-one-how-queer-erasure-plagues-craft-beer).
5. There have been vocal critics of the Whiteness and maleness of craft beer in the past, see Infante, Dave. 2015. "There are almost no black people brewing craft beer. Here's why." *Thrillist*. Accessed 2/1/21 (https://www.thrillist.com/drink/nation/there-are-almost-no-black-people-brewing-craft-beer-heres-why).
6. Mayorga-Gallo, Sarah. 2019. "The white-centered logic of diversity ideology." *American Behavioral Scientist, 63*(13): 1789–1809.
7. Hop Culture. "Beers with(out) beards keynote w new Belgium." October 11, 2020. (https://www.youtube.com).
8. Regan 2020.
9. Pomranz, Mike. 2017. "Brewer's association is trying to make offensive beer names a thing of the past." *Food & Wine*. Accessed 2/28/21 (https://www.foodandwine.com/news/brewers-association-trying-make-offensive-beer-names-thing-past).
10. Wolinski, Cat. 2019. "Hop take: The beer industry grapples with racism, again." *VinePair*. Accessed 2/28/21 (https://vinepair.com/articles/beer-industry-racism/).
11. Mayhugh, Jess. 2015. "Flying dog wins six-year raging bitch case." *Baltimore*. Accessed 2/28/21 (https://www.baltimoremagazine.com/section/fooddrink/flying-dog-wins-six-year-raging-bitch-case).
12. The authors of this book were recipients of a Craft X EDU scholarship to attend the Great American Beer Festival in 2019 and participate in a professional development program hosted by Craft X EDU.

13. Iseman, Courtney. 2020. "How Eugenia Brown is empowering women of color to join the beer industry." *October.* Accessed 2/28/21 (https://oct.co/essays/road-to-100-eugenia-brown).

14. The aftermath of this event is still ongoing as of the writing of this book. For more information, see Demmon, Beth. "Sweeping accusations of sexism, assault rock the craft beer industry." *Vinepair.* Accessed 7/1/21 (https://vinepair.com/articles/sexism-assault-beer-industry-ratmagnet/).

15. Chapman and Brunsma 2020.

16. Su, Ting. "Building the collective—How breweries can better prioritize diversity." *Good Beer Hunting*, January 9, 2020. Accessed 9/1/21 (https://www.goodbeerhunting.com/blog/2020/1/6/building-the-collective-how-breweries-can-better-prioritize-diversity).

17. It has proved difficult for businesses and public figures to remain silent on sweeping social movements such as the Me Too movement and Black Lives Matter.

18. It is worth noting that this interview took place in January of 2020, just before many U.S. states mandated the closures of all on-premise business in breweries and restaurants. Ironically, the neighborhood brewery model suggested by this brewer was particularly hard-hit by the pandemic: one Albuquerque-based brewery owner that does not can or bottle his products told us his monthly sales were down by 80% during much of 2020.

19. Roth, Bryan. "Will work for beer, Pt.1—The dollars and sense of the industry." *Good Beer Hunting*, April 26, 2018. Accessed 11/1/20 (https://www.goodbeerhunting.com/sightlines/2018/4/26/will-work-for-beer-pt-1-the-dollars-and-sense-of-the-industry).

20. See Depalma, Lindsay J. 2021. "The passion paradigm: Professional adherence to and consequences of the ideology of 'do what you love.'" *Sociological Forum*, 36(1): 134–158.

21. Based on Payscale.com information for "brewer" in 2021. Ziprecruiter also reports similar salary figures. Further, these numbers are consistent with our personal correspondences with many assistant brewers and head brewers in craft beer.

22. Crowell, Chris. 2020. "Anchor Brewing Workers officially ratify union contract—details here." *Craft Brewing Business.* Accessed 2/28/21 (https://www.craftbrewingbusiness.com/news/anchor-brewing-workers-officially-ratify-union-contract-details-here/).

23. As queer feminist scholar Jodi O'Brien warns, institutionalized efforts to make change "from within" risk getting coopted for the purposes of the organization itself. This is why "diversity initiatives" often fall short of their original goals, channeled instead into smaller niches of progress such as diversity hires or short-term branding strategies to fit the times. Diversity remains a concept that everyone agrees with on paper but is far more challenging to implement in practice. See also Mayorga-Gallo 2019.

Epilogue

Smack in the middle of writing this book, the COVID-19 pandemic swept across the globe, thrusting the beer industry into an unprecedented crisis. Starting in March of 2020, the majority of U.S. breweries were either required by the government to close their doors to the public or did so voluntarily. The sudden shuttering of brewery taprooms as well as other commercial settings where beer is typically consumed, such as bars, restaurants, sporting venues, and theme parks, came with an economic cost that was sudden and severe. Breweries furloughed workers as they watched keg inventory expire and go to waste. A survey conducted in April of 2020 by BA indicated that over half of brewery owners thought they would have to shut down permanently within three months should business lockdowns continue (the average brewery reported a 65% drop in on-premise sales during this time).[1] By July of 2020, two out of three breweries in Texas reported they did not think they could survive until the end of the year without outside financial assistance. While some government aid has flowed to small breweries, they continued to face on-again, off-again business restrictions due to health concerns related to COVID-19 well into 2021.

As we discussed in the concluding chapter, breweries, beer organizations, and industry groups have used this difficult moment as an opportunity to reflect on the state of the industry and grapple with issues of social justice and worker empowerment. But many of these same companies remain in survival mode themselves, reeling from the economic disaster of a pandemic that is still unfolding as this book goes to press. To be sure, these issues are intertwined in important ways: many commentators have observed that the anger and emotion that characterized America's summer of racial reckoning in 2020 was exacerbated by pandemic-related social isolation and frustration.

The way out of these dual crises in the longer term requires re-invigorating the industry in social, cultural, and economic terms.[2]

In the pages that follow, we highlight the resilient, resourceful, and unexpected ways breweries and other industry organizations have navigated the pandemic. "The crisis has forced the industry through several generations of maturation, and changes we didn't expect to hit for years have become the norm in a matter of weeks," writes beer journalist Jonny Garret. "How drinkers and businesses respond to these changes will in turn set the course for decades."[3] Many breweries have doubled down on their community support while innovating creative business solutions custom-fit for this era. Their actions embody the essence of what craft beer represents: authenticity, integrity, and a focus on community (see chapter 4). As a result of these efforts, by the spring of 2021, far fewer breweries have been forced to shutter than initial survey reports would have predicted.

INNOVATING FOR THE GREATER GOOD

With demand for draft beer down and hand sanitizer up, many small brewers and distillers around the country decided to answer a call they never asked for. "We were hearing reports that sanitizer was in short supply," explains John Gozigian, co-owner of La Reforma brewery in Albuquerque, New Mexico. "We also knew that we had the equipment sitting around and were capable of making it. We did so in order to help out how we could." La Reforma quickly repurposed their existing distilling equipment to create an entirely new product: a cleaning supply (see Figure 8.1). They, like many other breweries and distilleries, began to offer "hand-crafted" sanitizer to customers at minimal markup, if any at all. Some breweries even donated a portion of these products they made to first responders who were facing shortages of sanitizer and other PPE (personal protective equipment) at the time.

Matt Simonds, the owner of Albuquerque-based Broken Trail Distillery and Brewery, was reportedly the first distiller to make sanitizer in the state in March of 2020. He explained how he arrived at the decision to do so:

We were discussing at work that day the ridiculousness of selling Purell on ebay for hundreds of dollars. That evening, it hit me that this pandemic was real and thought—if we could put this together and give it out to people, that would be pretty awesome. So I started researching. I was probably up until 3 a.m. scouring the internet and my old chemistry textbooks to see what it would take to do this. It was important that the sanitizer be done correctly, quickly, and cheaply. The next morning, I hit the telephone. I was reaching out to suppliers for chemicals, containers, all the components to make this happen. By noon, David Rosebeary,

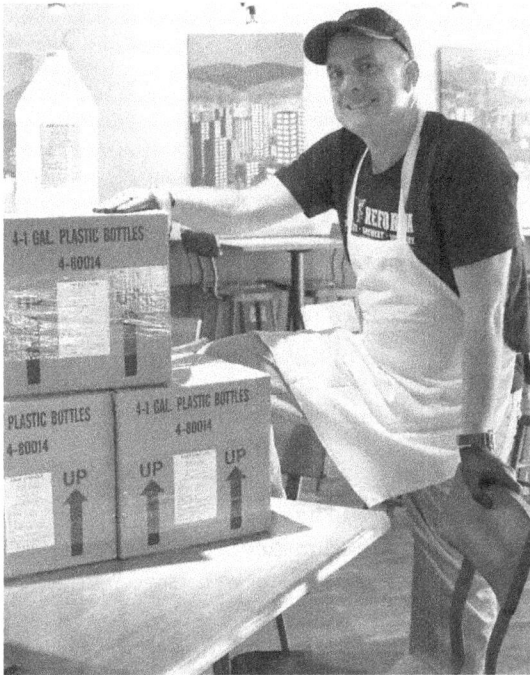

Figure E.1   La Reforma Brewing Company Co-Owner Jeff Jinnett with His House-Made Sanitizer. Many small breweries and distilleries around the United States found creative ways to use their resources for public good during the pandemic. *Source*: Courtesy of La Reforma Brewery.

our brewer, and I were batching it up. By 2 p.m. that afternoon (Thursday), we had free sanitizer available at our Uptown Tasting Room. Hand Sanitizer might not be our best beer, but the effort is one I'm most proud of.[4]

Matt's response showcases how quickly he and his small company were able to pivot their business strategy to be part of the solution on the ground.[5] Some beer distributors and breweries without distilling capacity also joined in the industry-wide effort to produce sanitizer. Staring down hundreds of kegs of beer going bad in their warehouse (if not more), these companies partnered with local distilleries to donate their product and turn it into alcohol-based cleaning supplies.[6] Producing hand sanitizer has been an innovative way that breweries and their industry partners have been able to contribute to a broader community response to the coronavirus pandemic.

Other craft breweries have teamed up to produce charity beers in support of vulnerable workers hit hard by layoffs and financial struggles during the pandemic. In March of 2020, Brooklyn-based Other Half Brewing Co launched a global collaboration project known as "All Together Now." In an open letter posted to their website, the owners of Other Half Brewing Co wrote:

Dear breweries of the world,

> There is an inextricable link that binds together everyone in the hospitality industry. Brewers, servers, bartenders, bussers, dishwashers, GMs, buyers, chefs, owners—we are all in this together. In this industry, when one of us struggles, the rest of us pick them up. It's baked into who we are.[7]

The brewery shared the recipe, artwork, and name for All Together Now publicly as "open source" material for other breweries to use, provided that a portion of proceeds from sales of the beer went towards supporting hospitality and service workers. The built-in flexibility of the initiative allowed participating breweries to team up with a wide range of charities and fundraisers in their local communities. In all, more than 700 breweries in 51 countries around the world signed up to participate.

The support from consumers for these types of charity beer initiatives during the pandemic has been resounding. Many breweries reported selling out of their run of All Together Now in a matter of weeks if not days.[8] In the wake of the success of All Together Now, other craft beer groups have launched similar charity-based collaborations. For instance, the Colorado Brewers Guild and the Left Hand Brewing Foundation teamed up to form the Colorado Strong Fund, which kick-started a charity beer called "Colorado Strong Pale Ale" in which the founding organizations agreed to donate the ingredients for the beer to participating breweries in order to raise funds to support local workers affected by COVID-19. More than 100 Colorado-based breweries participated in this effort while popularizing the hashtag #ColoradoStrong.[9]

Collaborative relief efforts such as All Together Now and Colorado Strong illustrate the capacity of those in the world of beer to enact a resilient response to a crisis transcending both industry and place. Brewers, consumers, and advocates alike have tapped into what sociologist Michael Ian Borer has described as the "translocal" dimensions of the craft beer scene—shared values and ties across disparate locations—to channel a collective response for a good cause.[10]

Organizations have also managed to rise to the moment by innovating new ways of operating during the pandemic. These strategies have required bold leadership decisions as well as the creative repurposing of organizational resources. In April of 2020, with the pandemic still in full swing, the Brewers Association was forced to do the unthinkable: the BA decided to cancel the annual Craft Brewers Conference (CBC) that was supposed to be held in San Antonio, Texas, and expected to draw upwards of 5,000 attendees. Every year, CBC represents the biggest gathering of beer industry professionals in North America. Canceling this in-person event meant issuing millions of dollars in refunds to conference goers, eliminating speaker panels and workshops planned months in advance, and absorbing a large part of the overhead costs for booking the conference venue. Following news of the in-person conference closure, the BA announced that a large chunk of CBC programming would be moved online, to be held in virtual meeting rooms and live-streamed events. Under this new format, planned conference attendees—including the authors of this book—would still be able to access many of the same professional events from the comfort and safety of their own homes. Further, the BA decided to open up attendance to the 2020 virtual event at no cost to individuals not registered for the conference. Through this gesture of goodwill, the BA seized on the opportunity to make the retooled event as inclusive as possible.

To be sure, the online CBC conference likely operated at a substantial financial loss (these numbers were not disclosed by the BA). But the BA's decision to invest and adapt to unprecedented circumstances also resulted in a series of innovations that have pushed the beer industry in directions that might have taken years to achieve otherwise. For example, the online conference featured guided video beer tastings sessions with Advanced Cicerones® from around the world and up-close access to industry luminaries who appeared on live video feeds and virtual "happy hours." It allowed conference sponsors and other industry advertisers to gain brand exposure by hosting these sessions, many of which featured viewer counts in the thousands (as opposed to dozens, which would be the norm for in-person conference events). CBC organizers managed to score a win for the craft beer community by proving how adaptive and innovative the BA could be in its support of its brewery members. It also set up the BA to be at the forefront of new technologies that are set to become a fixture for how we experience craft beer long after the pandemic subsides.

These remain incredibly trying times for breweries and brewery workers. The effects of the pandemic have been hardest on small companies that are underresourced—just as it has been hardest on workers who are underprivileged and unable to weather a sustained loss of their jobs. Fortunately, many in the world of beer have found new sources of resiliency and solidarity. They do so not by facing this struggle alone but, rather, "all together now." In beer, as in society, these uncertain times remind us that we forge our history through adaptation and change, both of which pair best with a strong sense of community.

NOTES

1. Watson, Bart. 2020. "Brewery sales dropping sharply, many set to close." April 7, 2020. *Brewers Association.* Accessed 7/21/21 (https://www.brewersassociation.org/insights/brewery-sales-dropping-sharply-many-set-to-close/).

2. Iseman, Courtney. 2020. "Craft beer is responding to covid and racism through communal initiatives." *Vinepair.* Accessed 3/2/2021 (https://vinepair.com/articles/craft-beer-community-covid-racism/).

3. Garrett, Jonny. 2020. "Final gravity—What will be left of beer culture after covid-19?" *Good Beer Hunting*, July 1, 2020. Accessed 2/28/21 (www.goodbeerhunting.com).

4. This interview was first featured on Dark Side Brew Crew. See Dark Side Brew Crew. "Hand sanitizer is the newest hot product from Brewstilleries around the state." April 3, 2020. Accessed 10/1/20 (https://nmdarksidebrewcrew.com/2020/04/03/hand-sanitizer-is-the-newest-hot-product-from-brewstilleries-around-the-state/).

5. Sadly, in November of 2020, Broken Trail Distillery and Brewery announced it was closing permanently amid ongoing, government-mandated closures.

6. This is based on an interview with a local distillery owner in Albuquerque, New Mexico.

7. All Together Beer. Accessed 9/15/20 (https://alltogether.beer/).

8. Iseman 2020.

9. A popular charity slogan in beer has been #BreweryStrong, initially the brainchild of Rob Callaghan of Tuckahoe Brewing Company to help provide aid to people in the brewer, bar, and restaurant industry. Schmid, Tristan. "Colorado brewers guild and the left hand brewing foundation announce creation of the colorado strong fund." *Colorado Brewers Guild.* Accessed 3/2/21 (https://coloradobeer.org/colorado-strong-pale-ale/).

10. Borer 2019.

Appendix

Key Terms

18th Amendment (United States): the amendment of the U.S. Constitution that established the prohibition of alcohol in the United States. The 18th Amendment was ratified on January 16, 1919, to go into effect the following year.

21st Amendment (United States): the amendment of the U.S. Constitution that repealed Prohibition (18th Amendment). Ratified December 5, 1933. The 21st Amendment ended a thirteen-year federal ban on the production and sale of alcohol within the United States.

Alcohol myopia: impacts of alcohol to limit information processing capacity and limit our attention on immediate events (myopia means nearsightedness).

Alcoholic Fermentation: the process of breaking down sugar into alcohol and carbon dioxide. This is why an old saying reads: "Brewers make wort, yeast makes beer."

Aroma (beer): our perception of a beer's smell, based on olfaction. We perceive the aroma of a beer through inhalation (orthonasal olfaction) and exhalation (retronasal olfaction).

Appearance (beer): our perception of the visual information about a beer, such as its color, clarity, and carbonation level.

Beer Geek: a person who devotes considerable time, energy, and resources to tasting, acquiring, and learning about beer. Beer geeks represent a subset of the larger beer scene though they have an outsized role in shaping demand for "rare" and valuable beers (see "whale").

Beer Psychology: a framework for understanding our beer experiences from a psychological lens. A fundamental premise of beer psychology is that our personal experiences with beer are influenced by intrapersonal, interpersonal, social, and environmental forces.

Beertender: a person who serves beer in a brewery taproom, or a bar that serves only beer.

Big Beer: large, corporate-owned breweries and the mass-produced products made by these companies. Big Beer, also known as "macro" beer, is considered the opposite of craft beer.

Black, Indigenous, and People of Color (BIPOC): a term replacing "people of color" that acknowledges the experience of Black people and Indigenous Peoples.

Brewers Association: the national organization for craft brewers in the United States.

Brewers Guild (state): a business association comprised of professional brewers and breweries within a given region. Brewers guilds help promote the industry and advance the interest of its members.

Cellarperson: a brewery worker responsible for the upkeep of brewed beer through the process of fermentation, racking (transferring), and carbonating in tanks.

Cicerone®: a beer professional whose knowledge about beer has been certified by the Cicerone® Certification Program. The title of Certified Cicerone® is the second level of the four-level certification program, which from lowest to highest are: Certified Beer Server, Certified Cicerone®, Advanced Cicerone®, and Master Cicerone®.

Cishet: a descriptor that signifies that a person is both cisgender (their gender identity corresponding with their sex assigned at birth) and heterosexual.

Controlling Images: coined by Patricia Hill Collins, controlling images are dominant-negative images of members of a particular group in society, such as Black men as dangerous criminals. Controlling images function as ideological tools that perpetuate the subordinate position of members of these groups.

Craft Beer: as defined by the Brewers Association, craft beer is a beer that is made by a brewery that is "small" and "independent" (see entry for "craft brewery"). More informally, craft beer is the opposite of the products of Big Beer (see entry).

Craft Brewery: according to the Brewers Association, the qualifications of craft brewery are twofold: a brewery that produces less than six million barrels a year and is independently owned (less than 25% corporate ownership). The BA's definition of a craft brewery has changed over the years. Notably, the definition used to include the criteria of being "traditional," which meant having a flagship beer made predominantly using traditional ingredients such as malted barley or wheat.

Crafty Brewery: a Big Beer-owned and operated brewery that masks as a craft brewery.

Craftwashing: the use of craft beer's aesthetics and branding by a larger corporation, particularly the emphasis on handcraftsmanship and small-scale production.

Cultural Appropriation: the adoption of an element of one culture by a person, group, or business not of that culture for personal gain.

Cultural Capital: cultural knowledge that aligns with the elite classes within a society. Acquiring cultural capital typically involves socialization within elite institutions.

Culture (beer): the values, norms, and meanings associated with a given society. In the world of beer, culture manifests as drinking practices as well as how beer is discussed and valued.

Distributor: a wholesale business operation that buys beer from producers (breweries) and delivers it to retail establishments (bars and retail stores).

Division of Labor: the assignment of different jobs to different groups of workers within a given group, such as a specific workplace or society as a whole.

Equity: as a form of social advocacy, equity is just and fair inclusion within society where all people can participate, prosper, and reach their full potential. Note it does not equate to equality.

Head (beer): beer foam. An unstable phenomenon on the top of the beer caused by proteins, lipids, and carbon dioxide that influences our beer experience, particularly aromas and mouthfeel.

Homebrewing: any noncommercial brewing operation. Usually associated with brewing beer in small batches (5–10 gallons) with specialized homebrewing equipment or home-made brewing equipment.

Hops: one of the four primary ingredients of modern beer. Hops are the flower clusters of a plant called *Humulus lupulus*. They contribute to beer's characteristic bitterness, aromas, and flavors. Hops also help prevent spoilage and improve a beer's head retention.

Importer: a wholesale business operation that buys beer from producers and ships it internationally to sell to select retailers and distributors.

Job Segregation: the distribution of workers across and within occupations, based on demographic characteristics such as race, gender, class, and age. Also known as occupational segregation.

Lacing: the residue of beer foam that adheres to clean glassware with beer poured in it.

LGBTQIA+: an acronym that stands for Lesbian, Gay, Bisexual, Transgender, Queer, Intersex, Asexual. The "+" at the end acknowledges that there are non-cisgender and non-straight identities which are not included in the acronym.

Malted Barley: one of the four main ingredients of beer, which provides the main source of fermentable sugar for alcoholic fermentation and the color of beer. (See malting for the process)

Malting: a process of transforming grains into malts through steeping, germinating, and drying. The process modifies the physical structure of grains to allow enzymes to synthesize or activate.

Master Brewer: someone who develops beer recipes, brands, and collaborations in a professional brewery. Sometimes known as a "brewmaster," this person is responsible for managing the overall brewing operation, brewhouse labor, and vision at a brewery.

Mouthfeel: the physical sensation of beer when we drink it. Mouthfeel takes into account the body, carbonation, astringency, creaminess, and alcoholic warming of a beer. Along with appearance, aroma, and taste, mouthfeel contributes to our overall perception of a beer.

Oligarchical Control (business): a large share of a given commercial market by a small number of companies. Oligarchical control makes it difficult for small companies to compete.

Overchoice: an impairment of decision making and choice behavior due to an abundance of options.

Privilege(s): unearned advantages within a given society due to one's social characteristics, such as race, class, gender, and sexuality. Privileges can be intersectional in the sense that they can be multiple and overlapping (e.g., a White, college-educated, cisgender woman).

Production of Culture (theory): the ways in which cultural objects are produced and ascribed with meaning within a given system. Examining beer culture from this perspective requires assessing how beer is made, distributed, sold, regulated, and consumed.

Prohibition: a term for government policies that make the commercial sale and production of alcohol illegal. Prohibition is most often associated with the historical period of U.S. Prohibition, which spanned from 1919 to 1933. See 18th Amendment, 21st Amendment.

Racialization: the extension of racial meaning to a social practice or group. We see this in common assumptions about craft beer being for White people, or cheap malt liquor associated with African Americans.

Social Capital: for an individual, one's ties to others can provide them with access to material and symbolic resources. For a group, the level of trust and closeness is exhibited by members of that group.

Social Identity: a person's sense of who they are based on their group membership(s), such as race or ethnicity, family, or professional craft brewer. Social identity has two components: the identity that an individual puts forth and how others perceive that individual.

Social Power: the capacity to do or change something to your will. Having social power means having your authority recognized by others in society. In other words, it's not only about how we view our power but also about how the world around us respond to our actions.

Social Organization of Labor: demographic patterns associated with a job or industry. While the beer industry as a whole is overwhelmingly male and white, women are disproportionately employed in customer service jobs, such as in the taproom.

Taste (physiological): gustatory perceptions of sweetness, saltiness, sourness, bitterness, umami, and fat.

Taste (cultural): having a "refined" palate for beer or any other cultural good. Taste is a culturally constructed phenomenon, meaning the kinds of tastes that are valued highly in a society are learned through socialization.

Taproom (brewery): an area of a brewery open to the public where beer can be legally served to customers and consumed on premise. Taprooms typically require a special "on-premise" alcohol license.

Whale (beer): a rare beer usually released by a craft brewery that is already subject to considerable hype among beer geeks.

Whiteness (theory): the ways in which White people, their customs, culture, and beliefs operate as the standard by which all other groups in society are compared. Whiteness is typically examined in the context of U.S. and European societies, though some scholars argue that these same standards have been widely disseminated today, making Whiteness a global phenomenon.

Yeast: one of the four basic ingredients of beer. Yeast converts fermentable sugar into ethanol and carbon dioxide. While there are many strains of yeast, the primary yeast strain used for beer is known as "Brewer's yeast" (*Saccharomyces cerevisiae*).

References

Acitelli, Tom. 2014. "How World War I affected beer." *All About Beer Magazine*. Accessed 9/15/20 (http://allaboutbeer.com/world-war-i-beer/).

———. 2013. *The audacity of hops: The history of America's craft beer revolution*. Chicago: Chicago Review Press.

Acker, Joan. 2006. "Inequality regimes: Gender, class, and race in organizations." *Gender & Society*, 20(4): 441–464.

Ajzen, Icek. 2020. "The theory of planned behavior: Frequently asked questions." *Human Behavior and Emerging Technologies*, 2(4): 314–324.

Alcademics. Temporary Page. Accessed 2/1/20 (https://www.alcademics.com/).

All Together Beer. Accessed 9/15/20 (https://alltogether.beer/).

Allworth, Jeffrey. "'Craft beer' means ... Anything Boston beer wants it to?" *Beervana*. October 31, 2018. Accessed 7/1/21 (https://www.beervanablog.com/beervana/2018/10/31/craft-beer-is-basically-anything).

Almiron, Paula, Francisco Barbosa Escobar, Abhishek Pathak, Charles Spence, and Carlos Velasco. 2021. "Searching for the sound of premium beer." *Food Quality and Preference*, 88: 104088.

American Psychological Association. "Resilience." Accessed 9/15/20 (https://www.apa.org/topics/resilience).

Anderson, Elijah. 2015. "The white space." *Sociology of Race and Ethnicity*, 1(1):10–21.

Appadurai, Arjun. 1990. "Disjuncture and difference in the global cultural economy." *Theory, Culture & Society*, 7(2–3): 295–310.

Ariely, Dan, and Jonathan Levav. 2000. "Sequential choice in group settings: Taking the road less traveled and less enjoyed." *Journal of Consumer Research*, 27(3): 279–290.

Ascher, Bernard. 2012. *Global beer: The road to monopoly*. Washington, DC: American Anti- trust Institute.

Attwood, Angela S., Nicholas E. Scott-Samuel, George Stothart, and Marcus R. Munafò. 2012. "Glass shape influences consumption rate for alcoholic beverages." *PLoS One, 7*(8): e43007.

Baker, Jeff. 2017. "Flattery or unfair? 'Vermont' beer pops up out of state." 3/17/17. *Burlington Free Press*. Accessed 2/23/21 (https://www.burlingtonfreepress.com/story /life/food/2017/03/17/flattery-foul-play-vermont-beer-pops-up-out-state/99252424/).

Barajas, Jesus M., Geoff Boeing, and Julie Wartell. 2017. "Neighborhood change, one pint at a time: The impact of local characteristics on craft breweries." In N. G. Chapman, J. S. Lellock, and C. D. Lippard (eds.), *Untapped: Exploring the cultural dimensions of craft beer*. Morgantown: West Virginia University Press.

Becker, Howard S. 1953. "Becoming a marihuana user." *American Journal of Sociology, 59*(3): 235–242.

———. 2008. *Art worlds: Updated and expanded*. Berkeley, CA: University of California Press.

Beers With(out) Beards Keynote w/ New Belgium. Accessed 2/28/21 (https://www .youtube.com/watch?v=2lxjHknFpOo&feature=emb_logo).

Bell, Emily. "Why good bars don't serve your beer in a frosted glass." *Vinepair*. Accessed 7/1/21 (https://vinepair.com/wine-blog/why-good-bars-dont-serve-your -beer-in-a-frosted-glass/).

Bell, Emma, Gianluigi Mangia, Scott Taylor, and Maria L. Toraldo. (Eds.). 2018. *The organization of craft work: Identities, meanings, and materiality*. Routledge.

Bennett, Judith. 1996. *Ale, beer, and brewsters in England*. Oxford, UK: Oxford University Press.

Bennett II, James. 2021. "We're reclaiming beer because it's ours." *Eater,* February 23, 2021. Accessed 2/23/21 (https://www.eater.com/22262702/beer-culture-in -america-black-brewers-history).

Bennet, Sarah. 2016. "Wholesale wars: The battle for the future of beer distribution." *Beer Advocate*. Accessed 7/1/21 (https://www.beeradvocate.com/articles/13526/ wholesale-wars-the-battle-for-the-future-of-beer-distribution/).

Benzecry, Claudio E. 2009. "Becoming a fan: On the seductions of opera." *Qualitative Sociology, 32*(2): 131–151.

Berger, Peter L., and Thomas Luckmann. 1967. *The social construction of reality: A treatise in the sociology of knowledge*. Garden City, NY: Doubleday.

Betancur, Maria I., Kosuke Motoki, Charles Spence, and Carlos Velasco. 2020. "Factors influencing the choice of beer: A review." *Food Research International,* 137: 109367.

Beverland, Mike B. 2005. "Crafting brand authenticity: The case of luxury wines." *Journal of Management Studies*, 42(5): 1003–1029.

Beverland, Mike B., and Francis J. Farrelly. 2010. "The quest for authenticity in consumption: Consumers' purposive choice of authentic cues to shape experienced outcomes." *Journal of Consumer Research, 36*(5): 838–856.

Bodnár, Vivien, Krisztina Nagy, Adam Cziboly, and Gyorgy Bárdos. 2021. "Alcohol and placebo: The role of expectations and social influence." *International Journal of Mental Health and Addiction, 19*: 2292–2305.

Bonilla-Silva, Eduardo. 2010. *Racism without Racists*: Color-blind racism and the persistence of racial inequality in the United States. Lanham, MD: Rowman & Littlefield Publishers.

Boothby, Erica J., Margaret S. Clark, and John A. Bargh. 2014. "Shared experiences are amplified." *Psychological Science, 25*(12): 2209–2216.

Borer, Michael Ian. 2019. *Vegas brews: Craft beer and the birth of a local scene.* New York: New York University Press.

Bourdieu, Pierre. 1993. *The field of cultural production.* New York: Columbia University Press.

Bourdieu, Pierre. 1984. *Distinction: A social critique of the judgment of taste.* Cambridge, MA: Harvard University Press.

Brady, Jennifer. 2018. "Toward a critical, feminist sociology of expertise." *Journal of Professions and Organization*, 5: 123–138. doi: 10.1093/jpo/joy004.

Brewers Association. 2020 Industry Statistics. Accessed 09/1/2020 (https://www.brewersassociation.org/).

———. 2019. *Draught beer quality manual* (4th ed.). Brewers Association.

———. "Brewers Association releases the Top 50 brewing companies by sales volume for 2020." Accessed 7/1/21 (https://www.brewersassociation.org/press-releases/brewers-association-releases-the-top-50-brewing-companies-by-sales-volume-for-2020/).

———. "Brewers Association releases annual growth report for 2019." Accessed 7/1/21 (https://www.brewersassociation.org/press-releases/brewers-association-releases-annual-growth-report-for-2019/).

———. "National beer sales & production data." Accessed 7/1/21 (https://www.brewersassociation.org/statistics-and-data/national-beer-stats/).

Calagione, Sam. 2005. *Brewing up a business: Adventures in entrepreneurship from the founder of Dogfish head craft brewery.* John Wiley & Sons.

Campbell, Colin. 2005. "The craft consumer: Culture, craft, and consumption in a postmodern society." *Journal of Consumer Culture, 5*(1): 23-42.

Campbell-Meiklejohn, D. K., Kanai, R., Bahrami, B., Bach, D. R., Dolan, R. J., Roepstorff, A., and Frith, C. D. 2012. "Structure of orbitofrontal cortex predicts social influence." *Current Biology*, *22*(4): R123–R124.

Cantazarite, Lisa. 2000. "Brown-collar jobs: Occupational segregation and earnings of recent-immigrant Latinos." *Sociological Perspectives, 43*(1): 45–75.

Carroll, Glenn. 1985. "Concentration and specialization: Dynamics of niche width in populations of organizations." *American Journal of Sociology* 90:1262–83.

Carroll, Glenn and Anand Swaminathan. 2000. "Why the microbrewery movement? Organizational dynamics of resource partitioning in the U.S. brewing industry." *American Journal of Sociology, 106*(3): 715–762.

Carvalho, Felipe R., Qian J. Wang, Raymond Van Ee, and Charles Spence. 2016. "The influence of soundscapes on the perception and evaluation of beers." *Food Quality and Preference*, *52*: 32–41.

Chapman, Nathaniel G. and David Brunsma. 2020. *Beer and racism.* Bristol: Bristol University Press.

Chapman, Nathaniel G., J. Slade Lellock, and Cameron D. Lippard. 2017. *Untapped: Exploring the cultural dimensions of craft beer.* West Virginia University Press.

Chapman, Nathaniel G., Megan Nanney, J. Slade Lellock and Julie Mikles-Schluterman 2018. "Bottling gender: Accomplishing gender through craft beer consumption." *Food, Culture & Society.* DOI: 10.1080/15528014.2018.1451038.

Cicerone® Certification Program. "About Cicerone." Accessed 7/1/21 (https://cicerone.org/us-en/about-cicerone-0).

———. "Tasting together: NEIPA with master Cicerone pat fahey." *Youtube.* Accessed 7/21/21 (https://www.youtube.com/watch?v=2s_tSkx5Hpo).

Cinelli, Melissa D., and Robin A. LeBoeuf. 2020. "Keeping it real: How perceived brand authenticity affects product perceptions." *Journal of Consumer Psychology*, 30(1): 40–59.

Collins, Nancy L., and Lynn Carol Miller. 1994. "Self-disclosure and liking: A meta-analytic review." *Psychological Bulletin, 116*(3): 457–475.

Coors Brewing Company. Accessed 2/20/21 (https://www.coors.com/Process).

Cowan, Nelson. 2001. "The magical number 4 in short-term memory: A reconsideration of mental storage capacity." *Behavioral and Brain Sciences*, 24(1): 87–114.

Craft Beer and Brewing. "Ale wives." Accessed 9/15/20 (https://beerandbrewing.com/dictionary/C1O0mFMSGP/).

Craft Beer and Brewing. "The history of beer." Accessed 2/8/21 (https://beerandbrewing.com/dictionary/UqfrcsPoAI/).

Craftbeer.com. "Seek the Seal™." Accessed 7/1/21 (https://www.craftbeer.com/breweries/independent-craft-brewer-seal).

Craft Beverage Modernization and Tax Reform Act. Accessed 9/15/20 (https://www.beerinstitute.org/wp-content/uploads/2016/11/S.-1562-Craft-Beverage-Modernization-and-Tax-Reform-Act-of-2015-One-Pager.pdf).

Crowell, Chris. 2020. "Anchor brewing workers officially ratify union contract—details here." *Craft Brewing Business.* Accessed 2/28/21 (https://www.craftbrewingbusiness.com/news/anchor-brewing-workers-officially-ratify-union-contract-details-here/).

Cruwys, Tegan, Kirsten E. Bevelander, and Roel C.J. Hermans. 2015. "Social modeling of eating: A review of when and why social influence affects food intake and choice." *Appetite, 86*: 3–18.

Currid-Halkett, Elizabeth. 2017. *The sum of small things: A theory of the aspirational class.* Princeton, NJ: Princeton University Press.

Curtis, Matthew. "The Emperor's New Gueuze: A Wild Revival in a Post-Appellation Age." *Good Beer Hunting*, May 16, 2018. Accessed 7/1/21 (https://www.good-beerhunting.com/blog/2018/5/12/the-emperors-new-gueuze-a-wild-revival-in-a-post-appellation-age).

Dahl, Melissa. "The annoying psychology of how your friends influence the beer you order." *The Cut.* Accessed 2/1/21 (https://www.thecut.com/2016/09/the-annoying-way-your-friends-influence-the-beer-you-order.html).

Daniels, Ray. "Why pour beer into a glass?" The Cicerone Certification Program. Accessed 3/1/21 (https://www.cicerone.org/us-en/blog/why-pour-beer-into-a-glass).

Dark Side Brew Crew. "Hand sanitizer is the newest hot product from brewstilleries around the state." April 3, 2020. Accessed 10/1/20 (https://nmdarksidebrewcrew.com/2020/04/03/hand-sanitizer-is-the-newest-hot-product-from-brewstilleries-around-the-state/).

Darwin, Helana. 2018. "Omnivorous masculinity: Gender capital and cultural legitimacy in craft beer culture." *Social Currents, 5*(3): 301–316.

De Cosmi, Valentina, Silvia Scaglioni, and Carlo Agostoni. 2017. "Early taste experiences and later food choices." *Nutrients, 9*(2): 107.

De Groot, Jasper H., Monique Smeets, Annemarie Kaldewaij, Maarten J. Duijndam, and Gun R. Semin. 2012. "Chemosignals communicate human emotions." *Psychological Science, 23*(11): 1417–1424.

Deener, Andrew, 2012. *Venice: A contested bohemia in Los Angeles.* University of Chicago Press.

Demmon, Beth. "Sweeping accusations of sexism, assault rock the craft beer industry." *Vinepair.* Accessed 7/1/21 (https://vinepair.com/articles/sexism-assault-beer-industry-ratmagnet/).

Depalma, Lindsay J. "The passion paradigm: Professional adherence to and consequences of the ideology of 'do what you love.'" *Sociological Forum, 36*(1): 134–158.

DeSoucey, Michaela. 2010. "Gastronationalism: Food traditions and authenticity politics in the European Union." *American Sociological Review, 75*(3): 432–455.

Domínguez-Quintero, Ana M., M. Rosario González-Rodríguez, and Jose L. Roldán. 2019. "The role of authenticity, experience quality, emotions, and satisfaction in a cultural heritage destination." *Journal of Heritage Tourism, 14*(5–6): 491–505.

Drinks Maven. "The iceman pour." Accessed 2/23/21 (https://drinksmaven.com/2017/03/the-iceman/).

Du Gay, Paul. 1996. *Consumption and identity at work.* Thousand Oaks, CA: Sage.

Durkheim, Emile. 1915. *The elementary forms of the religious life.* New York: Free Press.

Elevate. Accessed 8/18/20 (https://www.elevatebeer.com/).

Elliot, C.S. 2018. "Consuming craft: The intersection of production and consumption in north carolina craft beer markets." University of North Carolina at Chapel Hill. Dissertation.

Elzinga, Kenneth G., Carol H. Tremblay, and Victor J. Tremblay. 2015. "Craft beer in the United States: History, numbers, and geography." *Journal of Wine Economics, 10*(3): 242.

Enoch, Jamie, Leanne McDonald, Lee Jones, Pete R. Jones and David P. Crabb. 2019. "Evaluating whether sight is the most valued sense." *JAMA ophthalmology, 137*(11): 1317–1320.

Federal Reserve Banks. "Small business credit survey 2020." Accessed 2/26/21 (https://www.fedsmallbusiness.org/medialibrary/FedSmallBusiness/files/2020/2020-sbcs-employer-firms-report).

Field, Matt, Reinout W. Wiers, Paul Christiansen, Mark T. Fillmore, and Joris C. Verster. 2010. "Acute alcohol effects on inhibitory control and implicit cognition: Implications for loss of control over drinking." *Alcoholism: Clinical and Experimental Research, 34*(8): 1346–1352.

Fieldwork Brewing Company. "The meadows." Accessed 7/1/21 (https://fieldwork-brewing.com/beers/the-meadows/).

Florida, Richard. 2004. *The rise of the creative class and how it's transforming work, leisure, community and everyday life.* New York: Basic Books.

Frenette, Alexandre. 2013. "Making the intern economy: Role and career challenges of the music industry intern." *Work and Occupations, 40*(4): 364–397.

Friedmann, Harriet. 1992. "Distance and durability: Shaky foundations of the world food economy." *Third World Quarterly, 13*(2): 371–383.

Fritz, Kristene, Verena Schoenmueller, and Manfred Bruhn. 2017. "Authenticity in branding – Exploring antecedents and consequences of brand authenticity." *European Journal of Marketing, 51*(2): 324–348. doi:10.1108/EJM-10-2014-0633.

Frizzo, Francielle, Helison B. A. Dias, Nayara P. Duarte, Gabriela Rodrigues, and Paulo H. M. Prado. 2020. "The genuine handmade: How the production method influences consumers' behavioral intentions through naturalness and authenticity." *Journal of Food Products Marketing, 26*(4): 279–296.

Garrett, Jonny. 2020. "Final gravity—What will be left of beer culture after covid-19?" *Good Beer Hunting*, July 1, 2020. Accessed 2/28/21 (www.goodbeerhunting.com).

———. 2020. "A recipe for disaster: How lambic continues to redefine the beer world." Accessed 10/1/20 (https://www.goodbeerhunting.com/blog/2019/2/15/a-recipe-for-disaster-how-lambic-continues-to-redefine-the-beer-world).

Gately, Iain. 2008. *Drink: A cultural history of alcohol.* New York: Penguin.

Gatrell, Jay, Neil Reid, and Thomas Steiger. 2017. "Branding spaces: Place, region, sustainability and the american craft beer industry." *Applied Geography,* 90: 360–370.

Geertz, Clifford. 1973. *The interpretation of cultures.* New York: Basic Books.

Giancola, Peter R., Robert A. Josephs, Dominic Parrott, and Aaron A. Duke. 2010. "Alcohol myopia revisited: Clarifying aggression and other acts of disinhibition through a distorted lens." *Perspectives on Psychological Science*, 5: 265–278.

Girls Pint Out. Accessed 2/2/21 (http://www.girlspintout.org/about/).

Goffman, Erving. 1967. *Interaction Ritual: Essays on Face-to-Face Behavior.* Garden City, N.J.: 5–45.

Gohmann, Stephan F. 2016. "Why are there so few breweries in the South?" *Entrepreneurial Theory Practice 40*: 1071–1092.

Good Beer Hunting. 2020. "EP-255 Ray Daniels, Founder, Cicerone." Accessed 2/23/21 (https://www.goodbeerhunting.com/gbh-podcast/2020/2/6/ep-255-ray-daniels-founder-of-the-cicerone-program).

Granovetter, Mark. 1995 [1974]. *Getting a job: A study of contacts and careers.* Second edition. Chicago: University of Chicago Press.

Great American Beer Festival. "FAQ: Attendees." Accessed 7/1/21 (https://www.greatamericanbeerfestival.com/info/faq/).

Greene, C. M., Bahri, P., and Soto, D. 2010. "Interplay between affect and arousal in recognition memory." *PLoS One, 5*(7): e11739.

Gunaratne, T. M., Gonzalez Viejo, C., Gunaratne, N. M., Torrico, D. D., Dunshea, F. R., and Fuentes, S. 2019. "Chocolate quality assessment based on chemical finger-printing using near infra-red and machine learning modeling." *Foods*, 8(10): 426.

Hall, Elaine J., 1993. "Smiling, deferring, and flirting: Doing gender by giving 'good service.'" *Work and Occupations*, 20(4): 452–471.

Handwerk, Brian. "Celebrating 500 years of German's beer purity law." *Smithsonian Magazine*, April 22, 2016. Accessed 7/1/21 (https://www.smithsonianmag.com/history/celebrating-500-years-germans-beer-purity-law-180958878/).

Hannaford, Steve. 2007. *Market domination!: The impact of industry consolidation on competition, innovation, and consumer choice*. Westport, CT: Praeger.

Hayden, B., Canuel, N. and Shanse, J. 2013. "What was brewing in the Natufian? An archaeological assessment of brewing technology in the epipaleolithic." *Journal of Archaeology Method Theory* 20: 102–150. doi.10.1007/s10816-011-9127-y.

Healy, Jack. 2013 "A Montana loophole leaves a bitter taste with bar owners." *The New York Times,* April 20, 2013. Accessed 2/22/21 (https://www.nytimes.com/2013/04/21/us/montana-loophole-leaves-bitter-taste-among-bar-owners.html).

Hefty, Jennifer. 2019. "New Belgium founder: Sale 'not the last chapter' for Fort Collins Brewer." *Coloradoan*, November 19, 2019. Accessed 2/21/21 (https://www.coloradoan.com/story/money/2019/11/19/new-belgium-brewing-company-founder-kim-jordan-letter-fort-collins-beer/4238705002/).

Hertz, Julie. 2019. "The diversity data is in: Craft Breweries have room and resources for improvement." *Brewer's Association*. Accessed 11/1/20 (https://www.brewersassociation.org/communicating-craft/the-diversity-data-is-in-craft-breweries-have-room-and-resources-for-improvement/).

Hess, Alexander. 2014. "Companies that control the world's food." *USA Today*, August 16, 2014. Accessed 2/21/2021 (https://www.usatoday.com/story/money/business/2014/08/16/companies-that-control-the-worlds-food/14056133/).

Hicks, Joshua A., Rebecca J. Schlegel, and George E. Newman. 2019. "Introduction to the special issue: Authenticity: Novel insights into a valued, yet elusive, concept." *Review of General Psychology*, 23(1): 3–7.

Hieronymus, Stan. 2015. "How craft became craft." *All About Beer Magazine*, 36(1). Accessed 3/1/21 (http://allaboutbeer.com/article/how-craft-became-craft/).

———. 2012. *For the love of hops: The practical guide to aroma, bitterness and the culture of hops*. Boulder, CO: Brewers Publications.

Higgs, Suzanne, and Helen Ruddock. 2020. "Social influences on eating." Pp. 277–291 in *Handbook of eating and drinking: Interdisciplinary perspectives*, edited by Herbert Meiselman. New York: Springer Nature.

Hindy, Steve. 2014. *The craft beer revolution: How a band of microbrewers is transforming the world's favorite drink*. New York: Palgrave MacMillan.

———. "Free craft beer!" New York times opinion section, March 30, 2014. Accessed 9/15/20 (https://www.nytimes.com/2014/03/30/opinion/sunday/free-craft-beer.html).

Holl, John. 2019. "Patience for a pint: The art and science of the slow pour." July 16, 2019. *Beer & Brewing*. Accessed 2/23/21 (https://beerandbrewing.com/patience-for-a-pint-the-art-and-science-of-the-slow-pour/).

Homstrom, Peter. 2016. "The law that changed oregon's beer culture forever." *Portland Monthly*, July 2015. Accessed 2/22/21 (https://www.pdxmonthly.com /eat-and-drink/2016/03/the-law-that-changed-oregons-beer-culture-forever-june -2015#:~:text=In%20early%201985%2C%20the%20House,Brewpub%20Bill %2C%E2%80%9D%20HB%202284).

Howard, Philip H. 2014. "Too big to ale? Globalization and consolidation in the beer industry." In *The geography of beer* (pp. 155–165). Dordrecht: Springer.

Hop Culture. "Beers with(out) beards keynote w new Belgium" October 11, 2020. (https://www.youtube.com).

Infante, Dave. 2015. "There are almost No black people brewing craft beer. Here's why." *Thrillist*. Accessed 2/1/21 (https://www.thrillist.com/drink/nation/there-are -almost-no-black-people-brewing-craft-beer-heres-why).

Inside Beer 2018. "Japan: New Beer Taxation to turn beer and malt industry upside down." Accessed 2/20/21 (https://www.inside.beer/news/detail/japan-new-beer -taxation-to-turn-beer-and-malt-industry-upside-down.html).

Iseman, Courtney. 2020. "How Eugenia brown is empowering women of color to join the beer industry." *October*. Accessed 2/28/21 (https://oct.co/essays/road-to -100-eugenia-brown).

———. 2020. "Craft Beer is responding to covid and racism through communal initiatives." *Vinepair*. Accessed 3/2/2021 (https://vinepair.com/articles/craft-beer -community-covid-racism/).

Iyengar, Sheena S. 2010. "The art of choosing [Video]." TED Conferences. Accessed 7/1/21 (https://www.ted.com/talks/sheena_iyengar_the_art_of_choosing).

Kalev, Alexandra, Frank Dobbin, and Erin L. Kelly. 2006. "Best practices or best guesses? Assessing the efficacy of corporate affirmative action and diversity poli-cies." *American Sociological Review*, 71: 589–617.

Kanter, Rosabeth M. 1977. *Men and women of the corporation*. New York: Basic Books.

Koontz, Amanda and Nathaniel Chapman. 2019. "About us: Authenticating identity claims in the craft beer industry." *Journal of Popular Culture*, *52*(2): 351–372.

Lam, Tammy. 2014. "Brew free or die: Comparative analysis of U.S. and E.U. craft beer regulations. *Cardozo Journal of International and Comparative Law*, *23*(1): 197–xviii.

Leonardelli, Geoffrey J., Cynthia L. Pickett, and Marilynn B. Brewer. 2010. "Optimal distinctiveness theory: A framework for social identity, social cognition, and intergroup relations." In *Advances in experimental social psychology* (Vol. 43, pp. 63–113). Academic Press.

Lynn, Barry. 2012. "Big beer, a moral market, and innovation." December 26, 2012. *Harvard Business Review*. Accessed 2/28/21 (https://hbr.org/2012/12/big-beer-a -moral-market-and-in).

Maguire, Jennifer. 2019. "Wine, the authenticity taste regime, and rendering craft." In *The organization of craft work*, edited by Emma Bell, Gianluigi Mangia, Scott Taylor, and Maria L. Toraldo. New York: Routledge.

Maguire, Jennifer S., Jessica Bain, Andrea Davies, and Maria Touri. 2015. "Storytelling and Market Formation: An Exploration of Microbrewers in the UK."

In N. G. Chapman, J.S. Lellock and C. D. Lippard (Eds.), *Untapped: Exploring the cultural dimensions of craft beer* (pp. 236–260). Morgantown: West Virigina University Press.

Malone, Trey and Jason L. Lusk. 2019. "Mitigating choice overload: An experiment in the US beer market." *Journal of Wine Economics, 14*(1): 48–70.

Mayhugh, Jess. 2015. "Flying dog wins six-year raging bitch case." *Baltimore.* Accessed 2/28/21 (https://www.baltimoremagazine.com/section/fooddrink/flying -dog-wins-six-year-raging-bitch-case).

Mayorga-Gallo, Sarah. 2019. "The white-centered logic of diversity ideology." *American Behavioral Scientist, 63*(13): 1789–1809.

McCullough, Michael, Joshua Berning, and Jason L. Hanson. 2019. "Learning by brewing: Homebrewing legalization and the brewing industry." *Contemporary Economic Policy, 37*(1): 25–39.

McGann, John P. 2017. "Poor human olfaction is a 19th-century myth." *Science, 356*: 6338.

McPherson, Miller, Lynn Smith-Lovin, and James M. Cook. 2001. "Birds of a feather: Homophily in social networks." *Annual Review of Sociology* 27: 415–444.

Michener, Willa, and Paul Rozin. 1994. "Pharmacological versus sensory factors in the satiation of chocolate craving." *Physiology & Behavior, 56*(3): 419–422.

Mirabito, Adrian, Marcus Oliphant, George Van Doorn, Shaun Watson, and Charles Spence. 2017. "Glass shape influences the flavour of beer." *Food Quality and Preference, 62*: 257–261.

MolsonCoors. "2020 Sustainability Reporting." Accessed 8/18/20 (https://www.mol-soncoors.com/sustainability/sustainability-reporting).

Moss, Philip and Chris Tilly. 2001. *Stories employers tell: Race, skill, and hiring in America.* Russell Sage Foundation.

Mouly, Anne-Marie and Regina Sullivan. 2009. "15 memory and plasticity in the olfactory system: From infancy to adulthood." *The neurobiology of olfaction* (p. 367).

Mouw, Ted. 2003. "Social capital and finding a job: Do contacts matter?" *American Sociological Review, 68*(6): 868–698.

Mrkva, Kellen, Jairo Ramos, and Leaf Van Boven. 2020. "Attention influences emotion, judgment, and decision making to explain mental simulation." *Psychology of Consciousness: Theory, Research, and Practice, 7*(4): 404.

Murakami, Sakura. 2018. "New definition of beer gives japanese breweries license change." Accessed 2/28/21 (https://www.japantimes.co.jp/news/2018/03/31/business/new-definition-beer-gives-japanese-breweries-license-change/#:~:text=The%20change%20in%20definition%20gives,they%20were%20less%20heavily%20taxed).

National Public Radio. "Good beer doesn't just taste better, it sounds better too." Accessed 7/1/21 (https://www.npr.org/2021/05/27/1000991501/good-beer-doesnt -just-taste-better-it-sounds-better-too).

Neckerman, Katherine and Joleen Kirschenman. 1991. "Hiring strategies, racial bias, and inner-city workers." *Social Problems 38*(4): 433–447.

Noel, Corinna, and Robin Dando. 2015. "The effect of emotional state on taste perception." *Appetite, 95*: 89–95.

Noel, Josh. 2018. *Barrel-aged stout and selling out: Goose Island, Anheuser-Busch, and how craft beer became big business*. Chicago, IL: Chicago Review Press.

Noronha, Shilpa. 2020. "Artisan spotlight: Danielle French of Brasserie Cantillon." *Arcadian Fare*. Accessed 2/1/21 (https://www.arcadianfare.com/blog/artisan-spot-light-daniellefrench-cantillon).

Notte, Jason. "Opinion: Anheuser-Busch InBev shuts out craft beer brewers by hoarding hops." *MarketWatch*. May 12, 2017. Accessed 2/15/2021 (https://www.market-watch.com/story/anheuser-busch-inbev-shuts-out-craft-beer-brewers-by-hoarding-hops-2017-05-11).

Nugent, Anne. 2005. *The global beer market: A world of two halves*. London, UK: Euromonitor International. Accessed 8/1/20 (http://blog.euromonitor.com/2005/02/the-global-beer-market-a-world- of-two-halves.html).

Nurin, Tara. "The pay-to-play scandal in the beer biz: How far it goes nobody knows." *Forbes*. March 16, 2016. Accessed 2/15/2021 (https://www.forbes.com/sites/taranurin/2016/03/31/the-pay-to-play-scandal-in-the-beer-biz-how-far-it-goes-nobody-knows/?sh=307b5363b0d5).

O'Carroll, Cliona. 2005. "'Cold beer, warm hearts': Community, belonging and desire in Irish pubs in Berlin." In T. Wilson (Ed.), *Drinking cultures* (pp. 43–64). Oxford, UK: Berg.

Ocejo, Richard. 2017. *Masters of craft: Old jobs in the new urban economy*. Princeton, NJ: Princeton University Press.

Ocvirk, Miha, Natasa K. Mlinarič, and Iztok J. Košir. 2018. "Comparison of sensory and chemical evaluation of lager beer aroma by gas chromatography and gas chromatography/mass spectrometry." *Journal of the Science of Food and Agriculture*, 98(10): 3627–3635.

Ogle, Maureen. 2007. *Ambitious brew: The story of American beer*. San Diego: Harcourt.

Oliver, Melvin L. and Thomas M. Shapiro. 1996. *Black wealth/white wealth: A new perspective on racial inequality*. New York: Routledge.

Pager, Devah. 2003. "The mark of a criminal record." *American Journal of Sociology*, 108(5): 937–975.

Patagonia Provisions. Accessed 8/18/20 (https://www.patagoniaprovisions.com/pages/why-beer).

Paules, Greta F. 1991. *Dishing it out: Power and resistance among waitresses in a New Jersey restaurant*. Philadelphia: Temple University Press.

Paulsen, Krista E. and Hayley E. Tuller. 2017. "Crafting place: Craft beer and authenticity in Jacksonville, Florida." In N.G. Chapman, J.S. Lellock and C.D. Lippard (Eds.), *Untapped: Exploring the cultural dimensions of craft beer* (pp. 105–123), Morgantown: West Virigina University Press.

Pedulla, David. 2020. *Making the cut: Hiring decisions, bias, and the consequences of nonstandard, mismatched, and precarious employment*. Princeton, NJ: Princeton University Press.

Peiskar, Natasha. Brewers lectures. Spring session, March 2021.

Pellechia, Thomas. "Off-premise alcohol sales are up, with hard seltzer especially a boom." *Forbes*. Accessed 2/21/21 (https://www.forbes.com/sites/thomaspellechia

/2020/06/03/nielsen-cga-alcohol-dollar-sales-report-is-good-with-conditions/ #3770ebd51729).

Pershan, Caleb. "Inside the members-only world of online beer trading." *Eater.com*, May 4, 2020. Accessed 7/1/21 (https://www.eater.com/beer/2020/3/4/21157606/ rare-craft-beer-trading-america-facebook-private-groups-invite-only).

Peterson, Richard A., and Narasimhan Anand. 2004. "The production of culture perspective." *Annual Review of Sociology,* 30: 311–334.

Peterson, Richard A. and Roger M. Kern. 1996. "Changing highbrow taste: From snob to omnivore." *American Sociological Review,* 61: 900–907.

Peterson, Richard A. 1990. "Why 1955? Explaining the advent of rock music." *Popular Music, 9*(1): 97–116.

Petzel, Zachary W., and Jeffrey G. Noel. 2020. "Don't drink and drive, it's a prime: Cognitive effects of priming alcohol-congruent and incongruent goals among heavy versus light drinkers." *Journal of Health Psychology.* DOI: 1359105320934166.

Pomranz, Mike. 2017. "Brewer's association is trying to make offensive beer names a thing of the past." *Food & Wine.* Accessed 2/28/21 (https://www.foodandwine.com /news/brewers-association-trying-make-offensive-beer-names-thing-past).

Powers, Madelon. 1999. *Faces along the bar: Lore and order in the workingman's saloon, 1870-1920.* Chicago: University of Chicago Press.

Ray, Victor. 2019. "A theory of racialized organizations." *American Sociological Review, 84*(1): 26–53.

Reas, Emilie T., Gail A. Laughlin, Donna Kritz-Silverstein, Elizabeth Barrett-Connor, and Linda K. McEvoy. 2016. "Moderate, regular alcohol consumption is associated with higher cognitive function in older community-dwelling adults." *Journal of Prevention of Alzheimer's Disease, 3*(2): 105–113.

Regan, Holly. 2020. "All in the (chosen) family, part one — how queer erasure plagues craft beer." *Good Beer Hunting.* November 24, 2020. Accessed 2/28/21 (https://www.goodbeerhunting.com/blog/2020/11/23/all-in-the-chosen-family-part -one-how-queer-erasure-plagues-craft-beer).

Reinoso-Carvalho, Felipe, Silvana Dakduk, Johan Wagemans, and Charles Spence. 2019. "Dark vs. light drinks: The influence of visual appearance on the consumer's experience of beer." *Food Quality and Preference,* 74: 21–29.

———. 2019. "Not just another pint! The role of emotion induced by music on the consumer's tasting experience." *Multisensory Research, 32*(4–5): 367–400.

Reinoso Carvalho, F., Velasco, C., van Ee, R., Leboeuf, Y., and Spence, C. 2016. "Music influences hedonic and taste ratings in beer." *Frontiers in Psychology,* 7: 636.

Remmers, Carina, Sascha Topolinski, and Johannes Michalak. 2015. "Mindful (l) intuition: Does mindfulness influence the access to intuitive processes?" *The Journal of Positive Psychology, 10*(3): 282–292.

Ridgeway, Cecilia. 2011. *Framed by gender: How gender inequality persists in the modern world.* Oxford: Oxford University Press.

Ridzik, Agnieszka and Victoria Ellis-Vowles. 2019. "'Don't use "the weak word"': Women brewers, identities and gendered territories of embodied work." *Work, Employment, and Society* 33(3): 483-499.

Riello, Marianna, Maria Paola Cecchini, Alice Zanini, Miguel Di Chiappari, Michele Tinazzi, and Mirta Fiorio. 2019. "Perception of phasic pain is modulated by smell and taste." *European Journal of Pain, 23*(10): 1790–1800.

Risse, Lenora. 2018. "The gender qualification gap: Women 'over-invest' in workplace capabilities." *The Conversation.* Accessed 4/26/21 (https://theconversation .com/the-gender-qualification-gap-women-over-invest-in-workplace-capabilities -105385).

Rivaroli, Sergio, Jörg Lindenmeier, and Roberta Spadoni. 2019. "Attitudes and motivations toward craft beer consumption: An explanatory study in two different countries." *Journal of Food Products Marketing, 25*(3): 276–294.

Rivera, Lauren A. 2012. "Hiring as cultural matching: The case of elite professional service firms." *American Sociological Review, 77*(6):999–1022.

———. 2015. *Pedigree: How elite students get elite jobs.* Princeton, NJ: Princeton University Press.

Rodgers, Diane M. and Ryan Taves. 2017. "The epistemic culture of homebrewers and microbrewers." *Sociological Spectrum, 37*(3): 127–148.

Roth, Bryan. "Distress in delivery." *Good Beer Hunting*, March 7, 2018. Accessed 9/1/20 (https://www.goodbeerhunting.com/sightlines/2018/3/7/distress-in-delivery -pt-1-why-distributors-need-to-adapt).

———. "Will Work for Beer, Pt.1—The Dollars and Sense of the Industry." *Good Beer Hunting*, April 26, 2018. Accessed 11/1/20 (https://www.goodbeerhunting .com/sightlines/2018/4/26/will-work-for-beer-pt-1-the-dollars-and-sense-of-the -industry).

Royster, Diedre A. 2003. *Race and the invisible hand: How white networks exclude black men from blue-collar jobs.* Berkeley: University of California Press.

Sarkissian, Alex. "Missoula and beer: A history." *Missoula Independent*, April 29, 2010. Accessed: 7/1/21.

Schmid, Tristan. "Colorado Brewers guild and the left hand brewing foundation announce creation of the Colorado strong fund." *Colorado Brewers Guild.* Accessed 3/2/21 (https://coloradobeer.org/colorado-strong-pale-ale/).

Scott-Sheldon, Lori A., Kate B. Carey, Karlene Cunningham, Blair T. Johnson, Michael P. Carey, and MASH Research Team. 2016. "Alcohol use predicts sexual decision-making: A systematic review and meta-analysis of the experimental literature." *AIDS and Behavior, 20*(1): 19–39.

Sewell, S. L. 2014. "The spatial diffusion of beer from its Sumerian origins to today." Pp. 23–29 in *The Geography of Beer*, edited by Mark Patterson and Nancy Hoalst-Pullen. New York: Springer.

Sexton, Josie. 2015. "Brewers running out of names." *Coloradoan.* Accessed 9/15/20 (https://www.coloradoan.com/story/news/2015/02/24/beer-names-brewers-get -legal-trouble/23971025/).

Shikes, Jonathan. "Q&A: Todd Alstrom talks about beer advocate's influence and his move to Denver." *Westword*, August 6, 2013. Accessed 7/1/21 (https://www .westword.com/restaurants/qanda-todd-alstrm-talks-about-beer-advocates-influ-ence-and-his-move-to-denver-5736577).

Sierra Nevada Brewing Company. Accessed 8/18/20 (https://sierranevada.com/map/chico-sustainability-map/#).

Smart Barley. Accessed 8/18/20 (https://www.smartbarley.com/en/home.html#about).

Solar United. Accessed 8/18/20 (https://www.solarunitedneighbors.org/).

Solarte, Shana. "My Road to Cicerone®: Loy Maierhauser of MAP Brewing Company." Cicerone® Certification Program. Accessed 7/1/21 (https://www.cicerone.org/us-en/blog/my-road-to-cicerone-loy-maierhauser-of-map-brewing-company).

———. "My Road to Cicerone®: Michelle Tham of Labatt Brewing Company." Cicerone® Certification Program. Accessed 7/1/21 (https://www.cicerone.org/us-en/blog/my-road-to-cicerone-michelle-tham-of-labatt-brewing-company).

———. "My Road to Cicerone®: Toni Boyce of Beer Kulture." Cicerone® Certification Program. Accessed 7/1/21 (https://www.cicerone.org/us-en/blog/my-road-to-cicerone-toni-boyce-of-beer-kulture).

Spence, Charles. 2014. "Noise and its impact on the perception of food and drink." *Flavour*, *3*(1): 1–17.

———. 2020. "Wine psychology: Basic & applied." *Cognitive Research: Principles and Implications* 5: 1–18.

Spence, Charles, and Wang, Qian Janice. 2015. "Sensory expectations elicited by the sounds of opening the packaging and pouring a beverage." *Flavour*, *4*(1): 1–11.

Spinelli, Sara, and Sara R. Jaeger. 2019. "What do we know about the sensory drivers of emotions in foods and beverages?" *Current Opinion in Food Science*, *27*: 82–89.

Stack, Martin. "A concise history of America's brewing industry." *EH.net*. Accessed 7/1/21 (https://eh.net/encyclopedia/a-concise-history-of-americas-brewing-industry/).

Swagerty Jr., Daniel L., Ann D. Walling, and Robert M. Klein. 2002. "Lactose intolerance." *American Family Physician*, *65*(9): 1845–1850.

Tomaskovic, Donald and Dustin Avent-Holt. 2019. *Relational inequalities: An organizational approach*. New York: Oxford University Press.

Tsing, Anna. 2011. *Friction: An ethnography of global connection*. Princeton, NJ: Princeton University Press.

Tuttle, Brad. 2017. "Here's why craft beer pioneer Lagunitas says it sold itself to Heineken." *Money.com*. May 5, 2017. Accessed 2/15/21 (https://money.com/craft-beer-lagunitas-heineken).

United Nations Educational, Scientific, and Cultural Organization. "Beer culture in Belgium." Accessed 7/1/21 (https://ich.unesco.org/en/RL/beer-culture-in-belgium-01062).

Van Doorn, George, Justin Timora, Shaun Watson, Chris Moore, and Charles Spence. 2019. "The visual appearance of beer: A review concerning visually-determined expectations and their consequences for perception." *Food Research International*, 126: 108661.

Van Munching, Philip. 1997. *Beer blast: The inside story of the brewing industry's bizarre battles for your money*. New York: Random House.

Vartanian, Lenny R. 2015. "Impression management and food intake. Current directions in research." *Appetite*, 86: 74–80.

Ventura Alison K. and John Worobey. 2013. "Early influences on the development of food preferences." *Current Biology*, *23*: R401–R408. doi: 10.1016/j.cub.2013.02.037.

Vinepair. "The Definitive Timeline of Craft Beer Acquisitions." Accessed 2/15/21 (https://vinepair.com/craft-beer-sales/).

Waldinger, Roger and Michael Lichter. 2003. *How the Other Half Works*. Berkeley, CA: University of California Press.

Wallace, Andrew. 2019. "Brewing the truth': Craft beer, class and place in contemporary London." *Sociology, 53*(5): 951–966.

Warhurst, Chris and Dennis Nickson. 2009. "'Who's got the look?' Emotional, aesthetic, and sexualized labor in interactive services." *Gender, Work and Organization, 16*(3): 385–404.

Watson, Bart. "Evolving Beer's supply chain in an era of climate change." *Brewers Association*. Accessed 9/15/20 (https://www.brewersassociation.org/insights/evolving-beers-supply-chain-in-an-era-of-climate-change/).

———. "Brewery sales dropping sharply, many set to close." *Brewers Association*. April 7, 2020. Accessed 7/21/21 (https://www.brewersassociation.org/insights/brewery-sales-dropping-sharply-many-set-to-close/).

Wedekind, Claus, Thomas Seebeck, Florence Bettens, and Alexander J. Paepke. 1995. "MHC-dependent mate preferences in humans." *Proceedings of the Royal Society of London. Series B: Biological Sciences, 260*(1359): 245–249.

Wei Xie, Wei Xiong, Jie Pan, Tariq Ali, Qi Cui, Dabo Guan, Jing Meng, Nathaniel D. Mueller, Erda Lin, and Steven J. Davis. 2018. "Decreases in global beer supply due to extreme drought and heat." *Nature Plants*. DOI: 10.1038/s41477-018-0263-1.

White, Rob, Harry Shuckman, Josh Kaplan, and Amanda Ross. "A definitive list of trashy beers and what they say about you as a person." *The Tab*. Accessed 7/1/21 (https://thetab.com/us/2017/09/08/what-your-choice-pisswater-beer-71630).

Wilgus, Jeremy. 2018. "Japan's craft beer seen 25 years in the making." *Japan Times*. Accessed 9/15/20 (https://www.japantimes.co.jp/life/2018/10/06/food/japans-craft-beer-scene-25-years-making/#.XnurNtNKjs0).

Williams, Alistair. 2017. "Exploring the impact of legislation on the development of craft beer." *Beverages, 3*(18). doi:10.3390/beverages3020018.

Williams, Christine. 1991. *Gender differences at work: Women and men in nontraditional occupations*. Berkeley: University of California Press.

Williams, Cristine L., and Catherine Connell. 2011. "Looking good and sounding right": Aesthetic labor and social inequality in the retail industry. *Work and Occupations, 37*(3): 349–377.

Wilson, Eli R.Y. 2016. "Matching up: Producing proximal service in a Los Angeles restaurant." *Research in the Sociology of Work*, 29: 99–124.

———. 2020. "Pandemic inequality: Assessing the fallout in the restaurant industry." UCLA Institute for Research on Labor & Employment blog. Accessed 9/15/20: https://irle.ucla.edu/2020/04/15/pandemic-inequalities-restaurant-industry/.

————. 2021. *Front of the house, back of the house: Race and inequality in the lives of restaurant workers.* New York: New York University Press.

Wingfield, Adia H. and Renee S. Alston. 2014. "Maintaining hierarchies in predominantly white organizations: A theory of racial tasks." *American Behavioral Scientist, 58*(2): 274–287.

Withers, Erik T. 2017. "Brewing boundaries of white/middle-class/male-ness: Reflections from within the craft beer industry." In N.G. Chapman, J.S. Lellock and C.D. Lippard (Eds.), *Untapped: Exploring the cultural dimensions of craft beer* (pp. 236–260). Morgantown: West Virigina University Press.

Witteman, Cilia, John Van den Bercken, Laurence Claes, and Antonio Godoy. 2009. "Assessing rational and intuitive thinking styles." *European Journal of Psychological Assessment, 25*(1): 39–47.

Witz, Anne. 1992. *Professions and patriarchy.* London: Routledge.

Wolinski, Cat. 2019. "Hop take: The beer industry grapples With racism, again." *VinePair.* Accessed 2/28/21 (https://vinepair.com/articles/beer-industry-racism/).

WWJ News. "Craft beer conversation: Girls pint out brings women together over brews." *WWJ Newsradio.* Accessed 6/01/21 (https://www.audacy.com/wwjnews-radio/articles/craft-beer-conversation-girls-pint-out-detroit).

Yazdiha, Hajar. 2017. "The relationality of law and culture: Dominant approaches and ne directions for cultural sociologists." *Sociology Compass.* DOI: https://doi.org/10.1111/soc4.12545.

ZipRecruiter. "Brewer." Accessed 2/15/21 (https://www.ziprecruiter.com/Salaries/Brewer-Salary).

————. "Assistant Brewer." Accessed 7/1/21 (https://www.ziprecruiter.com/Salaries/Assistant-Brewer-Salary).

Index

Note: Page locators in italics refer to figures.

About the Authors

Eli Revelle Yano Wilson is an assistant professor of Sociology at the University of New Mexico. He is the author of *Front of the House, Back of the House: Race and Inequality in the Lives of Restaurant Workers*. His research broadly examines how race, work, and culture, intersect in the new urban economy.

Asa B. Stone is a social psychologist with a professional mission to elevate the appreciation for human capacity through science, education, and advocacy. They research the intersection of climate crisis and social justice as an affiliate assistant professor of the Resilience Institute and the Department of Geography and Environmental Studies at the University of New Mexico. Their ongoing research on beer includes the impacts of climate change on lambic production and cultural heritage.

www.ingramcontent.com/pod-product-compliance
Lightning Source LLC
Chambersburg PA
CBHW071413290326
41932CB00047B/2846